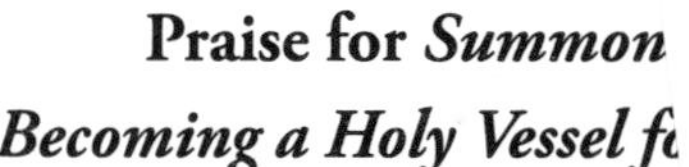

Praise for *Summon*
Becoming a Holy Vessel f… …orld

"Lama Cynthia Jurs is, to me—and clearly to thousands of others—the embodiment of feminine wisdom. The particular wisdom stream that flows through her is precisely the water we need to save and sustain life on Earth. Her new book tells a magnificent story in fresh, accessible prose—not simply as one woman's chronicle of her spiritual adventures, but as a light to guide our own steps as we stand up and speak out on behalf of this beautiful, broken world."

—Mirabai Starr, author of *Wild Mercy: Living the Fierce and Tender Wisdom of the Women Mystics*

"In total dedication to her path, Jurs embarked on an epic journey of service for all living beings. Her trials, challenges, passion, healing and dedication are laid bare in what is truly a beautifully written offering. This remarkable book stands as a model for each of us to heed our innermost calling to serve the Earth, no matter the outcome."

—Dahr Jamail, co-editor of *We Are the Middle of Forever: Indigenous Voices From Turtle Island on the Changing Earth* and author of *The End of Ice: Bearing Witness and Finding Meaning in the Path of Climate Disruption*

"This is the story of a remarkable adventure that is underway in our time, beginning with one woman's question. The question had ripened within her for a decade, since our times together facing nuclear weapons and the challenge they represent to all life on Earth. The response she receives ignites an adventure which, thanks to her courage, moves out across the planet, engaging countless people from all backgrounds. As I took part and watched it unfold, my initial incredulity turned to awe, my inner cynic silenced by tears. Whatever power the Earth Treasure Vases possess to heal our broken world, the real miracle for me is what they awaken and inspire in virtually everyone who accepts the call to fill them with prayer and place them within our larger body, the sacred living body of Earth."

—Joanna Macy, eco-philosopher and author of *World as Lover, World as Self*

"An unexpected metamorphosis is coursing through the great religions of the world, as their acolytes grapple with the calamitous dwindling of countless animals, plants, and once-flourishing places at the hands of a civilization that segregates material, earthly life from the realm of the spirit, and conceives the Sacred as a bodiless realm hidden above or behind sensuous nature. The metamorphosis has perhaps gone farthest within Buddhism, where some courageous and far-seeing teachers now call attention to the many-voiced Earth as the immanent presence of the Holy, as the very wellspring of all awakening.

"Those who are enacting this new Dharma Gaia commonly draw inspiration from the late Thich Nhat Hanh (radiant in his fierce simplicity and boundless heart), or from the passionate activist and bodhisattva Joanna Macy, or the great wilderness poet and Zen adept Gary Snyder. To their names we must now add that of the humble and vivacious Cynthia Jurs, who long ago pledged her life—body and soul—in service to the animate Earth.

"We greatly need the stalwart scientists who labor to fathom what's happening to our climate and oceans, as we hugely need the many valiant activists fighting for the well-being of other species and the continued flourishing of forests, rivers, and soils. Yet we also need fearless impresarios of magic faith like Cynthia Jurs, who work steadfastly to dissolve our collective callousness, and to replenish the mystery that binds the human heart to the heart of the world."

—David Abram, author of *The Spell of the Sensuous: Perception and Language in a More-Than-Human World* and *Becoming Animal: An Earthly Cosmology*

"Let Lama Cynthia take you on an astonishing pilgrimage across the globe! In her timely book, deeply rooted in women's ways of knowing and healing, Cynthia addresses the abuses of the patriarchy and offers her inspiring insights and spiritual illumination, all while planting prayers and sacred offering vases into the brilliant heart of Mother Earth. Through her devotion and perseverance, she trusted and followed her visions and intuition over and over again, taking on increasing challenges as she divined her way around the world, opening her heart to the powerful lessons of this mythic journey. This is an authentic spiritual book to be treasured. It is filled with profound healing, hard-won wisdom, and boundless love—a beacon and guide for us all!"

—Trudy Goodman, founding teacher, InsightLA

"*Summoned by the Earth* is a spiritual adventure story of dedication and courage. I found it simply wonderous how the ritual of planting these small vases creates a magical communion and generates inspired blessings in communities across the world."

—Jack Kornfield, author of *A Path with Heart*

"This is a story about one of the most remarkable lives of service I have ever witnessed. It is a story of courage, of deep transformation, of mysticism and magic, of humility and right action on behalf of our struggling planet. Cynthia is one of those inspirational souls who answered a call and stepped into it with her whole being. Her story is a path laid generously for each of us to savor, consider and then hold as a torch in our own lives."

—Clare Dubois, founder of TreeSisters

"Cynthia Jurs' subtle, brave, nakedly written, and impassioned book *Summoned by the Earth* challenges us all to listen to the Earth crying and act urgently. Cynthia's exploration of her own quest, inspired by an old lama in Nepal, to place Earth Treasure Vases in sacred sites all over the world is original, poignant and profoundly inspiring. Seekers and sacred activists of all kinds will learn a great deal from this humble master of truth and from how she worked to honor her own unique assignment against extreme odds. Read this book and give it to everyone you know."

—Andrew Harvey, author of *The Hope: A Guide to Sacred Activism* and *Radical Regeneration* (with Carolyn Baker)

"This book is a prayer from Mother Earth. Cynthia Jurs leads us on a powerful and heart-opening journey of becoming an Earth Holder, an Earth Protector. Through her own experiences of spiritual transformation, she shows us how we can each heal our precious Earth and soothe the suffering of her inhabitants by quieting our minds and listening to the deepest guidance within each of us. When we follow this wisdom, collaborating with others in community, we fulfill our true purpose: to awaken and make our world whole."

—Kaira Jewel Lingo, author of *We Were Made For These Times* and *Healing Our Way Home*

"Why do we ask questions? To invoke the powers of creation and to invite the union of our will with the Mysteries within creation. In this most remarkable saga, Cynthia Jurs inspires a way of knowing that comes from searching one's heart for the questions that open doors between worlds. *Summoned by the Earth* guides our heart into believing the impossible, becoming certain again of the lost wisdom of Earth and remembering what we can do to recover what is lost in time, between the veil and our willingness to ask. The opportunity to treasure Earth allows us to be the vessel for the healing that results in this intimacy of heart and the inner life of Earth. We will remember that we are on both sides of the veil, asking and giving in the full cycle of life."

—Orland Bishop, author of *The Seventh Shrine: Meditations on the African Spiritual Journey: From the Middle Passage to the Mountaintop* and founder of ShadeTree Multicultural Foundation

"I have known Cynthia as my sister in the Dharma for nearly forty years. She was one of the first Western lay Dharma teachers to be ordained by Venerable Thich Nhat Hanh, whose teachings on building community and bringing the spiritual dimension into our actions reverberate throughout this marvelous tale. We can all take inspiration from Cynthia and participate by practicing mindfulness and planting our pure intentions for Mother Earth by our way of living and relating with each other and all living beings. Thinking globally, acting locally, may all who read this book discover their heart's mission and join in one great action of humanity to bring healing to our precious planet."

—Sister Chân Không, True Emptiness, Senior Nun in the Order of Interbeing of Thich Nhat Hanh and author of *Learning True Love*

"Buddhism, feminism, and Earth spirituality converge in this highly engaging and moving tale of courage, healing, and redemption. Cynthia's path shows the way toward a more intimately sacred relationship between humanity and Earth."

—Charles Eisenstein, author of *The More Beautiful World Our Hearts Know Is Possible* and *Climate: A New Story*

"I am filled with awe and inspiration after reading *Summoned by Earth*. Cynthia's breathtaking devotion to Gaia brings forth a painful but crucial reckoning with the brutality of the patriarchal separation of spirit and matter, and the dire consequences of a spirituality that ignores the living, breathing source of us all, Gaia herself. Cynthia's is a story about the immense collective healing potential that actualizes when one human heart awakens and commits her life to love, to Gaia and her sacred assignment. Following her journey as she reconnects with her ancient calling as Gaia's priestess, we are all invited in through the temple doors to retrieve our primordial belonging with our splendorous Mother. This book is a guiding light for those of us wishing to birth a new paradigm of the divine feminine as embodied wisdom in action. I bow a thousand times."

—Chameli Gad, Goddess wisdomkeeper and founder of Awakening Women Institute

"Human civilizations from ancient Greece to India and Tibet have honored the Earth through healing rituals. Cynthia Jurs' work with the Earth Treasure Vases unites Buddhist wisdom with environmental activism in acknowledging our essential role as healers and protectors of Mother Earth, Gaia. Her book, *Summoned by the Earth*, reconnects us with our earthly origins while inspiring urgent, compassionate action on behalf of all of Nature."

—Dr. Nida Chenagtsang, founder, medical director and principal teacher of the Sowa Rigpa Institute of Tibetan Medicine

"This beautiful book by author and Buddhist teacher Cynthia Jurs is a powerful rendering of a life, a path, a vision, and a mission. Her practice with the Earth Treasure Vases is a rare ritual offering of feminine energy in our imperiled world. In fact, the story Cynthia tells is itself a treasure."

—Roshi Joan Halifax, abbot of the Upaya Zen Center, and author of *Standing at the Edge: Finding Freedom Where Fear and Courage Meet*

"Cynthia Jurs has walked the talk of planetary service like few people have. Her epic book brings forth an extraordinary global family, including people from all continents, faiths, and political perspectives, united in their love and care for our Earth. Through her thirty-plus years of global pilgrimage, she has woven a magnificent planetary mandala of prayers, a living source of refuge we can all draw upon and align with. Cynthia has breathed new life into an ancient Tibetan Buddhist tradition by sharing it with such reverence and freshness to cultures around the world. She has also made a major contribution by adapting traditional Tibetan Buddhist practices into a more Earth-centric approach that resonates strongly with the needs and concerns of our times. She is a living bodhisattva, and I'm honored to call her my friend."

—David T. Nicol, author of *Subtle Activism: The Inner Dimension of Social and Planetary Transformation*

"In an era of unprecedented, earthly change, Cynthia Jurs' timely book brings spiritual insight to the necessary synthesis of human flourishing and environmental renewal. As both guardian and guide, she reveals a path of healing and regeneration that reveres time-honored traditions while forging a viable and visionary future."

—Ian A. Baker, PhD, author of *The Heart of the World: A Journey to Tibet's Lost Paradise*

"*Summoned by the Earth* is a treasure teaching for our time. It is rare to find a book that truly transforms you upon reading, and *Summoned by the Earth* is such an offering—an extraordinary living mandala of transmission and healing. The depth of Cynthia Jurs' forty years of Buddhist practice is reflected in these pages, along with a deeply human and, in moments, heartbreakingly raw story. It is also a powerful revelation of the feminine face of Buddhism, true medicine as we collectively awaken to the urgency of reconnecting with our sacred path back to the wisdom of our precious Mother Earth. The dawn of a new era has come."

—Sarah Drew, author of *Gaia Codex*

SUMMONED BY THE EARTH

BECOMING A HOLY VESSEL FOR HEALING OUR WORLD

CYNTHIA JURS

FOREWORDS BY
ROBERT A.F. THURMAN
&
LAMA TSULTRIM ALLIONE

PROSPECTA PRESS

Copyright © by Cynthia Jurs 2024

All rights reserved.
No portion of this book may be reproduced in any fashion, print, facsimile, or electronic, or by any method yet to be developed, without the express written permission of the publisher.

Paperback ISBN 978-1-63226-132-8
eBook ISBN 978-1-63226-133-5
Limited Edition Hardcover (Hors de Commerce) ISBN: 978-1-63226-131-1
Audiobook ISBN 978-1-959162-47-6

Published by Prospecta Press
An imprint of Easton Studio Press
PO Box 3131
Westport, CT 06880
(203) 571-0781
www.prospectapress.com

Book and cover design by Barbara Aronica
Front cover photo ©2023, "Pink Full Moon Over Santa Fe Baldy," by Ed MacKerrow / In Light of Nature
Front cover art by Gonzalo Rescalvo / Abzzolum Digital Art
Crop Circle photos by Steve Alexander / Temporary Temples
Center of the Mandala and World Map of Earth Treasure Vase Locations by Tracy H. Seidman and Marty Peale

Manufactured in the United States of America

A project of Alliance for the Earth

CONTENTS

Dedication xv

Foreword by Robert A.F. Thurman xvii

Foreword by Lama Tsultrim Allione xxi

Notes on Language and Perspective xxiii

Prologue xxv

Section One: Answering the Call

Map of the Center of the Mandala 2

Chapter One: The Path 3

Chapter Two: Stepping Stones 18

Chapter Three: The Terma 37

Chapter Four: The Bomb in My Backyard 51

Chapter Five: The Mandala Begins 66

Chapter Six: Pilgrimage 79

Section Two: Hearing the Cries of the World

Chapter Seven: Planetary Acupuncture 97

Chapter Eight: A Thousand Arms 101

Chapter Nine: Twenty-One Taras 115

Chapter Ten: The Sound of the Bell in Africa 122

Chapter Eleven: Do Not Close Your Eyes Before Suffering 143

Chapter Twelve: Reckoning 148

Chapter Thirteen: The Heart of . . . Darkness? 156

Chapter Fourteen: Poison into Wisdom 175

Section Three: Becoming a Holy Vessel

Chapter Fifteen: Taking Refuge in the Earth 187
Chapter Sixteen: Sacred Time 195
Chapter Seventeen: Offerings 210
Chapter Eighteen: Becoming a Holy Vessel 223
Chapter Nineteen: Listening to the Elders 234
Chapter Twenty: Welcome to Country 241

Section Four: Collective Awakening

Chapter Twenty-One: Indra's Net 261
Chapter Twenty-Two: Sacred Activism 267
Chapter Twenty-Three: Mother Gaia 284
Chapter Twenty-Four: Head over Heels 289
Chapter Twenty-Five: Buddha Gotami 314
Chapter Twenty-Six: The Oracle's Message 324

Epilogue 341
Acknowledgments 347
Endnotes and Citations 357
Glossary 381
Earth Treasure Vase Locations 399
Resources 405
About the Author 409

For this beautiful blue-green planet we call home,
I give my life to you.

And to all of you who are reading this now
and to all who may come along next,

may our love be the resource we draw from
to restore harmony to the web of life.

FOREWORD

by

Robert A.F. Thurman

Summoned by the Earth is like an incredible dream. It is the amazing tale of how a wonderful human woman makes a heroic effort to save our precious Mother Goddess Buddha Bodhisattva Gaia, through decades of creative, courageous, and intelligent service, indivisibly from her own practice toward and performance of enlightenment.

The book recounts Cynthia Jurs' whole life, her great sadhana of love and determination and commitment. It makes nonduality truly alive in our dreaded times and strengthens my trust in life and my conviction that our future generations will experience the resplendent glory of a restored and fruitful Earth. As I read the book, my gratitude to Cynthia overwhelmed me—at many points in the story, I shed tears of relief, in awe of the inconceivability of her miraculous accomplishments.

Her retinue is unforgettable—from the sage Marian Naranjo of Santa Clara Pueblo, Christian Bethelson, Neema Namadamu, Dr. Mukwege, and the Pygmy communities in Congo, the Kogi in Colombia, the Aboriginal People and their songlines and her Mumma Aunty Margaret in Australia, Ani Pema Chodron and Lama Ngawang Tsultrim in Nepal, her acupuncturing husband Hugh, the amazing craftspersons who made the beautiful boxes for the Earth Treasure Vases and many others who were lifted on Cynthia's wings.

Recently, while reading aloud my friend Tom Cleary's monumental translation of the *Buddha-Avatamsaka, Huayen, Flower Ornament Sutra*, I had a kind of epiphany about Mother Gaia, Prithivi Devi, when reading one of the excruciating passages describing the enlightening being (Tom's choice for bodhisattva), about how life after life the bodhisattva gives her flesh and blood to cannibals and ghouls, her head and limbs and eyes, etc., because s/he cannot bear that any beings suffer from hunger. I realized that of course the most natural thing for a bodhisattva at the inconceivable liberation stage to do is actually to become a planet, a Mother Earth, and so become able to feed billions of animals and humans, etc., for millions of years. I came to recognize that Gaia, Mother Earth, whom the Buddha gratefully touched at the moment of his perfect enlightenment, is not merely a goddess; she herself is also a buddha-bodhisattva, just like Tara, Avalokiteshvara, Manjushri, or Samantabhadra!

Just then a mutual friend of Cynthia's handed me her awesome book! I immediately became absorbed in her "she-roic" accomplishments, her determined planting of the Earth Treasure Vases so laboriously and artfully, as well as her Lama-ship, her Tara/Gaia fusion and innovative tradition founding, with her mantra;

OM GAIA MANDALA SIDDHI PHALA BHRUM AH.

In sum, I find *Summoned by the Earth* utterly exemplary and inspiring. I support Cynthia and her vision 100 percent, and I think her new tradition of Mother Gaia is very important. I will follow it and defend it. And I know that many other women and men will joyfully rise with me in defense of life and be deeply inspired by Cynthia and her inconceivably liberating deeds. I believe that her courageous bringing of the enlightening Dharma literally down to Earth is a true implementation of Guru Rinpoche's miraculous Earth Treasure Vase tradition in this time of planetary crisis. Thank you, Cynthia, from the depths of my heart!

Robert A.F. "Tenzin" Thurman
Jey Tsongkhapa Professor Emeritus of Buddhology
Columbia University
Cofounder of Tibet House US
Woodstock, New York, 2.2.22

FOREWORD

by

Lama Tsultrim Allione

When I first met Lama Cynthia Jurs in the mid-1980s, she was like a lightning rod for the Earth changes, the profound disruption that was coming. A few years after our pilgrimage to Mount Kailash in 1988, she went up into the Himalayan mountains of Nepal to meet Lama Charok Rinpoche and ask what she could do to help the struggling Earth.

She received the instruction that she should bury Earth Treasure Vases containing sacred relics and prayers all around the world as a way to heal the injuries Mother Earth was sustaining. Since getting her "assignment," Lama Cynthia has focused on burying these sacred offering vases at key points on the Earth. It has been a long inner and outer journey for Mother Gaia, requiring years of self-sacrifice and difficult travel, including to some potentially dangerous places.

Now the Earth is literally on fire and we face the onslaught of rampant consumerism, pollution, destruction of forests, and fossil fuel emissions. There is no way to measure exactly how the vases have made a difference or what their impact has been. But the vases act as activators of Gaia's acupuncture meridians to bring healing and stabilization, and the immeasurable blessing power of the relics and intentions they contain, is certainly contributing to healing our Great Mother, Gaia.

I am reminded of the story of the great Dzogchen teacher Changchub Dorje, told by his devoted disciple Chogyal Namkhai Norbu Rinpoche. Changchub Dorje was building new stupas even as the Chinese army was invading the area of Tibet where he was building them. They were destroying every stupa they came across. He was asked why he would build new stupas when it was obvious that they would soon be destroyed.

He replied, "The very act of the building of stupas is vastly beneficial. Even if they are destroyed the day after completion or during construction, the intention and act of building them is of great benefit. Therefore, I will build them."

May the vast intention of Lama Cynthia's journey with the Earth Treasure Vases, and the communities that now hold them, benefit all beings everywhere, especially our precious Great Mother, Gaia.

Lama Tsultrim Allione
Encinitas, California
August 11, 2023

NOTES ON LANGUAGE AND PERSPECTIVE

In the writing of this book, I sought not to objectify the Earth, making a concerted effort to refer to Earth as Gaia, as a living being, as Mother Earth. As much as possible I dropped "the" before "Earth," but in some cases, for ease of reading, I did not do so. In addition, I have chosen to capitalize Earth throughout, out of respect for the one who gives us life.

It has been important for me to relate to Mother Earth as "Her"—a feminine embodiment of great wisdom who deserves our utmost respect. I have been motivated by the necessity to contribute to healing the feminine and overcoming the devaluing of Earth by a patriarchal worldview.

I struggled with the same issue around referring to "the Buddha" or "Buddha." Since the word "Buddha" generally means "one who is awakened," I referred to "the Buddha" when identifying Buddha Shakyamuni, the historical figure in whose footsteps we are following. When referring to Buddha nature, which we all have, I did not include "the."

Writing this book has required weaving the stories of many besides myself. I have done my best to tell these stories accurately and faithfully, and to represent events honestly. To the best of my ability, I have received approval from those whose stories I have told. To protect a few identities some names have been changed.

With respect for Aboriginal and Torres Strait Islander's cultural values, I'd like to draw attention to the fact that this work contains the names, images and words of people who are deceased.

Lastly, I have waded deeply into complex dharma teachings and layers of ancient myths. The interpretations I have come to are my own.

PROLOGUE

These times of collective suffering are virtually impossible to fathom, and we are filled with anguish. Buddhist teacher and eco-philosopher Joanna Macy says, "The loss of certainty that there will be a future is, I believe, the pivotal psychological reality of our time."[1]

Contemplating our death or that of a loved one, or even the end of an era, is one thing, but now, individually and collectively, we are faced with the possible end of life as we know it. There has always been the reassuring thought that even if we die, the trees we love would endure, the lake would be there for our children's children to enjoy. Now, we confront losses so sweeping that they are simply incomprehensible.

Everyone with eyes to see and a heart that cares knows that the body of our Mother Earth is being abused beyond recognition. It pains many of us physically to feel what the Earth has to endure. Bearing witness to Earth's suffering, we often find ourselves personally embodying the issues that are calling to be healed collectively.

Thich Nhat Hanh, the Vietnamese Zen master, was once asked, "What do we most need to do to save our world?" He replied, "What we most need to do is hear within us the sounds of the Earth crying."[2]

And so it was with me. Hearing within myself the sound of the Earth crying, I hoped to find a way to soothe those tears. I sought a path of service, and then found myself on an actual path climbing high into the Himalayas more than thirty years ago—one that would prove to be life-changing.

Incredibly, the path I found led to the proverbial old wise man in a cave. Carrying my anguish for Mother Earth, I could hardly believe I had been given this opportunity. Questions I had yet to formulate or speak aloud burned in my heart, along with deep yearnings for a larger purpose. But it wasn't until I was walking up that path into the mountains of Nepal that my life's guiding question crystalized.

Undertaking a spiritual pilgrimage, we ask ourselves to clarify what we are seeking. What unanswered question is probing us, pushing us on to this path? Once our direction is clear, even if we have no idea how we will get there, the universe can respond and clues start to come in. It's as if a magnetic force is drawing to us whatever we need to fulfill our intention.

I was compelled to make this pilgrimage but only had a vague sense of those larger forces pushing me along. When I reached the old man in his cave, there was a moment that came, as surely it must when we are touching the mythic dimensions of our lives, and I was invited to ask him my question. In response, I was given an impossible assignment, nearly as formidable as weaving straw into gold.

Had I known what it would take, what this journey of a lifetime would ask of me, and how I would be stripped of most all I held dear, I might never have undertaken it. Traveling into remote regions of the world to fulfill my assignment, with no guidelines and no one to tell me how, tested me again and again. It was an alchemical rite of passage that took me beyond my ideas of what to do and how to do it, and as a result, I moved into wholly new inner and outer terrain.

I learned to listen—to myself, yes, but also to the land, the Ancestors, the elders, activists, and regular folks all around the world who care about this beautiful blue-green planet we call home. I had to make relations with strangers, overcome my fears, and reach out across our differences with respect and humility, to fulfill the sacred task I had been given by the old wise man in the cave. Gropingly, I felt my way from an objectified woman of privilege to a servant of peace and healing. Time and time again, I had to let go and trust that Earth, Herself, was guiding me. Slowly, my life was tempered into a living prayer to Gaia.

In the end, the path that led to a cave at the rooftop of the world wound around the entire planet. I traveled from the Americas to Asia and Europe, from Africa to Australia, passing through disillusionment and despair to elation and deep fulfillment. I lost the path. I fell off the path. And still, I kept hearing that call, responding to a summons from the Earth.

Perhaps you hear it, too?

This is my story, my attempt to articulate a path of awakening that is responsive to the call of these times. I offer it to you, that we may find our way together.

SUMMONED BY THE EARTH

SECTION ONE

ANSWERING THE CALL

The Center of the Mandala

The First Five Earth Treasure Vases in the Center and Four Directions of the Rio Grande Bioregion

CHAPTER ONE

THE PATH

I am on the path, walking up the steep stones of the high Himalayas. The path climbs and climbs, and I wonder, as I stumble along, What am I doing? At home in Santa Fe, New Mexico, my life has recently fallen apart; my marriage has ended. I feel lost and confused, and here on this path halfway around the world, I am trying to find the way. Luckily, my traveling companions know where to go. It is 1990, and they are taking me to the hermitage of a 106-year-old Buddhist lama who lives in a remote cave at thirteen thousand feet in a faraway corner of Nepal.[1]

The moment I heard about this journey from my friend Jim Casilio, a devoted student of Tibetan Buddhism, I knew I had to go. I had been studying Zen Buddhism for almost a decade and was fascinated by Tibetan Buddhism, but had only recently become a student of Namkhai Norbu Rinpoche, Jim's teacher. As I climbed the arduous trail at an altitude where the blue sky stings and the snowy peaks ring out in crystal clarity, I realized I was being given a once-in-a-lifetime opportunity to meet the proverbial old wise man in the cave . . . and sure enough, I could ask him a question.

As my companions and I trekked up the trail for days on end, I prepared myself to meet the old lama, known formally as His Eminence Kushok Mangdon and personally as Charok Rinpoche

(Rinpoche meaning "precious teacher" and Charok, the place he resides). Charok Rinpoche was the teacher of Ngawang Tsultrim Zangpo, Jim's Sherpa friend who was also a lama and was guiding us on the trek. Lama Tsultrim had grown up in Nepal under Charok Rinpoche's care and looked upon him as his root teacher, having been his student since he was a small boy. He loved him as a father and was excited to see him again, as was Lama Tsultrim's mother, who traveled with us. She had not visited Charok Rinpoche for thirteen years. Even at sixty, she was stronger than the rest of us when it came to trekking.

It was November: nature was pulling in for the long winter. Still, the paths and trails were soft and welcoming. The days were full of good omens and auspicious signs, according to Lama Tsultrim, and the moon was in our favor. It seemed like a dream as I walked through that graceful landscape and thought about meeting an old wise man who had lived in the same place for more than one hundred years—a place unspoiled by "progress," with nature still intact. Here was someone whose unique perspective and experience could shed light on the situation we were in, living on the Earth at this time. I was filled with emotion and could not escape the sense of impending danger, even in this peaceful place.

What a remarkable chance to receive guidance from a holy man who had known only the protected valleys and mountaintops of Nepal, though he had traveled vast realms through the power of his compassionate awareness and expanded consciousness. What would his perspective be? And what could I learn from him that I could share with others to help make this Earth a better place for all? I hoped I was worthy to meet him.

One step, one breath; higher and higher into that rarefied air I climbed. With each step a clearer awareness dawned of the moment I was in. But what would my question be for the Rinpoche? I had no idea. My mind was a swirl of so many things at once: everything I cared about, everything I'd ever heard about enlightenment, all my ideas and worries, questions about life and the meaning of it. What should I possibly ask him? The leaves on the giant rhododendron trees along that rocky path nodded, and the prayer flags greeting us along the way waved their colorful hands. I was inspired to keep going by the prayers in the wind and on rocks carved with mantras invoking the compassion of Chenrezig and the companionship of Tara, the savioress, who is said to come when called—beloved deities venerated in that part of the world.

Along the way we stopped to purchase provisions to bring to the Rinpoche. The two Sherpa porters who accompanied us marched up the mountain in their flip-flops, carrying heavy baskets on their backs undeterred, while I followed behind with the others, my head down, breathing heavily.

At a certain point in our ascent, I knew I must find a question for Charok Rinpoche that would not just be meaningful to me but would bring an answer helpful to others who could never travel to such a place. To be given the chance to ask a question of an old wise man in a cave was quite an opportunity, and I felt a responsibility to everyone whom I imagined traveled with me on that mountainous path. I ached with the awareness that I was somehow part of something much larger than myself that I did not understand.

Walking up the path, my heart had to work hard to push the blood and pump the muscles to make the high-altitude climb, and I became aware of the Earth talking to me in my blood and bones. Once again, I sensed the terrible challenges our planet was facing, and felt Her calling for attention in each cell of my body. A deep longing for Earth's health and safety came into my heart and mind, and I asked myself, *What can I do to bring healing and protection to the Earth?*

This was the question I had been looking for.

As the question arose, I knew something important was awakening in me, but I didn't know what. I only knew that I cared—deeply. With each step and each beat of my heart, it became more and more clear just how much I love this Earth—and how worried I was about Her survival. I sensed I had found what had propelled me halfway around the world and up those high mountains. It was all I could think about.

We left the main trail and climbed steeply up several thousand feet more. When we reached an altitude of thirteen thousand feet, we found a collection of cave dwellings that was our destination. We walked through magical cedar and juniper forests strewn with big boulders, on soft paths padded with fallen leaves, past little streams. We could not see where we were going from below, but once we arrived, we discovered prayer flags flying all around and a marvelous homestead among the rocks and trees.

The holy man Charok Rinpoche lived in a "house" built under an enormous rock overhang—actually a large cave with a painted door, a few windows, and two rooms. One room was the kitchen-living-sleeping room, and the other was the gompa, a small temple painted with the peaceful and wrathful deities of the bardo, or realms it is said we traverse after death, reminding us of the journey that awaits us all.

We were welcomed by Rinpoche; his daughter, Ani Pema Chodron, a nun in her fifties who had served him devotedly all her life; and his little grandson, Ngawang Tenzin Trinle, age five, the son of his son who had died unexpectedly a few years before. All around Rinpoche's home were other caves, some fixed up like his, and others, like the one my fellow travelers and I used, just caves. Yogis had come here to live and practice over many generations. Now that Rinpoche was so old, his little grandson was everyone's hope for the future and for the lineage to be maintained. He was being trained.

Charok Rinpoche had lived his entire 106 years in the Solukhumbu region of Nepal, with the last several years spent here in his cave retreat. He was a tiny man; I was told he used to be over six feet tall. His eyes were mostly closed, though it seemed he could make out light and dark. I thought he was very beautiful, with a long white beard and long fingers on big, graceful hands. The kitchen we gathered in was black from all the smoke collecting over the years. Ani-la, his daughter, brought us butter tea and later chang, a fermented grain drink. She hovered over us and said insistently, "Please, drink! More, more, more!"

Rinpoche mostly sat in a four-by-five-foot box next to the fire where he meditated and slept—sitting up.[2] He appeared to melt into his robes and cushion as if he had no legs at all, his head, chest, and arms rising out of the folds of the worn burgundy cloth he dressed in. Yet he managed to get up and move his body with the help of his grandson, who was almost always at his side. His life had been dedicated to the practice of meditation, his mind sharpened by living amid the elements of earth and sky. In spite of his advanced years, he was totally lucid and didn't miss a beat; his perceptions were quick and finely tuned. I was overwhelmed by his example—I could see that the years of meditation had resulted in his gaining awareness in old age, not losing it, as is so often the case with elders in Western culture. If nothing else, just to meet someone so old in this lifetime, who was such an example of graceful aging, was reason enough to have come all this way.

I watched him sitting there in the loose folds of his robe, and it seemed he was already very close to the end: bones thinly covered in flesh, so little left. In the blink of an eye, he would give it up, and his earthly remains would be carried up into the rocks to be burned as an offering. A stupa would then be built in his honor, and the little boy with the runny nose would take over his seat.

We lived with Charok Rinpoche for several weeks, walking among the lichen-draped pines and well-worn paths. We spent our days in our little cave-camp in the mornings, then around noon we would walk up to Rinpoche's cave and spend the afternoon with him. He and Lama Tsultrim would talk, Lama's mother would tell stories, and Ani-la would feed us Sherpa stew made from the dried-meat carcass we had brought for them.

I wondered when I would be able to speak directly to Rinpoche about my question. How could I ever adequately express what was in my heart and on my mind? Then one day, sitting outside on a small terrace, the opportunity arose. It was sunny and warm after lunch, and Rinpoche turned to us and asked, "What is it like where you come from? Do you have places for retreat in America?"

I told him about our lives in the West, struggling to find the words to bridge the differences in our experience. I told him about what was happening to our world, how the Earth was in peril. And I shared my deep concern about the radioactive poisoning around Los Alamos National Laboratory (LANL), the birthplace of the atomic bomb, just across the Rio Grande Valley from Santa Fe, where I lived.

It took some explaining—especially about the half-life of uranium and the amount of time it takes for this deadly substance to deteriorate. He listened carefully and seemed to understand the severity of the problems we faced. I told him about the way nature has been poisoned and ravaged and about the values of our "civilized" world. I shared with him how people are getting sick with cancer as a result of contaminated water and land, and that these substances affect the entire web of life.

"This is the reality we are living in now. The climate is changing. Everything has changed—the lifespan of radioactive waste is 250,000 years! What are we to do, Rinpoche, to face the hopelessness of this overwhelming situation? What can we do to bring healing and protection to the Earth?"[3]

He asked if there were any people where I came from whose lives were dedicated to spiritual practice. "Even just one person can bring benefit to the whole area around where they live," he said. Then he looked directly into my eyes and murmured, "But you, you need to get some Earth Treasure Vases and put them in the ground. They will do that work."

What did he mean by Earth Treasure Vases? I couldn't imagine what those were, much less how they could help. But Charok Rinpoche went on to tell me about the ancient tradition of the Sa Chü Bumpa—literally, "vessels giving life-essence to the Earth." He said that the lamas from every lineage all over the Himalayas make Earth

Treasure Vases and consecrate them through their prayers. Inside are placed many different kinds of offerings, sacred relics, precious substances, and medicines. Once consecrated and sealed, the treasure vases are then ritually buried in special places to bring healing and protection to a whole area.

Later that night, Lama Tsultrim told me more. He recounted how during the eighth century in Tibet, there lived an extraordinary visionary, teacher, and prophet considered to be a second Buddha named Padmasambhava who predicted times of great deterioration and suffering for our planet in the future. One of the healing remedies he offered was the practice of the Earth Treasure Vases. He foresaw that the very essence of the elements of life—fire, water, air, earth, and space—would be threatened and become so depleted due to our obsessive consumption and materialistic fixation that they would lose their vitality. The five poisons of greed, anger, jealousy, pride, and ignorance, which cause much suffering for us humans, would gain such a hold on our collective consciousness that we would completely forget our basic goodness.

But Charok Rinpoche and Lama Tsultrim both insisted the Earth Treasure Vases had the power to restore that lost vitality to the elements and bring long life, reduce warfare and violence, enhance peace and prosperity, and even reconnect us to our innate wisdom. They told me that the vases had the power to remove negativity, purify and pacify the environment, and bring harmony and healing even over great distances, affecting the hearts and minds of those who came within their sphere of influence. They knew the Earth Treasure Vases would point the way for us to realize that we are each a small part of a vast, interdependent whole.

Charok Rinpoche assured me, saying, "The vases will help greatly. You should learn more about this practice. In fact," he said, "you should definitely get some made and put them in places of need. The abbot of Tengboche Monastery, several days' walk away, can make the vessels for you. You should go there and ask for his help."

I thought to myself, How can this be true? And anyway, he doesn't really understand! We're talking about 250,000 years of radioactivity and birth defects! How can a clay pot in the ground make any difference to the physical substance of the Earth? But I felt it would be quite disrespectful to say this to him directly. So I kept quiet and thought more deeply about what he was prescribing. It seemed that the tradition of the Earth Treasure Vases asks us to recognize that the healing of the environment may take place on many levels at once, not just the physical. Maybe the Sa Chü Bumpa contained some wisdom or formula that really could help the Earth in these times. At least it was worth a try.

Rinpoche continued, "Everything comes from the Earth. The Earth is what gives us everything, so it is good to do this now. Even war and bad illnesses won't come to countries if such a bumpa is there. The vase transforms the poison. Put them all around the area and it will help. Even putting one is enough."

I was inspired, and we immediately made plans to visit the abbot of Tengboche and ask for his help. But before our departure, we were to receive the initiation and blessing of long life from Charok Rinpoche. Long life for us and for the Earth as well, I prayed.

When the day came for the long-life ritual, Lama Tsultrim prepared me to receive the initiation by conducting a ceremony for me to formally take Charok Rinpoche as my teacher and make vows to take refuge in the Three Jewels. These "jewels" refer to the Buddha (the Teacher), the Dharma (the Teachings) and the Sangha (the Community) in the Buddhist tradition. He symbolically cut some of my hair and gave me the spiritual name Sherab Zangmo, which means "Good Woman of Wisdom." The little boy escorted us into the small gompa where we sat along the wall while Rinpoche performed the initiation. Lama Tsultrim sat close to the feet of his teacher, the picture of devotion, weeping quietly throughout. With Rinpoche's grandson always nearby, we watched the passing on of the old traditional ways that go back thousands of years.

When Charok Rinpoche was finished, we all helped him out of the gompa. Many hours had passed, and stepping outside, we found our little mountainside refuge completely enshrouded by mist. The light cast a strange glow on the land, yet I felt as if my vision had cleared. I saw with fresh eyes, and it seemed my cells had been rearranged as I savored the otherworldly light on the landscape around us. We watched the high mountain peaks in the distance appear and disappear in and out of the mist that hung over the valley, like a vision of a god realm. A perfect half-moon shone brightly above us.

We set out for a very long two-day walk to Tengboche Monastery the next day. We arrived late in the afternoon as more foggy mist laid over the monastery grounds and surrounding mountains of Everest, Lhotse, and Ama Dablam. Because we had been sent by Charok Rinpoche, and Lama Tsultrim's father was the abbot of a respected monastery called Tolu Tharling Gompa in the Solu region of Nepal, we were well received and invited to meet Tengboche Rinpoche the next morning.

The abbot of Tengboche, Ngawang Tenzin Zangpo Rinpoche, entered the sitting room, briskly swishing his bright orange shawl over his burgundy robes. He had a thick head of graying hair, and refined features. We bowed and offered the traditional white silk khata scarves of respect. He smiled broadly when I told him Charok Rinpoche sent us and asked if he would help by making the Earth Treasure Vases. "Of course! How many do you need?" he inquired.

My mind stopped. The world situation was completely overwhelming. Should I ask for seven thousand, seven hundred . . . or seven? "I don't know . . . twenty-five?" I stammered.

"Oh, yes, yes—no problem!" he answered.

It is the tradition for Earth Treasure Vases to be crafted by the lamas inside the monasteries and to be filled with specific offerings and sacred substances, then sealed and consecrated over many months before they are taken out into the countryside to be buried. Once the pots are filled and sealed, they should never be opened: they are to be quietly buried intact in an unmarked location. But the abbot was concerned about customs and security officials opening them as the pots traveled around the world. So he made a highly unorthodox suggestion: the lamas would mix the most sacred substances directly into the clay and consecrate the empty pots, then give them to me and my community at home to fill, seal, and plant in the ground.

It was a radical departure from tradition on the part of the lamas to allow us to do this work, as normally this kind of ritual activity was carried out only by ordained monks behind closed monastery doors. I questioned him: "Isn't there a practice I need to learn before undertaking this?"

"No, no!" he told me again and again. "Just put them in the ground; they'll do the work." Really? I could not believe it.

With a twinkle in his eyes, the abbot excused himself momentarily and shuffled off, gathering his shawl in his arms and sweeping it over his shoulder. When he returned, he reached into the folds of his robes and brought out the most sacred of medicines and relics. Because the vases were for sites that had been severely poisoned, he said, "We need to give everything we can. These are my most powerful offerings. They will be mixed directly into the clay."

He showed us "precious pills" that had been made from the eyes, tongues, and hearts of realized practitioners. He told us that these parts of the body do not burn when they are cremated—a sign that the body, speech, and mind of such great masters have become fully enlightened. There were other miraculous medicines and substances he said he would include, some of which he showed us. He told us he would gather hundreds more relics like this to mix into the clay of the Earth Treasure Vases.

It would take a year to gather the relics, craft the vases, and accomplish the practice to prepare the vases and empower them for our use. Lama Tsultrim promised to oversee the process and make arrangements to get the vases to us. The abbot made sure we knew that when planting the vases, there would be nothing special to do—that the vases themselves would do the work. He said to place them in the ground carefully and protect them well, but to leave their resting places unmarked.

I was moved to tears at the unconditional collaboration the abbot of Tengboche offered us, immediately recognizing a great need and responding without a moment's hesitation. I left our meeting feeling undone and could not control my tears. He had given so much. Lama Tsultrim's mother took my hand and led me down the steps. How grateful I was to have her motherly presence close by.

We met with Tengboche Rinpoche once more the next day before we left. Smiling a lot, we acknowledged what we planned to do and our commitment to do it. I struggled to express the inspiration I had received from him, the gratitude I felt, and the hope that had been kindled in me to face our despoiled Earth with a possible antidote. We prayed our efforts might benefit beings for many years to come and truly serve our beloved planet. As we left, I gave him a beautiful clear crystal to symbolize our intention and bond.

After our auspicious meeting with the abbot, we headed down the trail toward civilization once again. I walked the path as if assisted by an invisible energy supporting me. Everywhere I turned, I saw things I had not seen before. Each rock seemed alive; a clear light pervaded everything and cast a special glow on the land. Though we walked for hours, I was unaffected by the effort, as I was filled with joy and peace.

As we crossed the river and started up the other side of the trail, Lama Tsultrim hesitated at a big boulder. "This was where the first lama of the Khumbu stopped to get out of the rain," he explained. "He leaned against the rock, and his body was imprinted there." He pointed at a dent in the rock. As Lama Tsultrim told of the lama "flying through the Khumbu Valley on the back of a tiger," I was struck by the utter sincerity in his voice and became aware that these were a people who still believed in supernatural powers and lived in a world "behind the veil," one many of the rest of us left a long time ago. In that moment I knew the veil had lifted and I was on the other side, in a realm where it was possible to imprint a stone and fly on the back of a tiger. These things were possible . . . anything was possible. I remembered tales from long ago when we all lived like this—and it seemed this time was suddenly alive and well. As we continued walking, every stupa we passed reminded me of the enlightened awareness that permeates all that is, a portal into that other world.

I learned that this region of Nepal is known as a beyul—a hidden land where the veil between the worlds is thin. These hidden valleys, it is said, are themselves like concealed treasures waiting for the right time to be discovered. They are protected and lie beyond ordinary reality in a realm where sensitivity is heightened and spiritual understanding is nurtured. Food and shelter are supposed to be available without effort, and mystical texts, sacred images, and, some say, even the fountain of youth can be found there. In *The Way to Shambhala,* Edwin Bernbaum writes that Sangye Tenzin, a lama scholar who lived in the Khumbu region, told him, "'The real treasure concealed in a hidden valley is something intangible . . . What's really precious in a given place is the special blessings it gives.' This blessing he referred to is a kind of spiritual power or radiation that is supposed to have a positive effect on whoever is open to it . . . The spiritual influence of the place, something in the air or in the ground itself, will help to clear the mind and awaken the heart, the two basic prerequisites for attaining enlightenment."[4]

The Tibetan Buddhist scholar Ian Baker also writes about these places, which he encounters on his explorations. In his book *The Heart of the World: A Journey to Tibet's Lost Paradise,* Baker notes that these realms often "remain sealed from the outer world not only by towering mountains, dense jungles, and glacier-covered passes, . . . but by protective veils placed there by Padmasambhava. Only those with the karma to do so can enter the depths of the hidden lands."[5] Baker's teacher Chatral Rinpoche goes on to say, "The beyul that Padmasambhava established in Tibet are not literal arcadias, but paradises for Buddhist practice, with multiple dimensions corresponding to increasingly subtle levels of perception."[6]

Walking through the Khumbu in Nepal, I understood these were not just legends but stories describing real experiences and places. I was connecting with a lineage of transmission that was keeping them alive through people like Lama Tsultrim, who had not yet left that world behind in disbelief. I had entered rarefied air and I was grateful for the brief taste: I had been given a practice from this very place whose effects could not be measured on the basis of our contemporary conditioning.

Charok Rinpoche died the following year. I felt blessed to have encountered such a holy man and received his simple remedy: "Fill Earth Treasure Vases with offerings and prayers, seal them with your best intentions and plant them like seeds to bring protection and healing to the whole area. Just put them in the ground; they'll do the work."[7]

CHAPTER TWO

STEPPING STONES

The year after my pilgrimage to Charok, the vases arrived in painted metal trunks packed in shredded coconut fiber. Although the answer to the question I asked of the old lama had been given, I had no idea what to do with the Earth Treasure Vases. The magnitude of the world's problems was so overwhelming and the assignment so daunting that I put the trunks in my closet and tried to forget about them. I was not ready to take up the practice of burying the vases and fulfilling this mission.

I did not know it then, but my seemingly disconnected life experiences, adventures, and expeditions, both inner and outer, had, in fact, been taking me down the very path I needed to traverse. From stepping stone to stepping stone, across rough terrain and through dark forests, I was trying to find the way to fulfill my yearning for wholeness and meaning.

I sensed the Earth Treasure Vases would wait for me. First, though, I needed to understand a little more about the steps I had taken—before the vases would demand I put everything to work to fulfill the purpose of my life. I had not prepared my own vessel adequately and knew I needed to apply myself to the study and practice of the dharma.

Over the course of the next decade, I studied with many teachers in the Tibetan Buddhist tradition and practiced in the Zen tradition of Thich Nhat Hanh. I was soaking up the teachings—attending retreats, reading, studying, and practicing for many long hours. It was a time of feeding the deep spiritual hunger within me that was finally being nourished through the teachings of the lineage masters. I felt as if I had found an inexhaustible treasure trove of wisdom, and I did not need to look any further. It was thrilling to think I would never reach the end of what was being revealed. My love for the teachings only grew as I opened my heart and mind to the teachers whose capacity to illuminate the extraordinary path of the dharma, were speaking to me powerfully. As I devoted myself more and more to practicing the teachings I was being given, a new way of seeing was being born through dreams and insights that guided me on the path of awakening.

In 1993 I began the practices called ngöndro under the guidance of Gyatrul Rinpoche. A charming and traditional old gap-toothed lama with a great sense of humor, Gyatrul Rinpoche would become my most beloved Tibetan root teacher. Rinpoche had the habit of giving his students funny nicknames and was a terrible tease. My soon-to-be husband, Dr. Hugh Wheir, who was a veterinarian working to protect endangered sea turtles in Mexico at the time, was dubbed Turtle Dundee, and Rinpoche often called me Octopus for the paisley-patterned leggings I wore that looked like an octopus to him. Occasionally he also called me Sausage, but I never quite knew where that came from. He always kept us on our toes and never allowed us to take ourselves too seriously. Rinpoche's light-hearted touch opened the door for me to begin the ngöndro practices under his guidance.

In the Tibetan tradition, once one has decided upon a lineage to practice in, one is encouraged to go into retreat and complete one hundred thousand repetitions each of the four sections of ngöndro practice. These so-called "preliminary" practices establish a strong foundation for the dharma teachings to take root in one's life. They are profoundly transformational and require a huge commitment of time and attention over many years.

During my first solo ngöndro retreat, much became clear as I practiced deeply, no longer dipping in my toes, but now jumping in and getting wet. One night after many days of intensive practice (four two-hour sessions a day), I vividly dreamed of countless people in my life going back over many years. In the dream I understood each of them and their situation in great detail. At first the dream sequences were quite normal; I made a connection to each individual and saw their truth and mine in relationship to them. But gradually these connections and associated images sped up so that eventually there was an endless progression of people and places and times passing through my awareness so quickly I could not keep up with, focus on, or attach to any of them. This continued for a long time until I understood that they were all fleeting and ungraspable, seemingly real but impossible to hold on to, however important I might have thought they actually were.

When I awoke in my retreat cabin, I attempted to write the dream down, but soon realized it would be impossible to capture it all. As I looked around the room, it was as if the dream continued: I was fixating on everything that appeared in rapid succession before my eyes, yet I could not grasp at anything or make it "real" by naming or labeling it.

I saw that my conditioned way of thinking invests all things, whether person, relationship, or object—animate or inanimate—with an identity as "other," projecting a separate identity onto *everything.* I saw that this is how we uphold our sense of self, identifying with "self" as the subject, and the object of our perception as "other"—an insidious habit of mind that labels everything, creating the separation between me and you, this and that—solidifying our sense of self until it becomes fixed and "real." But in that timeless moment I recognized how it is the nonexistent "I" who projects self-nature onto everything—and suddenly it all fell away and I was left with a sense of *non-self.*

The teachings call this the realization of being "empty of a sense of self." There was no separation between "me" and the arising of phenomena. Little "me"—the one who creates these separations in order to build up my sense of self—was momentarily seen for what it is: a fabrication perpetuating the illusion of being separate and alone.

I was beginning to see more and more clearly how my life was like a dream, and all that had come before that retreat in a little cabin way up on the side of a mountain in northern New Mexico was a synchronous succession of experiences arising in my life to take me where I needed to go. As I awoke from the dream, I sensed how all the stages of my life were connected and had led me to that very moment.

• • •

I came of age in Northern California during the heyday of the counterculture movement in San Francisco. Like all my friends, I started getting stoned at a young age. I smoked marijuana and hung out on Telegraph Avenue in Berkeley, near the university where the Free Speech movement was born, wearing hippie dresses I made from Indian bedspreads. I marched for peace against the war in Vietnam in Golden Gate Park and went to concerts at the Fillmore Auditorium. My parents were civic leaders in Oakland with a strong interest in local politics. Our home was a hub for political events and dinner parties ripe with interesting conversations. It was a privileged life, but not one without the awareness of other lives less so. Living in Oakland in the 1960s and early 1970s, it was impossible to overlook the gap between rich and poor and the segregation of Black and White. These issues were of great concern to my parents and that concern was instilled in me.

I appreciated my parents' community service, but somehow I did not feel I belonged in my family. I rejected my mother's deeply ingrained expectations that I fit in and rebelled against my upper-middle-class conditioning. Already a wider view was coming into focus, and as I watched my three older sisters devote themselves to getting married and having children, I yearned for a different life purpose and was grateful to have a choice about being a mother—or not. The planet was already overpopulated, and before bringing new lives into the world, I wanted to follow my own path, not the one laid out for me by society.

I was also compelled to find a way to fill the spiritual vacancy I felt but had no tools to address this in the context of my upbringing. Although she would never admit it, my mother had a spiritual connection to nature, even though she came from a long line of atheists. My father grew up in Christian Science but rejected that religion when his mother and brother both died young for lack of medical care. I was told I could go to church if I wanted to, but my parents were no help getting me there.

By the time I was sixteen, my rebellious nature had become so strong that I left my parents' home and moved into an apartment with an older friend, with the unexpected support of my father. I finished high school in San Francisco at seventeen and soon left the Bay Area, going as far away as I possibly could. I had no interest in college—I wanted to travel the world. Incredibly, my parents let me go.

With a pack on my back, I flew to Europe with a friend. Several months later, we joined my father and uncle, who was a great adventurer, on a dog-sledding expedition in Greenland. This was my first experience with an intact Indigenous culture, and I was thrilled. The shaman who drummed himself into a trance carried me with him into an altered state that lingered for years somewhere in the recesses of my little life. I had opened briefly to a vastly other world and tasted a different way of perceiving.

After Greenland, I was hired by the same adventure company we had used for the dog-sledding expedition, to work as a cook on trips taking tourists by Land Rover into the wilds of Afghanistan and Iran. It was 1973. I met up with the crew in Turkey, and we traveled overland on the old Silk Road, entering a world as far away from the world I came from as could possibly be. We had been in Afghanistan and Iran for some months and were preparing to meet our next group in Kabul when General Mohammad Daud Khan, brother-in-law to Afghanistan's king, Mohammed Zahir Shah, staged a coup and overthrew the monarchy. During the night, tanks rolled in to occupy Kabul's main square in a show of force. The next morning we went there and discovered women had placed fresh flowers in the gun barrels of all the tanks. It seemed like a pretty peaceful takeover, but we knew we had to get out.

I was sorry to leave Afghanistan. I had been entranced by the nomadic women in their black tents, decorated with striking silver jewelry studded with amber, garnets, or lapis lazuli. They wore dresses like the ones I had dressed in on Telegraph Avenue in Berkeley. They pulled me into their world, and a part of me yearned to stay. The dignity and fierce independence of the horsemen, riding Arabian stallions as fast as the wind, with turbans flying out across the desert, made a lasting impression.

We explored the northern route through the country to Mazar-i-Sharif alongside camel caravans and spent time in the lovely city of Herat near the border of Iran. We crossed through the center of Afghanistan on a track in the sand to visit the legendary Minaret of Jam. I shopped for vegetables in the market bazaars, and we camped every night under the stars for months on end. The incredible bluest-of-blue Band-e Amir lakes reflecting the red-desert cliffs in their still waters continues to appear in my dreams. And in Bamiyan, I saw towering Buddha statues carved in the rock with cave-like monastic cells tucked all around them. Sadly, that great wonder of the world has been destroyed by the Taliban, and Afghanistan has been tragically devastated by years of war.

Departing Kabul in July of 1973, we drove through the no-man's land separating Afghanistan and Pakistan, where guns of all kinds were being replicated for black-market trade, over the famous Khyber Pass. Our next group was flying into Islamabad, and we scrambled to arrange a different tour in northwest Pakistan. We headed for Hunza Valley, a faraway corner of the world close to the border of China known for the longevity of its people. The high mountains of the Karakoram stood sentinel above, and the Indus River flowed glacier blue-gray at their base, cutting through the enormous mountain ranges to create beautiful valleys untouched by time. Fruit trees blossomed in carefully cultivated terraces along the way. We passed through Gilgit and an unforgettable place called Chitral where the people are said to be descendants of Alexander the Great. It was the first time the people had ever seen the likes of us, and they were shy. But they welcomed us with a dance, and later showed us their village. The women wore long, dark handwoven dresses with silver chains draped like belts around their waists and numerous red beads around their necks. They had the most glorious long braids, plaited in all kinds of creative ways, into which they had tucked fresh pink carnations down the length of their hair for the occasion.

We traversed the Swat Valley, and for the first time I saw ancient stupas and tattered prayer flags flying in the hills. I wandered around in a kind of daze as if something was . . . different there. I sensed another world revealing itself to me briefly. It got my attention—a kind of recognition, perhaps, like something familiar I couldn't quite place. Years later, after I became a student of the Dzogchen teachings of Vajrayana Buddhism, I learned that the great saint Padmasambhava had been born in the Swat Valley. Here, in the land of Oddiyana,[1] I sensed for the first time a hidden realm I now know was a beyul. Something awakened in me that would be reawakened years later in Nepal on the trail descending from Tengboche and Charok.

Our group had one more tour before going home. From Pakistan, we were allowed to cross back into Afghanistan and travel on to Iran. In the old Persian capital of Isfahan, we had a night off from our duties with the group of tourists we were hosting, and after making sure the group was happily ensconced in a nice hotel, our crew went out to have a few beers in a local disco. I took to the dance floor with one of the drivers, a kindly mechanic from Wales who was my friend.

But I didn't realize that Jack, the man we worked for, who had become my lover, was insanely jealous. When we got back to the caravan park where we were camping, I sat up with a cup of tea after everyone else had gone to bed. Suddenly, Jack appeared in the darkness from around the side of one of the Land Rovers. In a moment that would become a marker in time, delineating my life before and after that fateful evening, Jack loomed over me, then leaned back and with all his force, kicked me in the face with his heavy boot. With the wind knocked out of me, I collapsed onto the ground. He bent down and grabbed me by the hair and dragged me into the bushes, where he proceeded to beat me wildly and attempt to strangle me. I screamed for my life, but even though the campsite was packed with people and our crew was all around, *no one came.*

It was my friend, the Welsh mechanic, who heard my screams from some distance away and came running as Jack pressed his big hands into my neck. I could no longer scream; I was unable to breathe. But the arrival of my friend got Jack off of me, and I ran away.

I locked myself in one of the vehicles. Jack tried to break in, but by then the others came to my rescue and prevented him. He threatened to leave me there on my own the next day, but was finally convinced to take me with them to Tehran. He had conditions: I would hide behind dark glasses to cover my black and blue face and promise not to speak to any of the members of our group. After the group disbanded, we were each left to pick up the pieces and make our way home. But the company we worked for had gone bankrupt and our departures were delayed for lack of funds. My mechanic friend, Taffy, took care of me until we could leave on our own. Not only was I unsafe around Jack, but in that culture, if I did not cover my head and face with a scarf and wear a long skirt, men would follow me and put their hands up my skirt on the street in broad daylight.

Finally, we received enough money to make the return trip overland to Europe. I got off in Greece to stay with the family my sister married into, then flew home to California in time for Christmas.

• • •

When I returned from Afghanistan, Pakistan, and Iran, I needed to recover from entering those other worlds—and almost losing my life. I could not tell my parents what had happened. I could barely talk at all. I was reeling not only from the incident with Jack but also from immersing myself in such another world for so long. My perspective was forever altered from having gone "as far away as I could." If I thought I did not fit in with my family before, now it was certain. There was no way they would ever understand what I had been through, much less be sympathetic. As a young woman still in her teens, I knew my experiences would not have been believed or supported. They did not want to hear these things—and they did not ask.

I needed to heal, so I migrated to the mountains of Colorado. I lived in an old log cabin in the uninhabited high country of Specie

Mesa. The old homestead on the mesa was known as Cowboy Heaven and had once been the last stop on the roundup before bringing the cattle to the train. It was a five-mile ski in the wintertime from the main road and twenty-five miles to the nearest town of Telluride. Together with my friend Janna, I hauled water from a crystal-clear spring at the bottom of a hill, carrying two jerricans down the steep slope and filling them slowly and carefully from the little pool in the ground that bubbled up from the base of the trees in a quiet aspen grove. In the fall, we brought in many cords of wood. Standing dead aspen burns quickly, but is easy to cut and bountiful. Together we chopped wood each winter to heat the cabin and cooked on an old wood cook stove. I remember the way the leaves on the aspen trees changed colors season to season: how tiny green buds would appear in the spring and unfurl themselves in the warmth, and how the stark white branches would catch the deep snow in winter and the tall snow drifts would wing around the wide porch of the big, warm cabin.

Janna and I became amateur herbalists. We gathered wild herbs in the pristine aspen groves, studied their medicinal properties, and set up a laboratory for our herbal healing work. We read poetry and studied the kabbalah and the cards of the tarot. Living at an elevation of ten thousand feet and wandering in the meadows at midsummer, ingesting magic mushrooms and dancing in handmade moccasins, I again entered another world and was opened to an awareness of something so much larger than myself. The veil of illusion lifted, and I saw the world of consensus reality for what it is. By living on the land, chopping wood, carrying water, and looking through different eyes, slowly, slowly, my broken body and damaged heart were repaired. That little piece of heaven did its work in me.

Living on the mesa was my first awakening to a spiritual path, a path of nature. Time in Colorado stretched out through the seasons for four years until, in the late 1970s, I knew it was time to return to California. I was interested in studying the healing arts, and the lamas had begun to come to San Francisco. In the 1950s and 1960s, many Tibetans fled their homeland due to an escalation of the long-standing conflict with the Chinese government. During this time, the teachings of the Vajrayana were brought out of Tibet and shared with the world. This great spiritual tradition became available where it was needed, and I was hearing its call.

The sixteenth Karmapa and his entourage performed the famous Black Hat ceremony, and when His Eminence Kalu Rinpoche arrived on the scene, I spontaneously took refuge with him. The dharma doors opened, and, in the presence of the lamas from Tibet, I tasted something I could not forget. I moved to Los Angeles to continue my studies of bodywork, and incredibly, the Indian Guru Sri Baba Muktananda moved in down the street. For months and months, I sat in his presence to get my daily dose of shaktipat.

My spiritual calling grew more intense in the early 1980s. I moved back to Northern California and began to study Zen. In spite of my restless nature, I learned to sit still. When I met Thich Nhat Hanh, who had been nominated for the Nobel Peace Prize by Dr. Martin Luther King Jr., my heart opened. He gave a talk in Berkeley, and I was deeply moved by the way he brought his dharma practice together with social activism. He spoke of "Engaged Buddhism" and counseled us to slow down in order to make peace with ourselves if we wanted to see peace in the world. I yearned for world peace, and Thich Nhat Hanh's teachings pointed the way.

At this same time, I was part of a small group inspired by the fifth-century-BC Chinese philosopher Mo Tzu, headed up by the former president of Oberlin College, Bob Fuller. We were working to understand the causes of war, but I cared more about peace. We traveled to Egypt, Israel, and Palestine. In Jerusalem, lying on the ground near the Wailing Wall, tired from all the talk, I was suddenly overcome with intense emotion and began to cry. The wails from the centuries of endless war that had taken place there permeated my awareness. Shaking with the screams I heard echoing through time, I felt the grass under my cheek and sensed the old rocks nearby holding the pain of the Earth, and I heard the land crying from centuries of violence. Deeply weary of the conflict in the world, this experience made me wonder, Are there any cultures that are peaceful? What can we learn from them?

Upon my return, I was motivated to organize a gathering to explore the causes of peace at the Ojai Foundation, a community directed at that time by Joan Halifax, now the Roshi of Upaya Zen Center in Santa Fe. Joan suggested we invite the very embodiment of peace, Thich Nhat Hanh, to open the Peaceful Cultures Council.

Forest fires were raging around the Ojai Foundation in Southern California the summer of 1985, and we were almost forced to evacuate. Instead, helicopters fighting the fires filled up with water directly below where we gathered on the hill with Thay. (Pronounced "Thai." Thay means "teacher," and it was what Thich Nhat Hanh was affectionately called.) Soot fell from the sky, and a dry, dangerous heat enveloped us in a tinderbox. Each time the choppers flew overhead, their deafening sound made it impossible for Thay to continue speaking. As he grew silent, breathing in and out with mindfulness, we realized how reminiscent the scene was of the war he had lived through in Vietnam.

Everyone who attended that retreat was transformed by meeting Thich Nhat Hanh—I certainly was. I believe it was his second visit to the country since the 1960s, when he had come to the US to teach at Princeton University and Columbia University and had met Dr. King. Upon his return to Vietnam, he was not allowed back in his own country and lived in exile in France until he was finally able to return to his homeland at the end of his life.[2]

When the retreat was over, I packed my bags and traveled to Asia for the first time, visiting India, Nepal, Thailand, and Ladakh. Bhutan was calling, too, as an example of a contemporary kingdom dedicated to maintaining peace, in part, through implementing the notion of "Gross National Happiness" into their system of governance. There, I met my first teacher of Vajrayana Buddhism, who took me under his wing and introduced me to the feminine deity Tara, who would become my great spiritual ally. World peace seemed elusive even in protected places like Bhutan, but as I immersed myself in Buddhist cultures, the practice of meditation became part of my path to inner peace.

On the way home after many months traveling in Asia, I stopped in France to see Thay, whose simple teachings and unforgettable presence had impacted me deeply. There were only a few people living at his new community, Plum Village, and we enjoyed intimate conversations over cups of tea in his simple hut. During the war in Vietnam, Thay had founded the Order of Interbeing for his lay students who were social activists.[3] I was invited to join the Order in a formal ceremony.

Thay rang the bell, invited us to breathe with awareness, and helped us to return to our true selves. The need to look outside was tempered as I learned to relax into the present moment as he so beautifully taught. It was time to look within.

But I mourned leaving Asia. I loved the Asian cultures and felt as if I had found my spiritual home in that part of the world. I did not yet realize that home is within. One day, Thay took me aside and told me, "Asia is here. Here is Asia," pointing to his heart.

As part of one's commitment to joining the Order of Interbeing, one agrees to take sixty days in retreat every year. These "days of mindfulness" can be a time to invite others to practice with us as a sangha. Thay gave me a little bell to begin and end periods of sitting and walking meditation, and the bell soon became a big part of my life. I started to lead meditations in California, and in 1987, when I moved to Santa Fe, I founded the Open Way Sangha to continue the practice in community.[4] I had found my path home within my awakening heart.

After a number of retreats with Thich Nhat Hanh in the US and France, in 1992 he suggested I travel to Vietnam with Joan Halifax and one of his senior nuns, Sister Annabel Laity, and to visit the spiritual home of his lineage on his behalf. We were his first Western students to visit his homeland since he had been exiled. It was a profound honor to travel there for Thay many years before he was allowed to return. By then I had met my husband, Hugh Wheir, who accompanied us.

Thay had given us the handwritten manuscript of his book *Transformation and Healing* to deliver to his root temple in Hue, along with a photo of him as a novice, which I carried. An elder nun, Sư

Bà, who had sewn his robes when he became a monk at age sixteen, looked after us. Thay had written ahead requesting we be served all his favorite foods, which he had listed. She and her nuns cooked us an unforgettable meal with twenty different dishes lovingly prepared. Hugh and I will always remember this as the most memorable meal of our lifetime, and when I commented to Sư Bà, "This is food for gods and goddesses," she replied, "No. This is food for monks and nuns!"

Hugh and I were married by Thich Nhat Hanh on May 1 of the following year, 1993, in Plum Village. Thay and the monks and nuns of Plum Village performed a beautiful, humble wedding ceremony and blessed us with their loving support.

The next year, I was informed that Thay wanted to make me a teacher. I did not think I was deserving and certainly did not feel ready. So, after going into retreat to contemplate his invitation and look deeply at this opportunity, as it was suggested I do, I told him, "No, thank you." But Thay's straightforward handwritten response via fax was:

Dear Cynthia,
It is the Teacher's responsibility to give the transmission and it is the student's responsibility to accept it.

Love and trust,
Thay

Needless to say, I accepted, and at six in the morning on August 11, 1994, in the lower hamlet at Plum Village, I was the first of twenty lay students that day to receive dharma transmission from Thich Nhat Hanh in the Lamp Transmission ceremony and become a dharma teacher, or dharmacharya.

• • •

While deepening my connection to Thay's Vietnamese Zen tradition, I also was pursuing my interest in the Tibetan tradition and became a student of Gangteng Tulku Rinpoche and Namkhai Norbu Rinpoche. Then His Holiness Dudjom Rinpoche entered my dreams very powerfully, and I had a fortuitous meeting with Gyatrul Rinpoche, the lama who called me Sausage. Gyatrul Rinpoche was Dudjom Rinpoche's representative in the West, and upon hearing my dreams, he insisted that I receive the transmission for the entire Dudjom Tersar lineage, which he offered to transmit. He came to Santa Fe, and, for a whole month, gave all the empowerments of the lineage to the large group of us who gathered in my living room.

It was during another ngöndro retreat, after much discipline and effort during an intense three-month practice period, that I found myself in a state of deep relaxation. I let go into the most exquisite sense of openness I had ever felt and realized that this is the state pointed to in the teachings when we are instructed to relax without effort and rest in awareness itself. In the Dzogchen teachings, this is referred to as rigpa, or the nature of mind.

Most of the time we make such an effort (about everything!)—such a big deal, as Gyatrul Rinpoche would say. But this is counterproductive. Of course, we must make an effort to train, but to sustain the "View" of rigpa and integrate it into our everyday lives, we must learn to relax completely. This is the key that lets in the light. And from that place of total relaxation and letting go, I became aware of the light in *everything*. I experienced *light* as the very nature and expression of love and compassion. This experience so completely overwhelmed me that it changed my life.

When I later spoke to Gyatrul Rinpoche, he confirmed my experiences, encouraged me, and told me to keep going. But "don't make a big deal," he said. Gyatrul Rinpoche had a knack for never letting any of us get away with thinking we were special. He taught me to remember that I am nobody, and when I can remember that, the teachings are able to penetrate this "old skin bag" in a useful way.

From all these experiences, a door of perception opened, and it was made clear to me that each of us has the capacity for enlightenment if we stay on the path and cultivate the ground of our being, which is none other than the awareness of non-self. With practice, it is as if the veil that separates us from the reality of pure energy lifts or is peeled away, and we see "as it is." This view is always here, never separate; it's just that we don't normally cultivate the conditions that make it accessible.

Looking deeply, we see there really is no place where I leave off and you begin. You may look like an old tree and I may appear as a bird in the clear blue sky. "Please call me by my true names," Thich Nhat Hanh once wrote, "so I can hear all my cries and laughter at once, so I can see that my joy and pain are one. Please call me by my true names, so I can wake up, and the door of my heart could be left open, the door of compassion."[5]

• • •

Despite the dark passages, through chopping wood and carrying water and the healing power of mindful breathing, along with the budding realization of how life is but a dream, I was eventually able to open to the light guiding me on the path of this life.

"Slowly, slowly, step by step, we shall arrive," Gyatrul Rinpoche used to say. And true enough, I began to find my way, stepping from stone to stone with surer and surer footing—the purpose of my life becoming clear.

It was time to take the Earth Treasure Vases out of the closet.

CHAPTER THREE
THE TERMA

It had been highly untraditional: Lama Ngawang Tsultrim Zangpo, who had guided me in Nepal, had followed the instructions of both Charok Rinpoche and the abbot at Tengboche, and after crafting the vases, gave me explicit directions to fill, seal, and bury the vases as I saw fit.

Still, when I unpacked the clay pots and set them on my altar at home, I was more and more overwhelmed by the assignment and the instructions to "put them in the ground—they'll do the work." I had no idea what to do and thought it couldn't be that simple. I wanted help, but the lamas I studied with were not interested. I came to feel that, to some of them, focusing my dharma on the Earth was a distraction from the main practices I was doing.

The practice of the Earth Treasure Vases, like many teachings in the Tibetan tradition, is considered a terma or "hidden spiritual treasure."[1] The Nyingma (Old School) lineage of Tibetan Buddhism holds that in the eighth century, the great teacher who brought Buddhism to Tibet, Padmasambhava, and his principal consort, Yeshe Tsogyal, concealed certain teachings to be revealed at the appropriate time in the future by "treasure revealers" known as tertöns. Padmasambhava made many prophecies about the future and knew that the world was not ready for all he had to transmit. So, in order to preserve the teachings and ensure their blessings would bring benefit to future beings, he and Yeshe Tsogyal concealed countless termas in the Earth and in the mindstreams of his disciples who brought them forth in later incarnations when the time was ripe.

When a terma's time has come, it may physically appear as a scroll or text. Sometimes, even a ritual implement or statue is uncovered in the ground, in a cave, embedded in a rock, or in a lake or stream. Termas can also appear to the tertön as a vision in the sky in front of them or in a dream. These visions and dreams catalyze the realization of a latent terma, and when the practitioner awakens, they bring it forth. In 1984 one of my teachers, Namkhai Norbu Rinpoche, received a terma in a dream. In a state of contemplation that resulted in automatic writing, he wrote the whole thing down. To confirm it was a terma, a few days later he wrote the whole thing down again. Comparing the two texts, they were exactly alike except for several differing words that shared the same meaning.

Many of the great masters of the Nyingma lineage were tertöns, and many of the texts studied and practiced today are termas, including the Earth Treasure Vase practice. Padmasambhava gave specific instructions for the creation of treasure vases to assist with the healing of the environment and the restoration of vital energy in future degenerate times when beings would suffer from sickness and disease, poverty and starvation, and weapons of mass destruction and war.

Before he left Tibet for the Copper-Colored Mountain at the end of his life, Padmasambhava concealed the terma of the Earth Treasure Vases and requested the dharma protectors to safeguard it until it could be brought forth to heal the environment during the dregs of time.

It was clear that time was now.

Although the Earth Treasure Vase practice has not been widely taught, it has been quietly carried out by all the various lineages of Tibetan Buddhism. The late Lobsang Lhalungpa, who was a Buddhist scholar and served the government of His Holiness the Dalai Lama in Lhasa before fleeing Tibet, once told me that Earth Treasure Vases were crafted, consecrated, and distributed on an annual basis in old Tibet. The late Dudjom Rinpoche, supreme head of the Nyingma lineage and a tertön, revealed an Earth Treasure Vase practice in 1929 when he was still a youth in Tibet. Another great lama of the Nyingma lineage who passed away in 1991, Dilgo Khyentse Rinpoche, recognized the Earth needed special assistance in these times and requested six thousand Earth Treasure Vases to be made. Today, these Peace Vases are being distributed through his dharma heir, Dzongsar Khyentse Rinpoche.[2]

It was after receiving the vases that I met Gyatrul Rinpoche, who transmitted all the terma teachings of Dudjom Rinpoche's entire lineage to me and my dharma community, the Open Way Sangha. I was struck by Gyatrul Rinpoche's comment at the time: "If we have encountered the teachings, we are all tertön. We have this memory."

Little did I know how the terma of the Earth Treasure Vases would ripen over the years. For me, the conjunction of my karmic connection to these teachings and my pilgrimage to meet the old wise man in the cave served to create a quickening for the terma to arise in my life and be put to work.

• • •

It took me five years to unwrap the Earth Treasure Vases and bring them out of their trunks in the closet into the light of day. The responsibility was almost unbearable, and yet I could not ignore the assignment I had been given. Then one day I was compelled to face them directly. All by myself, with no other helping hands, I carefully brought out all the vases, dusted them off, and set them on my altar. Several vases had broken in transit. Lama Tsultrim had gathered precious medicines and mixed these into the clay so every piece held promise, carrying healing for the Earth like a homeopathic remedy. I collected each little shard into the bottom of one of the broken vases for safekeeping, and counted thirty intact empty vessels.

Where in the world was I to begin? I brought a colorful globe onto the floor where I was hunkered down in front of the altar and spun it round and round. Gazing at the whole Earth in my hands, and the vases that had come to me, I called on all the spiritual forces I could imagine to help me see the way through my feelings of overwhelm about this enormous assignment. I did not know where to go with the vases, but I trusted there was something else operating that was inexplicably profound, which I could not yet fathom. So I did the only thing I knew to do: I placed the globe on my altar along with the vases and waited for clarity to come. I had asked the lamas to help guide the process for me. But they did not get involved. I realized I had to stop looking for an outside authority to tell me what to do and instead trust that, with all the teachings I had received, the strength of my own inner wisdom would guide me.

As a child I never knew how to pray and yearned to be taken under the wing of some divine being and instructed. I imagined her like an angel dressed in white, leaning in close to whisper in my ear from the branches of the big deodar tree outside my second-floor bedroom window. We didn't go to church in my family and no one talked to me about spiritual things. For years whenever I tried to pray, I felt so awkward, having never been taught how to open my heart to talk to the holy.

With the thirty vessels lined up before me, empty and needing to be buried, I longed for that angel at my window again. I wished for clear instructions to counter my uncertainty and was sure there was a "right" way to do this, if only I knew what that was. And all the while I felt the sense of urgency coming from the Earth; my heart grew wild with yearning to offer the vases in such a way that would truly make a difference. But still I felt so inadequate. I paced, I practiced, I wrote in my journal. I consulted the I Ching. I waited for guidance to come.

As challenging as my relationship with my mother had been, and in spite of my rebelliousness and my need to distance myself from her, she had given me the gift of an active and dependable imagination. And while she didn't bring me to church or teach me to pray, she connected me intimately to nature. Through her, I inherited a love for Mother Earth.

My mother's mother insisted on the living presence of fairies and elves, and my mother, Florence, passed this on to me. My grandmother had a special friend who drew and sculpted these magical beings, and my mom had a treasure chest on a high shelf where she kept the paper dolls of fairies, elves, and other wondrous creatures this friend of the family had made. They were, perhaps, her connection to the spirit world. She occasionally allowed me to pull them out of their manila envelope and play with them carefully. On the envelope, "Florence's Paper Dolls. Do not touch. Please note: a fine of $50,000.00 for touching" was written in her youthful hand. They came alive when I held them.

In the summer, she and I would go outside at dusk and build fairy houses with mossy rocks and fallen tree branches. We gathered flowers and offered the fairies tiny plates of cake and, in the tops of acorns, water that we imagined was a wine-like nectar. Often the fairies came and danced in the night while I was asleep. In the morning, I would find little notes written in a tiny scrawl, telling me about their adventures. They always made quite a mess and left cake crumbs everywhere!

My mother also celebrated the life of the Original Peoples of California and told me a lot about the Miwok who inhabited the land where we stayed each summer by Clear Lake. I found obsidian arrowheads along the shore and kept them in a shoebox—my own treasure chest. In the afternoons we would walk down the road to an old oak tree covered with thick green moss that we called the Wish Tree. She would lift me up onto a big wide branch and instruct me to close my eyes. "Where do you want to go?" she would ask. "How do you want to travel?" Then we'd go—by winged horse or flying carpet and sometimes by steamship or camel—to places like Persia or India, China or Timbuktu. Always Timbuktu. She instilled an excitement for adventure in me, and I was thrilled at the thought of traveling the world and exploring foreign cultures.

My mother made up many stories, painting elaborate pictures in my mind's eye through her telling. She loved to read out loud. Sometimes I pulled out her art books so she would talk about the great artists of our time as we poured over the reproductions. She read constantly, and when I was older, I remember her being terribly affected by Rachel Carson's *Silent Spring*. Whenever I was bored or didn't know what to do, Florence would suggest some creative activity to point me in a fruitful direction.

Because of my mother, I had a deep well of creative imagination to draw from, and without even realizing it, I slowly formulated a way to respond to the terma that had come to me. Paradoxically, since some of the lamas I studied with did not show much interest in the treasure vases, a space opened up for the practice to come alive in a new way. I was free to imagine, create, and even innovate in response to the vessels on my altar. In my meditations I began to see, to visualize, and to enact ways to feed the spirit of life on Earth through making sacred offerings that reflected my deepest wishes. Soon the vases and I would travel on pilgrimages to the lands that beckoned.

• • •

The vases slowly took on a life of their own, despite my feelings of inadequacy. It helped when others responded to my invitation to meet on the full moon to meditate with the pots. Our little Open Way Sangha, which was really just an informal collection of friends, took on a shared sense of purpose, and each month people brought their own imaginative and meaningful offerings that symbolized healing and protection for the Earth. We were quickened by droughts and fires and motivated by the lack of rain and snow in our region. Everyone sensed life was out of balance, and no one knew what to do. Maybe this was a remedy? We threw ourselves into it.

We were gardeners, construction workers, craftsmen and builders, artists and writers, doctors, nurses, and activists. Our meditation practice was a way to stay centered and find peace individually, but now we had a larger purpose. Everyone cared about the Earth and the ecosystems we loved and wanted to protect. After our practice, we would gather in the kitchen to be nourished by the food everyone brought: Elizabeth's warm polentas, David's hearty salads, Walter's homemade bread, plates of fruit, and, always, Joanna's chocolate cake. Our community spirit was well fed as we explored how we could work with this ancient terma in ways relevant to the challenges we faced today.

We chose the full moon as our time for meditation because the exact time of the full moon is a moment shared around the whole planet. It is said in many spiritual traditions that the effects of our prayers are multiplied many thousandfold during the time of the full moon. It is a powerful support for meditation, a time to come into alignment with the natural rhythms of the whole Earth and the entire cosmos.

In those early days, our full moon gatherings were experimental as we drew from the teachings and practices we had learned and applied them to working with the Earth Treasure Vases. We sat in a circle, the vases on a low altar in the center with candles placed in the four directions. Sitting in a circle was important to dispel any shred of hierarchy and bring us down to Earth, all on the same level. I always rang a bell to begin and told the story of meeting the old wise man in the cave.

As my apprenticeship to the little holy vessels commenced, I soon saw the need for a simple guided meditation that anyone from any culture or tradition could relate to. Drawing from various aspects of the Buddhist teachings, I gradually wove key elements of my dharma practice into a new guided meditation for the Earth Treasure Vases. These came to include:

Working with the Breath

As with many forms of meditation, the Earth Treasure Vase practice is carried on the breath. By resting our attention on the breath, we not only align ourselves with the life force of Mother Earth, but we also become present with our connection to both her beauty and suffering. Breathing with awareness throughout the meditation, we learn the basis of mindfulness, which is simply to be aware of what is happening as it is happening. By focusing on the breath, we bring our body and mind into oneness and enter the present moment. With the help of our breath as an anchor for our mind, we learn to stay with the visualization for healing the Earth and the feelings that may arise. The breath is the vehicle for the practice.

Meditation

The most important basis for the Earth Treasure Vase meditation became the cultivation of bodhicitta—our heartfelt wish to relieve suffering. The Tibetan Buddhist practice of tonglen facilitates this. Breathing in, we imagine taking in or receiving the suffering that is present in the world, whether sickness and disease, war, poverty, homelessness, pollution, droughts and floods, or any number of other circumstances. And breathing out, we send our love, compassion, and healing impulses to relieve the suffering of the world.

Tonglen means "taking and sending." We practice taking the awareness of suffering into our hearts to feel it completely. We do not reject or push it away. Rather, we embrace it and then imagine sending our heartfelt caring and loving kindness to alleviate that suffering in all the ways called for. Both the taking and sending are done on the breath. Breathing in, receiving; breathing out, sending.

The suffering we share with others opens the doorway to healing and liberation. Facing into the shadow of suffering, turning toward that which we might prefer to turn away from, we develop the capacity for healing. If we continue to ignore the dis-ease it only festers and grows stronger. Breathing through any reactivity, judgment, or fear that might arise, we train ourselves to stay present even in the face of that which we have aversion to so that the door to healing will open, the door of compassion.

Visualization

They say in the Buddhist teachings that there are eighty-four thousand "dharma doors," meaning there are just about as many ways onto the path as seekers searching for a way in. We each have to find our own way. The breath is one way to focus our hearts and minds in meditation. For some, visualization practices can also open that door.

Building on the foundation of mindfulness and tonglen, we were inspired by the Tibetan practices that utilize light in their visualizations as a way to connect with the spiritual forces of awakening.

By identifying with light as an expression of our being, we access an unconditioned place within us that is part of an evolutionary shift in consciousness. If we wish to evolve, focusing on our reactive emotions and feeding negative, destructive attitudes does not help. Resting in awareness and sending our love out on the breath in the form of light, we create the conditions for our wild creativity to emerge.

This is not in any way to bypass, avoid, or deny the darkness. In fact, the only way en*light*enment is possible is by going into the darkness, both inside and around us. The practice of the Earth Treasure Vases teaches us how to do this skillfully. As Thich Nhat Hanh would say, we "do not close our eyes before suffering," but face it, breathe into it, and feel it completely. This is a kind of alchemy, and it cannot be rushed. But once we have learned not to close our eyes before suffering, we can all the more powerfully radiate the light of our love to relieve the suffering of the world.

The inevitable suffering associated with shifting into a new time is greatly eased if we choose to focus on the light, and as we do, we build, through the power of our creative hearts and minds, a new cooperative, collaborative, living system that supports all life in peaceful coexistence.

We need each other to activate the feeling and substance of the light because it is . . . love. From love springs wisdom. It is our caring not for ourselves but for others to whom we are inextricably linked that catalyzes the healing, the awakening, and the shift to the next level of our evolution. This is the hero's journey, the path of the bodhisattva, the one with endless compassion for the Earth and all beings.

Prayers and Offerings

After meditating, we open one of the vases and pass it around the circle to receive people's offerings, giving everyone the opportunity to express their prayers and wishes and place a symbolic offering inside.

We have cried, laughed, and reached deep into our hearts to bring out the most meaningful wishes, intentions, and prayers we could muster, as if our lives depend on it. I have wiped my tears around the rim of many vessels, held the hands of countless friends, and gathered offerings everywhere I go, asking: "What would Mother Earth like now? What does Gaia need here? What is the special alchemy this particular location is calling for? What are the offerings that will make this Earth Treasure Vase complete?" I always ask with the greatest respect for the Tibetan teachings, but also wondering, What is called for here and now?

Ultimately, the practice teaches us to focus on our love and caring and to shine the light of our love out into the world. Instead of coming away from the meditation feeling heavy and depressed with the sorrows of the world, we come away feeling uplifted and joyful, in spite of how awful things are. The little holy vessels contain all our love and caring as seeds full of promise for the world. We, in turn, are strengthened with an awareness that something beautiful and meaningful is possible. Planting these seeds is the most important thing we can do in the face of oppression, negativity, terror, and injustice.

• • •

The practice would evolve in many ways over the years. I did the first written adaptation for the meditation as I sat in the old courtyard of the offices of Procuraduría Federal de Protección al Ambiente (PROFEPA), Mexico's environmental protection agency. My friend Georgita Ruiz was the director of PROFEPA in Oaxaca, and she was passionate about her job to protect one of the most biodiverse regions on the planet. Oaxaca is an agricultural paradise, and Georgita had a difficult time confronting oil and gas pollution, arresting sea turtle poachers on the coast, stopping the expansion of GMO agriculture, and breaking through the corruption that characterized most government agencies in Mexico. In 1997, she wanted us to bring an Earth Treasure Vase to the coast of Oaxaca after Hurricane Rick devastated the region.

As I waited for Georgita to finish one of her endless meetings, I realized that the group of Indigenous Mazatec healers I was going to share the guided meditation with that night at her invitation would not understand the practice as I first learned it unless I adapted it for them. So, with pen in hand, and a postcard of the Virgin of Guadalupe on my lap, in what felt like one gesture and one breath, I wrote down the bones of the guided meditation that had been slowly coming clear at home with Open Way Sangha. That night, I shared it with the group of curanderos (traditional healers) and friends who gathered at Georgita's to initiate the vase for the coast of Oaxaca. Their prayers confirmed the meditation had carried the spirit to their hearts.

Receiving the trust of the lamas who passed this practice on to me was the gift of a lifetime. That the vases came as *open* vessels was an even greater gift. I sometimes wonder what Charok Rinpoche and the

Abbot of Tengboche might have known about the future and what would be needed in our times. Perhaps our fumbling innovations at the Open Way Sangha were part of the way in which the terma itself asked to be realized? In any case, I'm sure that if the vases had been given to us already filled and sealed, the practice would never have taken us to the depths it has, nor would the effects have been as profound. And while I am reluctant to project magical powers onto the little holy vessels, it is unmistakable that the sacred medicines mixed into the clay imbued the vases with potent energies.

With the vessels in our midst, month after month, year after year, our sangha gathered to fill the seemingly empty pots in our own humble ways. Over and over, I saw that everyone has innate wisdom and caring within their hearts. No one of us has the answers—we are all in this together, in community. It has to be a group effort. As the vases made their way, warm hand to warm hand around the circle, we listened attentively to each person, taking in their prayers with full attention. As we did, the vases seemed to come alive, their purpose activated in new and creative ways. And always, we were aware that the vases we held in our hands were made from clay containing powerful sacred medicines connecting us to the great lineage masters of this ancient tradition. This connection seemed to empower us in our prayers and take them beyond anything ordinary into a mythic realm where anything is possible.

CHAPTER FOUR

THE BOMB IN MY BACKYARD

As I climbed that path to meet Charok Rinpoche, I was haunted by something deeply distressing. Even in that rarefied air, I could not shake the awareness of the bomb in my backyard.

An outpost of Indigenous sovereignty, breathtaking landscapes, spiritual teachings across many traditions, and the arts, New Mexico became my home in 1987. After moving here, I soon discovered that just across the Rio Grande Valley, thirty miles from where I lived, is the Los Alamos National Laboratory (LANL)—the birthplace of the atomic bomb.

New Mexico is famously known as the "Land of Enchantment." But from the conception of the first nuclear bomb to its horrifying conclusion, and the proliferation of nuclear weapons that continues, our beautiful state has become a factory for the deadliest weapons on Earth, and a dumping ground for the radioactive poison that is their by-product, altering the fabric of life here forever.

These are the unceded lands of the Tewa people. Surrounded by four sacred peaks, with six pueblos located on or near the Rio Grande, the Tewa's ancestral homeland has been stewarded by the Tewa people since time immemorial.[1] It is a place where two cultures with vastly different, if not opposing, values collide—the Pueblo people who ceremonially protect and care for their holy and sacred lands, and the conquistadors, colonizers, and scientists who claimed the region.

LANL is built on a dormant supervolcano in the midst of the Jemez Mountains within the Tewa world. Somewhere around 1.25 million years ago it erupted, sending ash all the way to Kansas and Utah.[2] Today, the lab sits on fault lines that indicate a major earthquake would not be unreasonable.

The effort to build the bombs was known as the Manhattan Project. It began in the 1940s during World War II when scientists moved to this remote part of New Mexico to construct the first two atomic bombs, named Fat Man and Little Boy, which were dropped on Hiroshima and Nagasaki, Japan, respectively. Since then, over the decades, LANL has dumped barrels of plutonium and other radioactive substances into the canyons and arroyos around the lab. Nowadays, the lab continues to manufacture plutonium pits and other components needed for weapons of mass destruction.[3] Much of the waste generated is currently stored above ground in, of all things, fabric tents in a place called Area G on the Pajarito Plateau.

The many canyons and arroyos coming off the Jemez Mountains have never been properly cleared of the waste from bomb-making discarded there for more than eighty years. This waste drains directly into the Rio Grande River. Watchdog groups suggest that the water pumped out of the Rio Grande for irrigation of crops and piped into Santa Fe for drinking water could be highly contaminated.[4] An enormous plume of hexavalent chromium and other toxic chemicals are polluting the underground aquifer for the entire region. In 2014, the plume was about one thousand feet below ground in the regional aquifer and measured a mile long, a half-mile wide, and one-hundred-feet thick.[5] Chromium levels have been dangerously above the drinking water standard set by the Environmental Protection Agency since 2018, and there has been a recent increase in concentration. When this will be cleaned up remains to be seen.[6]

Additionally, Indigenous communities of New Mexico and activists have long called for the end of this region being treated by the federal government as if it were a "sacrifice zone."[7]

In the spring of 1996, the Earth let me know in no uncertain terms that it was time to pull the vases out and put them to work. Right in my own backyard, the signs of climate change were revealing themselves, and an enormous forest fire was raging around LANL, bringing the lab's stockpile of radioactive substances at Area G dangerously close to exploding.

• • •

Before relocating to New Mexico, I had met a woman I immediately loved and respected—Buddhist teacher and eco-philosopher Joanna Macy. I was moved by the way she held her engagement with the issues of our time in the context of her dharma practice, much like Thich Nhat Hanh.

When Joanna was visiting the Tibetan community of Tashi Jong in northern India in 1980, she heard the ancient Shambhala Prophecy for the first time. This prophecy arose in the Tibetan Buddhist tradition twelve centuries ago. There are varying interpretations of the prophecy, but the version Joanna received was given to her by her spiritual friend Dugu Choegyal Rinpoche.

"There comes a time when all life on Earth is in danger," Rinpoche told her. "Great barbarian powers have arisen. Although these powers spend their wealth in preparations to annihilate each other, they have much in common: weapons of unfathomable destructive power and technologies that lay waste to our world.

"At this time," he said, "the Shambhala Warriors would rise up, go into the very heart of the barbarian power, and dismantle the weapons through the use of two weapons of their own: wisdom and compassion."

When Joanna heard this prophecy, she realized it was coming true in our time. "How do they train?" Joanna asked. Choegyal replied,

> *They train . . . in the use of two weapons . . . compassion and insight. Both are necessary . . . You have to have compassion because it provides the fuel to move you out there to do what is needed . . . But that weapon is very hot, and by itself is not enough. It can burn you out, so you need the other—you need insight into the dependent co-arising of all things. With that wisdom you know that it is not a battle between the good guys and the bad guys, for the line between good and evil runs through the landscape of every human heart. And with that insight, you also know that each action undertaken with pure intent has repercussions throughout the web of life, beyond what you can measure or discern. By itself, that insight can seem too cool, too conceptual to sustain you and keep you moving, so you need the heat of the compassion, our openness to the world's pain. Both are necessary to the Shambhala Warrior.*[8]

I heard this prophecy from Joanna and was deeply affected. The "weapons of unfathomable devastation" Choegyal spoke of were being produced in my homeland. And the power structure that supported this activity seemed impenetrable.

But if all things are connected, and each act affects the whole, perhaps an Earth Treasure Vase could help. If destruction and annihilation could be unleashed from this place, perhaps healing could be, too. I was determined: ground zero for the worst nightmare ever conceived would become the first location at the heart of the Earth Treasure Vase global healing practice.

• • •

In the teachings of the Five Buddha Families, the color white at the center of the mandala is connected to the element of space, which carries with it the habitual emotional reaction of ignorance—one of the five poisons that cause such suffering to ourselves and others. But when this energy of ignorance is faced with awareness and experienced for what it is, it is transformed.

The teachings say that even ignorance can be transformed into wisdom. They refer to the hidden jewel within our ignorance as the Wisdom of Vast Spaciousness. When this wisdom is awakened, it becomes possible to move out of our denial and the habitual tendency to ignore the realities of the challenging things we face like radioactive waste and nuclear war. And with awareness, we find ourselves in a place of spaciousness, where an open-hearted sense of responsibility arises that allows us to respond constructively instead of avoiding the situation.

Admitting the presence of radioactive waste, or "poison fire," as Joanna Macy calls it—and guarding and protecting it on behalf of future generations—is a deeply intelligent response to the legacy of radioactive waste we are passing forward. She calls this "Nuclear Guardianship."

This notion catalyzed the idea for me that an Earth Treasure Vase could serve as a guardian near LANL, vigilantly radiating out protective energies from the center of what would become our global healing mandala.

Wondering where exactly the first vase might find its home, I was told about a cave above LANL from an acquaintance who scribbled vague directions on a slip of paper. One day, I took off to find it. Much to my surprise, I found my way straight there even though it is hidden in the side of the canyon, a small slit in the rocks that opens into a large, deep cavern. Once inside, we can either feel as if we are entering into the belly of the beast or as if we are returning to the womb of the Earth from whom we were born.

Here, overlooking LANL, an Earth Treasure Vase could be sequestered above this repository of ultimate destruction and deadly poison to do its holy work.

• • •

Tewa elder Marian Naranjo of Santa Clara Pueblo reminds me in no uncertain terms that in northern New Mexico, we are living inside of the Tewa "church." This land holds powerful medicine.

Not far from Los Alamos, Santa Clara Pueblo is known for its pottery. Marian is a potter there and has also become an influential educator and activist representing those in her tribe whose health has been affected by the lab. Many members of the Pueblo communities in the area took jobs at LANL, entering into a relationship of financial dependency with the lab, and now their health is compromised.

The very ground that the Los Alamos National Lab was built upon was stolen by the US government from the Tewa people during World War II, taken by eminent domain. Since before the war ended with the dropping of bombs on Hiroshima and Nagasaki, some of the traditional lifeways have not been carried out because the people are denied access to their sacred lands.[9] Within the electric fences of this top-secret military-industrial complex and its high-level security forces, are the very places that the Tewa people need to go to make their prayers and offerings to maintain balance and harmony in the world.

When Indigenous people are not allowed to keep up their ceremonies in the places that they know are important for this purpose, we all suffer. Certain places have special jobs to do. The elders know that tending this sacred purpose is part of what keeps the web of life intact and flowing in harmony. Marian Naranjo has long been trying to teach us the path of right relations with the land and people here.

Over the years, I had always feared that a forest fire in this dry landscape would ignite Area G and the plutonium stored there. When that fated fire did come, first in 1996, then again in 2000, again in 2011, and yet once more in 2022, it was Marian and her community—along with several neighboring Pueblos—who were, once again, forced to make a sacrifice when the firefighters diverted the raging wildfire away from the lab and the enormous stockpile of waste, and onto Pueblo lands. All but one of the many natural springs in the Jemez Mountains above Santa Clara were destroyed.[10] The smoldering landscape after the devastating fires looked like a war zone.[11]

After the 1996 fire subsided in the fall, it was time to take the Earth Treasure Vase to the cave. I was grateful to have the support of the Tibetan monks from Gyumed Monastery in Dharamsala, who had arrived in Santa Fe to perform a number of ceremonies and rituals. Given the location of the vase and the powerful energies we were addressing with our prayers, it was good to have their help. The monks were warm and friendly and well versed in the Earth Treasure Vase practice.

Early one morning, a group of us met with the monks where they were in the process of creating a huge sand mandala. I brought the Earth Treasure Vase into a final ceremony to receive the prayers and offerings of everyone who came. When the vase was full, the monks took charge, and with expertise sealed the vase, wrapped the five colored silks around its neck, and carefully braided the colored cords around them, then stamped the cords onto the silk with golden sealing wax. We placed the vase inside a wooden box handmade by sangha member David Bacon, who had covered the box with sheets of copper to conduct energy underground, and then the vase was tightly packed with our homegrown dried lavender and secured for its job ahead.

The spiritual support provided by the monks was reassuring and generated a sense of confidence. When the vase was ready to go, we all climbed into vehicles and drove to the trailhead. An eerie feeling accompanied us as we hiked through the charred hillside still smelling of smoke from the fires. Gigantic old ponderosas and thousands of piñons and juniper trees were burned to the ground just above the sprawling laboratory below us. Nothing grew in that scarred landscape.

Local Tewa elder Vickie Downey accompanied us up the hill and down into the cave to assist the monks. Vickie held the Earth Treasure Vase tenderly and offered her blessings on behalf of the Native people whose ancestral homeland had been taken from them in the 1940s. Following this, the monks conducted an elaborate ceremony to further consecrate the vase and open the site by making offerings to the local spirits. The vase was then placed deep in the cave, where boulders were moved to allow it to be lowered down inside and completely hidden from sight.

When we came out of the cave after the ceremony was complete, it seemed the light was brighter and the walk downhill so much shorter.

• • •

After the burial of our Earth Treasure Vase guardian above Los Alamos, Joanna Macy stewarded another vase in the year 2000 and buried it adjacent to the National Tritium Labeling Facility at the Lawrence National Laboratory, overlooking the University of California, Berkeley.

Tritium is a radioactive form of hydrogen, which is soluble in water and easily absorbed by plants and animals. When tritium binds organically in this way, its toxicity increases a hundred fold.[12] The facility's emissions, as measured by the EPA, are sufficient to rank it as a Superfund site; nevertheless, it continues to operate.

In her book *World as Lover, World as Self,* Joanna points out that a terrible crime against future generations lies in the production of such radioactive waste. "Radioactivity produces not only disease, death, and sterility," she writes, "it affects the genetic code itself. Likened to a madman in a library, it can scramble and lose forever the blueprints for life crafted by our long evolutionary journey."[13]

Furthermore, radioactivity is invisible, making it impossible for future generations to know where the danger lies. "Each year, another twelve thousand tons of high-level waste are produced by the world's nuclear reactors. This waste contains isotopes that include Iodine-129 (with a half-life of more than 15 million years), Plutonium-239 (with a half-life of 24,000 years, but which decays into Uranium-235, with a half-life of 700 million years) and Neptunium-237 (with a half-life of more than 2 million years)."[14]

These inconceivable numbers boggle the mind. We simply do not have a long-term solution for the safe disposal of nuclear waste. It is a problem we are passing forward in time.

Recalling the monasteries that kept learning alive during the Dark Ages, Joanna conceives of a different approach to nuclear waste: "Communities with similar dedication will be needed to guard the centers of radioactivity we are bequeathing to tens of thousands of future generations. In my mind's eye I could see surveillance communities forming around today's nuclear facilities, . . . centers of reflection and pilgrimage, where the waste containers are monitored or repaired, and where wisdom traditions of our planetary heritage offer contexts of meaning and disciplines of vigilance."[15]

Joanna wrote to me after burying the vase in her care. "The whole process, from the ritual filling of the vase with prayers and intentions to its nighttime burial on the hillside by the fence along the facility, was stirring."

She goes on, "Each of us present that night, deeply engaged in every step, were grateful for this way to manifest our fierce caring and ground it in the sacred living body of Earth. The steep hillside above Berkeley and the Bay was eerily beautiful under the stars. In the night breeze we could feel the world breathing—and the hovering presence of past and future generations."

Another vase guardian was now doing its job in the land.

• • •

Joanna teaches us about "deep time"—the kind of time required to face the lifespan of radioactive substances. This always makes me think of that cave at the center of the Earth Treasure Vase Mandala. Here, in this powerful womb, time falls away, and all who come here enter a place of peace and receive a profound healing in communion with Mother Earth. Yet, when we emerge, we are immediately confronted by the presence of the military-industrial complex down the hill.

Over the years since burying that little clay pot in its depths, I have returned many times to this cave to make offerings and prayers. This has been key to keeping the practice alive and renewing my commitment to nuclear guardianship.

I continue to ask myself, What will it take to transform the Los Alamos National Laboratory? And as always, the task seems so daunting that it makes me want to shut down and space out, avoiding the great work of facing this terrifying beast with full presence.

This is exactly the emotional reaction the powers that be hope for so that they can continue their path of greed and aggression. I vow not to be caught by the poison of ignoring the truth that is here, and call upon the Ancestors of the land, the Buddhas, the bodhisattvas, and the elemental energies of "vast spaciousness" to help me wake up with everything I've got. Cultivating wisdom and compassion here is going to take a lifetime.

At a recent Feast Day at Santa Clara Pueblo, my friends and I brought food to share at Marian's and sat at her table, knowing we are all part of the healing. Marian is a living treasure filled with visions for her people that are taking root in her community.

This year, there were more dancers than I ever remember seeing before. The pueblo is growing fields of corn to feed the people. Marian and her extended community have recently built a special ceremonial Bread House and a Woman's House to teach the traditions that have not been practiced in the seventy years since the bomb was conceived. She says some of the Pueblo chiefs are watching and appreciate her efforts to renew the traditions, like making the sacred bread called "buwah" that she feeds them to nourish their spirits and keep their ceremonies alive. Marian's fingers are blistered from cooking this paper-thin bread on burning hot stones. Her back aches and her legs are numb from the hard work to bring back the old ways and pass them on. For me, it is she who carries the hope of the Earth Treasure Vase placed deep inside that cave above the Los Alamos National Lab.

Marian tells me about taking a visiting Japanese journalist to see the lab. Approaching Area G, she walked up to the locked gate, encountered a Native youth working as a guard and asked if she might be permitted to enter and offer prayers and cornmeal at one of the sacred sites inside. It is one of the many places the elders have not had access to since the lab was built. The young man heard her heart and asked his superior to allow her in.

Much to her surprise, she was granted entry. Marian's prayers and those of Kathy Sanchez, cofounder of Tewa Women United,[16] who was with her that day, marked a turning point for her. From that time, she has witnessed small openings in the armor of the military-industrial complex. Marian believes that when prayers and offerings can once again be made on the sacred lands of the people, the weapons of mass destruction and the poisoning of Mother Earth will naturally cease.

But restoring balance in the belly of the beast is no easy task. Cancer creeps into every dark corner, drug addiction claims the best of lives, and denial holds sway in the minds of the scientists who insist the lab is doing necessary and important work.

Joanna Macy is in her nineties now and carries a deep concern about the deadly radioactive waste stored in thousands of drums outside, under those fabric tents in Area G. These are eventually to be delivered to an underground cavern in southern New Mexico to be kept out of sight and out of mind. Joanna points out that given the tremendous lifespan of these toxic substances, people will simply forget about what has been left for future generations to contend with. She speaks of the importance of an oral history for future times, when the information stored in computers may no longer be accessible. It is easy to bury the past, place the poison underground, and forget about it. But if this knowledge is lost, we would be delivering future generations into a terrible ignorance.

I hold to Joanna's idea that the guardianship of the "poison fire" should be regarded as a spiritual practice passed from generation to generation, as a sacred responsibility to diligently stay aware and awake to what we are placing in the Earth and passing forward to future generations.

It occurs to me that in the Buddhist tradition, sutras are regularly chanted to teach what needs to be remembered. I realize that this is one way to pass along this knowledge as a spiritual practice. And I think, Who better to transmit this sacred knowledge than the First Peoples of this place, who already know how to keep an oral tradition alive and have survived for so long? I wonder, perhaps, if such a spoken-word sutra is an assignment for Native poets and Buddhist scholars to craft together.

• • •

In 2016, Marian Naranjo organized and led a ceremony inside the Valles Caldera as part of the annual Gathering for Mother Earth hosted by Tewa Women United. The caldera, situated just above LANL, is what remains of that supervolcano. The greatest power spot for the Pueblo people, the caldera, like so many sacred lands, was taken from them and privately held, preventing the people from carrying out their lifeways. But in 2015, the caldera was transferred to the National Park Service, and public access is now permitted.

Marian and other Pueblo people are reclaiming their connection to the land by making offerings and praying for the restoration of balance and harmony with Mother Earth. She says she doesn't know how, but she knows these prayers will be answered. Marian counsels us to "make a conscious decision about which energy of the unseen world you wish to feed: the life-giving forces of the ancestral spirit world or the forces of mass destruction?"

She observes, "Give thanks for your life. Be happy with this thought. Be happy with this feeling. Concentrate and feed this positive energy with your presence. Connect with the Ancestors. Have no doubt about their presence! Ask for permission to be among them and ask for their help to restore our Mother . . . Know that through serving the life-giving energies, real Peace will come to the World."

I join my prayers with Marian's that we may all hear the call to do our part as Shambhala Warriors in restoring balance and harmony to the Earth. May we sense the ways we are being uplifted when we listen beyond the din of the dominant culture to the winds that echo through the caves and carry the mountain bluebirds in flight. When we listen carefully, we may even be able to hear and feel the drumbeat on Pueblo Feast Days calling us to remember the earth under our feet and to dance.

CHAPTER FIVE

THE MANDALA BEGINS

The healing called for in relation to LANL was daunting. It seemed only right, then, that the next step would be to plant vases filled with prayers in each of the four directions of this region, to act as a support to the vase in the cave doing its powerful job.

Beyond political boundaries and borders, what defines a region are its rivers, the lifeblood of the ecosystem. Political boundaries have carved up the Earth artificially, disregarding living systems and separating cultures that once shared a relationship in the region they inhabit. Relating to an area as a bioregion is a way of reclaiming the land away from politics, toward a collaborative relationship of interbeing in our shared bioregions around the world.

Here in the southwestern United States, a once great river, the Rio Grande, flows from the Colorado Rockies to the Gulf of Mexico, and serves as the main artery defining our bioregion. Water is scarce, and this vital source of life is threatened at each and every turn. A precarious mix of unstable ecological forces collides here, with unchecked development, global climate change, and nuclear proliferation as active ingredients.

The teachings of the mandala principle found in Tibetan Buddhism inspired me to look upon our watershed as part of a vast mandala that encircles the whole Earth. A mandala is a geometric pattern that symbolically and metaphysically represents the universe, and at its most basic is made up of the center and the four directions. Each of the four directions and the center of a mandala can be seen to embody a quality or energy that is one aspect of the whole. When taken all together, these qualities make up a complete individual; when one part dominates, it takes the whole system out of balance.

In Tibetan Buddhist teachings, the five colors associated with each direction represent the elemental energies of earth, water, fire, air, and space. First arising as light and sound, then as color, these energies move from energy toward form and coalesce into the elemental energies, which are the building blocks of life. Each of us is composed of these elemental energies, and in these teachings we learn about the emotional qualities associated with each of the five elements. These emotions can either be expressed neurotically and reactively (as poisons), or, through the application of awareness, these poisons can be transformed into understanding and wisdom.

I instinctively felt this teaching could be applied not only to an individual, but also to a living system like a bioregion for the healing that is needed in relation to Mother Earth. I was inspired to plant the next four Earth Treasure Vases in each of the four directions of the Rio Grande bioregion. I saw that by honoring the directions within the land and placing the Earth Treasure Vases in relationship to each other this way, we could begin to create a global healing mandala.

Our sangha met, contributing an astounding variety of offerings to fill these four vases. It was clear to all who held them they had a purpose. The process of filling them with offerings and prayers at the time of the full moon, holding them with care, allowing them to guide us to where they could do the most good, taking them on the road, into forests, up mountains, and to the rivers of this land, opened us up. We were participating in the work of sacred activism and nurturing a relationship with each other and the Earth.

By fall of 1996, those four were ready to go, one for each of the four directions of the Rio Grande bioregion.

The healing had begun.

The North

In the northern direction of the mandala is the source of the Rio Grande River which bubbles up from the base of the Rocky Mountains near Creede, Colorado. According to the Tibetan tradition, it is thought that sources of rivers are excellent locations to bury a treasure vase as the flow of the river carries the prayers in the vase along its length, like the prayers written on the multicolored Tibetan prayer flags blowing in the wind that send healing mantras out in all directions.

Leslie Larsen, a bioregional activist who was working on behalf of the Rio Grande to link people and places along the river, volunteered to take responsibility for burying the Earth Treasure Vase there in October 1996.

It was a new moon and a solar eclipse the day we began the process. On our altar we lit candles and offered flowers and bowls of water. We also brought beeswax to seal this vase and send it on its way. After a meditation, a few final offerings were placed into the vase, including some pebbles from the path walked by Thich Nhat Hanh outside his hut at Plum Village. We melted the wax and brushed it over the cork to seal the pot. Five colored silks were arranged one by one over the cork with green on top since it was going north, dressing her nicely.

We remembered that the north is connected to the Karma Family and the element air. With green its associated color, this direction works with the transformation of jealousy or envy into the Wisdom of All-Accomplishing Activity. We needed this wisdom to do the job ahead and as we tied the fabric over the neck of the vase with the silken ties and dripped golden sealing wax onto the cords, we prayed for it to be accomplished well.

The vase was then lowered into a box crafted out of old-growth fir. "Very strong and long lasting," said carpenter David Bacon, who had made this box, too. We packed dried sage, lavender, and rose petals around the vase so it didn't move, and closed the lid. It fit like a glove.

With the vase secured in the passenger seat, Leslie drove to the Rio Grande Reservoir, the first dam on the river. She spoke of mountain peaks rising into the clear sky, the new morning sun streaking across the fields and valleys. "I was expecting to find the river gushing forth from the ground at the source, but discovered the Rio Grande comes from snowmelt, with many small streams joining to gather their waters and deliver them to give life to the watershed along the way.

"At the far end of the valley," she recounts, "where the river enters, you could see how she keeps her channel even under the lake. A green valley with two soaring pyramid peaks hovering above greeted the vase and me, and mountains formed a ring around us. It was clear that the vase wanted to be planted here at the first major confluence.

"There was a boulder topped with green lichen in a direct north-south axis with one of the peaks," she continued. "I set the gleaming copper box at the base of the boulder and quieted myself to hear where to dig. The sound of the river as it slipped over a bed of rock filled the air. The energies were very strong, like a song—not audible, but I felt it being sung." Leslie hung prayer flags and offered her intentions for accomplishing good outcomes—snows filling the mountains in winter, gentle warming and flowing waters in spring, a return of monsoon rains, health for all of nature, humans respecting the river and the life she brings, the pollution cleaned, the balance restored.

"The ground was yielding," she observed. She rang a bell and when the vase had been planted in the rich soil, she placed sod over the top so no trace of disturbance could be seen. "I could feel the vase's energy stretching out in all directions," Leslie concluded. "I had no idea that the power of these vessels to create renewal would be so tangible, but now I have no doubt. Maybe not this year, but in time, the balance will be restored."

I was grateful to Leslie for taking the first step to accomplish the Earth Treasure Vase Mandala to the north in the Rio Grande bioregion.

The East

In the Tibetan tradition, mountaintops are also powerful locations to plant a vase. To the east, we placed an Earth Treasure Vase on Mount Baldy above Santa Fe, or *Povip'In*, which means "Flower Mountain" in the Tewa language.

Baldy stands sentinel as the guardian of this land above where the Open Way Sangha practices. I feel the mountain's presence when we meditate on the full moon gatherings. The small river flowing through our little valley of Chupadero ten miles north of Santa Fe derives from the snowmelt and rains generated from Mount Baldy, just above us. The seasons unfold in relationship to the life force that Baldy provides—rain, snow, wind, and sun.

As Leslie was burying the Earth Treasure Vase to the north, a little group of us gathered at Open Way Sangha in the early morning with this Earth Treasure Vase at the exact time of the new moon solar eclipse.

David, who had crafted the copper-covered fir box for Leslie, made many more such boxes for the vases. He and his partner, Louise, and our friends Gretchen and Linda came together in a circle with Hugh and me. Gretchen arranged the silks so that each color showed—blue on top for the eastern direction—then we sealed the ties with the gold sealing wax. Linda, who is a gardener, brought a basket full of dried herbs and flowers to secure the vase inside—oregano, thyme, yarrow, sage, roses, and lavender. So many fragrances and life-giving beauty were packed all around the little clay pot. Everyone was joyfully amazed at what a beautiful gift to the Earth this was!

The vase rode in David's backpack up the slopes of Mount Baldy as our little group walked up the mountain's flanks to its 12,632-foot summit. In the eastern direction, in the mandala teachings, the color blue represents the element of water embodied by the Vajra Family and the transformation of the poison of anger or hatred into Mirror-like Wisdom. We were aware that our anger at what is happening to the Earth, our land and home, can be transformed by clearly seeing our own calling to stand up for this mountain and the life that it feeds.

We dug the vase into the side of Mount Baldy, overlooking the vast Rio Grande bioregion below. Heartfelt offerings were made to honor our mountain. The next day, when it rained, we knew the mountain had heard us.

The West

Full of naive enthusiasm, we then took an Earth Treasure Vase to the summit of a Tewa holy mountain in the Jemez Mountains to the west. Once part of the towering volcano that exploded some 1.25 million years ago, the expansive Valles Caldera is all that remains at the base of what is now the 11,561-foot-tall Chicoma Mountain, or *Tsikumu* (meaning "Flint Stone Mountain" in the Tewa language). We proceeded humbly and with great respect, not wanting to disrupt local customs, but motivated to add our prayers to this time-honored place of pilgrimage for Indigenous peoples.

All too aware of the painful legacy of what was done to the First Peoples of this area, we made our way up the mountain. The Tewa people were forced onto pueblos when the colonizers arrived, and their traditional ways of life were dishonored—first by the Spanish settlers and Euro-American colonizers, and then by the US government. This dislocation remains a tremendous source of ongoing suffering here.

According to the mandala teachings, in the western direction, what is called for is Discerning Awareness in order to transform the poison of desire or greed into wisdom. The element of fire lives here, and its color is red, connecting it to the Padma Family.

Hiking up through the gentle aspen groves to the top of Tsikumu, we prayed for this awareness to enlighten us all. The vase, dressed in red and carefully packed as the others had been, was respectfully buried under boulders looking down on the caldera and the Indigenous lands surrounding it. We did not linger but made our offering and left the vase to its rightful guardians in that place.

Marian Naranjo tirelessly invites us to be respectful and become aware of the mannerisms of her people, and to remember our place within this vast natural landscape still held sacred by the elders. Some years after the burial of the Earth Treasure Vase at Tsikumu, I was horrified to realize that we had not followed the proper protocol to seek permission from the elders to plant the vase on their holy mountain. I still feel ashamed to have been so blind and ignorant.

Marian had counseled me to take care when entering into the holy places of the Ancestors. When prayers and offerings have been made over many generations, these places take on a power that is not to be dismissed. One needs to approach Tsikumu with respect.

Blinded by my White privilege and the fear that time is running out, I would make many mistakes in the years to come as I brought vases to other sacred lands. The colonization of Indigenous cultures, land, and resources is a wound that has left deep scars in need of healing if we are to restore balance and harmony to the Earth. To ask the elders for their blessings requires humility, and to approach these places with the proper attitude requires respect. It takes time to build a relationship of trust. I had much to learn.

I pray the Ancestors of that land have heard our prayers and received our offering. Marian received my apology and has recognized our prayers as sincere. From this, we are in the process of building a relationship of trust, and she knows I would welcome the opportunity to make proper relations with her community elders.

Some years later when we returned, the vase had been absorbed into the mountain, its location impossible to discern. This vase brought me invaluable lessons about the importance of Discerning Awareness and how the fulfillment of our prayers for healing and protection can lead to difficult truths about our assumptions, particularly for those of us who are White. I have come to realize that an enormous part of healing the Earth is making reparations and offering respect to the elders in the lands we visit. To care for the land means we must also restore the trust between all our relations so that our offering is received sincerely.

The South

The mouth of the Rio Grande in the south called to my husband, Hugh, and me, and we decided the two of us would make the journey to where that Great River flows into the Gulf at the border between the United States and Mexico.

The sangha sealed this southern vase on the full moon of March 1997 during the exact time of a full lunar eclipse when the Hale-Bopp comet was visible. We dressed the Earth Treasure Vase with yellow on top for her connection to the south, representing the Ratna Family, the element of earth. She was beautiful.

The Rio Grande flows from southern Colorado through the state of New Mexico, and continues south all the way down the very big state of Texas to the ocean at the Gulf of Mexico. It is a long way to the ocean from Santa Fe.

Arriving in Brownsville, twenty-five miles from the *boca del rio*, we took a room for the night at the Holiday Inn next to the bridge that leads to Matamoros on the Mexican border. In the mandala teachings, the energy of the south calls for the Wisdom of Equanimity, for balance and harmony to nurture all beings. We realized that this vase had an even bigger task to do to address the issues of social justice and right relations between our two countries.

The river marks the border and has become a dangerous place instead of a beautiful natural boundary. Now a poisoned gateway where distrust and tensions are high, it leads to prison and detention camps. Here, the vase needed to embody not only our prayers for the Earth and the lifeblood of the planet, but also our strongest intentions for harmony with our neighbors on the other side of the border. Prayers here are for justice and compassionate action, for wisdom and foresight, reaching across these boundaries, walls, and prisons to restore trust.

In the morning paper, we discovered that with the new moon, the tides would be much higher than any other day, but there was a window between 9:00 and 11:00 a.m. when the tides would be low enough to accomplish our task. I lit incense and picked up our "traveling companion" from the hotel-room altar I had created with its Virgin of Guadalupe candle that burned all night. I held the vase close to my heart and kissed it. I did not want to let go, but the tears were of joy for this little living being I loved dearly, like a child. I talked to it, telling it about its important work and what we hoped and prayed for it to do. Hugh did the same, and we both felt our hearts open wide in the presence of the vase and the awareness of its task ahead. We lowered it into its copper box, packed it with herbs and flowers, and then made our way to the place where the fresh water meets the salt sea.

Synchronicities played out along the way as we entered a timeless moment. We drove the car right onto the wide sandy beach like others were doing. Trash littered the sand where old oil drums had washed up. With so much industry in South Texas, it is terribly polluted. Although we were slightly nervous we might get stuck, our rental car—auspiciously named Achieva—made it just fine.

Being observed burying our hidden treasure was a real concern, so we had to look for a safe and protected spot. A little way back from the beach, we found some dunes protected behind sparse trees and shrubs. This was our place to dig a hole, just like a turtle does to lay her eggs—so familiar to Hugh, whose nonprofit organization worked to protect endangered species including the sea turtles that nest in Mexico. Awareness of injustice continued to fuel our prayers as we contemplated the artificial separation of cultures and economic inequality. Ringing a bell and quieting our minds, we dug a nest for the vase three feet down, made our offering, covered our tracks, and departed.

The next morning, thanks to all the birds squawking loudly, we woke to see the dawn's light glowing pink and bright. We meditated in bed together, connecting with the vase and our sangha members back home who were with us in this endeavor, and after tea outside, as the tides rose during the exact time of the new moon, we made love. Our hearts were so open and our love so fully on the surface, we kissed and hugged and merged and came in an all-over, full-body orgasm, uncontained.

The image that filled my awareness was how feminine the hole we had prepared in the Earth to receive the vase seemed, and how masculine the act of entering her to deposit the vase into that dark opening felt. I imagined the waves crashing on the sand—coming together, meeting, filling, radiating out in all directions, and echoing into the dunes where the vase had been planted, sending vibrations over and over and over through the sand to meet and penetrate the vase, ignite its spirit, quicken and wake up its purpose, on and on endlessly. Our love was radiating out in all directions with the intention to be of benefit, and to live in balance and harmony.

• • •

Up and down, back and forth, north, south, east, west, above, and below—with our love permeating the vases and their intention taking up residence at the center of my life, it was becoming clear that this was my life's work, the thread to follow. Connecting earth and sky, water to mountains, Indigenous wisdom and Buddhist insight, our prayers were beginning to form a web of light mirroring the interconnected web of life. I was tending an ancient, well-worn tradition and supporting it to find new expression in a world hovering on the brink of extinction.

We had managed to establish the center and all four directions of our mandala of healing intentions within the sacred lands of the Rio Grande watershed. Now it was time to expand out into the rest of the world. Heeding the words of Charok Rinpoche, I had to trust that the first five vases were doing their job in the ground, and that now we could turn our attention to other regions where healing and protection was also needed.

The time of my wandering was at hand. It would be a journey of a lifetime that would take me from the Heart of Mother India to the Heart of Africa, and, with the help of a global community, into the Heart of the World.

CHAPTER SIX

PILGRIMAGE

My life began in earnest when I realized that the Earth Treasure Vase practice was my purpose, and pilgrimage was my path. "With each step a lotus blooms,"[1] Thich Nhat Hanh invites us to imagine, as we breathe in and out with each step of our walking meditation. With every step, we have the possibility to arrive into the present moment, where life actually happens.

Most of us are unaware of the real questions that guide our lives and put us on the path. It was a stroke of grace that I found my question to Charok Rinpoche walking up the trail in the Himalayas. I was on the path but had no idea why I was there until the question I carried with me became clear. Human beings are so often hurled along by forces outside ourselves, round and round and round. It is only when we begin to inquire into our true purpose, or we finally hear the small quiet voice within begging for attention, that we find ourselves on our true path.

Forming an intention to make a pilgrimage is a way to consciously enter into an inner dialogue and catalyze a new direction for our lives. And when we allow ourselves to be guided by a question or an intention on a journey—whether it's an inner or outer journey—the world opens up in ways we never dreamed of before.

I was beginning to learn how important it is to listen for the guiding questions of my life. And I was aware that each of us must discover our own unique path to realization. When we are in touch with the deepest questions that guide our lives, we can make our life's journey a conscious one. Living into the answers, a deep fulfillment is born. But this is no easy task. In the face of all that can arise in life or on a pilgrimage, a deep concentration is required to stay fully connected to our intention, to stay present and open to receive the guidance and direction we have called for. It is so easy to become distracted when familiar old habits vie for our attention. But in undertaking a pilgrimage, with each step we decide to leave all that behind and, as Thich Nhat Hanh taught, to enter the present moment. Even if we do not or cannot physically travel, the spiritual path is like a pilgrimage.

The practice of walking a spiritual path on pilgrimage also includes offering up our attachments and ideas so we can discover the hidden truths unavailable in our ordinary lives and be shown new ways of being. Setting out, as I would do time and again, to put myself consciously on the path, the path itself became the goal. I learned to understand the opportunity each moment holds to wake up and take whatever obstacles that arose as further opportunities to cultivate insight and transform the negative habits that blocked me from understanding.

On the path of pilgrimage, we can look into the mirror of everything that occurs as a teaching. Traveling outside our normal everyday reality, we develop a wider perspective and see so much more. If we have the courage to look suffering in the eyes and not turn away, we may notice our own reactivity. So often, I noticed my habitual reactive patterns that prevented me from being fully present and awake. Being open enough to meet the Buddha in whatever form he or she appears takes faith! But if I shut down, I knew I risked missing a moment of synchronous connection, of divine intervention, a moment where self and other dissolve, and another world opens up.

• • •

It was just such a pilgrimage that I made to India as I was beginning to travel beyond my own bioregion with this practice. I was in love with the buddhadharma and had immersed myself in retreats, studying and practicing deeply to accomplish the ngöndro, when my dharma brother Shantum Seth, a dharmacharya in Thich Nhat Hanh's lineage and a consummate guide to India, invited me to join him "in the footsteps of the Buddha." To carry an Earth Treasure Vase to all the places of the Buddha's life would be deeply fulfilling, and then to bury the vase at the source of the Ganges River, a profound offering.

Like the Buddha, India is also a great teacher. In Mother India, we are confronted by life, death, and everything in between. One cannot control the situation—things don't operate in the ways we Westerners might be used to. There is no hiding, little comfort, and when things don't go the way they do at home, we can only look at ourselves.

We were a week into our journey and our "Buddhapath" pilgrimage group was nicely settled into our comfortable bus driving on a country road outside of Varanasi when, suddenly, we heard a loud noise and the bus came to a screeching halt as the rear axle disconnected and rolled across the road into the ditch—just barely missing the oncoming cars, trucks, ox carts, rickshaws, bicycles, and pedestrians. All we could do from the state of shock we found ourselves in was to be grateful no one was hurt and wait by the side of the road for a new bus to take us onward.

But one fellow pilgrim, who was a litigation attorney, became more and more incensed. By the time we got to our hotel late that night, he was (understandably) ready to sue, until he realized the futility of attempting this in India. Instead, he was able to recognize his own reactive patterns, and this allowed him to enter more fully into the pilgrimage experience.

The heart of our pilgrimage was in Bodh Gaya, where the Buddha was enlightened. Today, the Buddha takes the form of hundreds of thousands of pilgrims from all over the world representing the diverse cultures that practice the dharma. To see the myriad faces of Buddhism and watch the many forms of practice pointing to the same source is to free our hearts and minds from our fixed views. Thai, Sri Lankan, Tibetan, Japanese, Korean, Burmese, Vietnamese, Western, and Eastern—chanting, bowing, prostrating, making offerings, or sitting in silence—and dressed in traditional robes of red, yellow, black, brown, pink, or white. It is a veritable United Nations of Buddhism at the hub of the wheel of the dharma where the Buddha sat until the realization dawned that all things are interdependent and empty of a separate self.

As is the tradition, we quietly walked around the towering enlightenment stupa that commemorates this great event, reciting mantras or breathing mindfully with each step in order to enter into the power of the place more fully. After our circumambulation, our group sat under a descendent of the original Bodhi Tree. Taking it all in, I felt the energy of devotion that permeates the stones we walked upon; I felt it in the rustling leaves of the trees filled with squawking birds and in the hearts of all the pilgrims there. Being in the proximity of so many other people practicing together and witnessing a collective aspiration taking so many forms was unlike anything I had ever seen or felt anywhere before.

But there, under the Bodhi Tree, I confronted a familiar feeling of being consumed by the habit of self-centeredness and asked myself, What would it take to overcome, break through, and tame this incessant ego of mine, this terrible self-clinging? What would it take for me to be free like the Buddha and . . . enlightened? A lot of practice and trust in the process, I thought.

As I finished the end of my meditation under that great tree, a leaf fell in front of me, and although I wanted to grasp it and keep it for myself, I continued to meditate and entered into a deeper state of awareness. When this timeless absorption passed, and the activities of life as usual came back into my awareness—all of which seemed so consuming and pointless—I yearned to stop being caught by distractions and, once and for all, give up the other activities in my life. Then I noticed myself grasping even at this urge to stop as I made plans about how and where I could prolong this experience. So I took another breath, and let go once again.

I told myself I must transform this attachment to "I," "me," and "mine" into a practice for the benefit of others. So with every step and each breath, I offered my pilgrimage to realize this intention. I began to see that we *are* interconnected, and there *is* an effect rippling out that brings positive results into the world. With this, I sensed I had at least momentarily arrived. I was home. And I was suddenly aware this was one of the happiest days of my life! Every detail was so vivid and full. I had found my place amid the crowd, and I prayed:

May I be of benefit to all beings throughout space and time.
May I rest in the lap of the Buddha.
May my feet be firmly on the Path.
May "I" surrender and allow "my" life to be lived as an offering.
May I do everything with Buddha Nature in my heart!

Then a voice inside said, It's starting to rain, Cynthia, you should go back to the hotel, but instead, I turned and went to the very seat of the Buddha's awakening, down the stairs to the Bodhi Tree and the Mahabodhi Stupa once again. Most everyone was leaving because of the rain, but I kept going. Eventually the rain pushed me under a portal where many Tibetans were gathered doing prostrations. It was crowded but it felt good to be close to others. I recited mantras and watched the rain. The man behind me kept going with his prostrations; blue parrots were flying overhead, enjoying the rain on their feathers.

As the rain let up, I went back out to circumambulate, walking round and round that original seat of awakening. The monk who was prostrating took it upon himself to clean the drains so the water didn't flood too much. Everyone seemed so happy; they didn't mind that it was wet, or that the butter lamps might not light later on. The rain was a purification, an auspicious blessing bringing us together. I continued around the periphery of the site and at the main temple I went inside to find many monks and laypeople sitting in meditation. I could feel a powerful, conducive energy and noticed an open spot in a back corner. I sat down. The longer I stayed, the deeper I went into meditation, and the more I felt, simply, *I am home.* A great love rose up in me for my fellow pilgrims and this diverse culture of the dharma. Everyone together at the hub of the wheel, in the presence of an enormous Buddha statue with Himalayan eyes, dressed in Thai robes. There were Sri Lankan offerings placed in Chinese urns—and the ever-present cameras held by Japanese visitors frequently snapping photos. I hunkered down on the dirty floor for a long time, mosquitoes hovering at my face but not biting. The rain had come again, and there was no point in going back out. I lost track of time . . .

Over what must have been more than three hours and many mantras, I found my rhythm and my voice and settled into the practice. There was a tiny Tibetan woman who sat to my side reading from a small book and doing mandala mudras from time to time. She was elderly and very sweet, and when I finally got up, she looked at me like she really didn't want me to go, and said, "Leaving?" There was a monk who did a long liturgy with great concentration and power. So many different people, each doing their own thing, and all the while, the sound of mantras humming. This time, this place, this sacred mandala, and such strong devotion to the dharma all around, brought Buddha Nature into my heart over and over and over, swelling inside me, so I no longer yearned to have it because it was simply there—not separate any more. In proximity to these other women and men, my extended dharma family, I felt such joy—like nowhere else on Earth!

Later, circling the stupa again after the rains stopped and before leaving at last, even my backpack, with the treasure vase held safely inside, felt lighter. I was comfortable and at ease. Whenever my mind wandered off into thoughts and plans, I brought it back and, with a breath, gave it up to whatever the Buddha had in store, not just for me but for all life—the beggars, the lovers, and all who are on the path to realizing the Way. With each step, I offered my life in service to the Earth, the Three Jewels. The Buddha was within my heart and the Bodhi Tree, too.

From Bodh Gaya, our pilgrimage continued to Sarnath where the Buddha "turned the wheel of the dharma," sharing those first teachings with his friends. Our group sat together in a circle on the wide expanse of grass adjacent to the large stupa that commemorates that famous event. A woman in our group was struggling terribly with being in India. The wife of a successful doctor, she had never traveled beyond her comfortable, privileged life in Pasadena, California. We listened to Bonnie reveal her discomfort with the beggars and lepers, the poverty and disease, as she cried unstoppable tears.

Then, a striking Indian woman dressed in a tattered orange and magenta sari made her way, barefoot, toward us. She held an open basket of fodder in one arm and carried a scythe in her other hand. Approaching from a long way away, she made a direct line for us as Bonnie cried and cried. The woman came closer and when she arrived, she circled around our periphery and plopped down right next to Bonnie. Bonnie tried to ignore her, but the woman stroked her tear-stained face, saying, "Why are you crying? Don't cry. You have everything and we have nothing, but we are happy. Don't cry." Bonnie was quite wrapped up in her own story, and it took her a while to even hear the woman, but the woman kept repeating the same words over and over, gently stroking her face and looking into her eyes with great kindness. "Don't cry. You are rich and we are poor, but we are happy." This encounter changed Bonnie—and us all—forever.

In India, the Buddha also takes the form of the myriad sense impressions—the cacophony of smells, sounds, tastes, sights, and feelings all demanding one's attention. There are beggars, from small children to the elderly, everywhere one goes, with hands outstretched. There are the disabled and deformed, crawling, hobbling, running, whining, and looking pleadingly with deep, dark eyes. Humanity is not sterilized or homogenized or hidden behind closed doors. There is such beauty in the bright colors of the saris, the flower offerings, the fragrant perfumes and spicy scents. There are ten thousand ways to practice compassion and slowly, the eighty-four thousand dharma doors open. Every beggar is a Buddha, and the woman with the scythe is surely a bodhisattva on the path with the perfect gesture to awaken understanding in Bonnie.

Stupas are teachers, too. As symbolic representations of the enlightened mind, they contain relics of the Buddha or other realized beings and often commemorate what happened at a particular location. They are powerful repositories of energy, made all the more so by the centuries of devotion that have been offered around them as pilgrims circumambulate their base, reciting mantras endlessly. At Bodh Gaya, the stupa towers into the sky, an elaborate pinnacle. In Sarnath, it sits firmly on the Earth, huge and full. Kushinagar's stupa honoring the Buddha's death melts back into the Earth, edges softened, covered by green moss, quiet and unadorned.

• • •

We had been in India for three weeks traveling to the places of the Buddha's life. In each of these sacred sites, we had done a ceremony to bless and fill the Earth Treasure Vase. With all the prayers and offerings contained inside the vase, a small group of us agreed to carry it far into the mountains to be planted at the source of the Ganges, where our deepest hopes and wishes could flow out along that powerful river to the Bay of Bengal.

It was while traveling in India that I began to see through the eyes of the Earth Herself—to see how she had been damaged, degraded, and disregarded. Up in the high Himalayas, the Ganges flows a clear, gorgeous, glacial blue-green, a primordial milk. But the Ganges is being dammed now, and the life force, or Shakti, of that sacred river is blocked and controlled to satisfy the greed of "civilization." Trash litters the landscape, and plastic bags have invaded an overpopulated country whose citizens are accustomed to discarding their garbage anywhere because it will be eaten by the ever-present cows, goats, and dogs. Near Sarnath, in Varanasi, the City of Light, people come to die on the shores of the Ganges, and their cremated remains are offered into the river to purify their past karma so as to ensure a better rebirth. Here, the river flows black and thick with toxic waste, yet, people still bathe and drink the purifying nectar of the holy river, the goddess Ganga.

In Varanasi we met Dr. V. B. Mishra, otherwise known as Mahant-ji, a respected religious leader of the Tulsidas Temple. Educated as an engineer, he founded the Sankat Mochan Foundation, which is dedicated to cleaning up the Ganges, against all odds. Mahant-ji received us at the temple and offered his heartfelt prayers into the vase along with the healing herb tulsi that grew on the temple grounds. Then feeding the vase with prasad from the main altar, Mahant-ji chanted his own prayers into the little holy vessel for the Ganges to be cleansed.

Our large pilgrimage group dwindled to six dedicated to making the final journey along the upper reaches of the Ganges with the intention of burying the Earth Treasure Vase as close to the spiritual source of the Ganges at Gangotri as we could get that time of year. The bustling town of Haridwar, the last stop on the train, is known as the Gateway to the Gods because from there, one enters the high Himalayas where Shiva lives and the Ganges originates. This area is a holy land for yogis and sadhus, many of whom walk hundreds of miles in order to sit and meditate on the glacier far above Haridwar where Ganga begins. They believe that the river is a living being, a goddess, and worship Her for Her power to purify negative karma throughout many lifetimes. Bathing in Her waters is said to bring purification of body, speech, and mind, and ensure a blessed rebirth.

As we traveled north along the Ganges with the vase, the river became our teacher. At Devprayag, two rivers meet—the Bhagirathi and the Alaknanda—and where they join, they become the Ganges. Just below this, the Tehri Dam, a gigantic operation to produce electricity, has destroyed a vast area of the land. The dam became a teacher too, as we witnessed the ill-conceived attempts to block the flow of the mighty Ganges, the lifeblood of India. Beyond Devprayag, we traveled another two days up along the Bhagirathi toward its source, considered to be the place where the wild goddess Ganga poured to Earth from the heavens as Shiva sat atop the highest peak. Ganga is said to have flowed through Shiva's dreadlocks and in this way, her wildness was tamed just enough to flow onto Earth.

Making our way into the steep mountains, winding up and up before we reached the end of the road, we stopped to meet with Nanima (Grandmother), who directed a small ashram along the shore of the river. Considered a kind of saint, having completely dedicated her life to her guru and his teachings, Nanima was yet another form of the Buddha on our pilgrim's path. We found her working in her garden, dressed in a white sari, head covered, her weathered face smiling widely to reveal decayed teeth and a warm open heart. She welcomed us onto the porch of her cottage where we talked, huddled close together around the Earth Treasure Vase. Nanima asked if she could hold the vase. She was quiet, then said, "It is full of healing . . . it has a great healing power in it." She meditated, then added, "I have joined my small contribution into it. Your love for the Earth and your desire to help, these are the most healing things of all."

Her heart, cleansed by a daily bath in the holy river high above Rishikesh, where she had spent many years with her guru, was a powerful example of strength and dedication, radiant beauty and clarity. She spoke to us of the damage to the Earth and the holy river, echoing what Charok Rinpoche said so many years ago—that even just one person who has realized the nature of truth will benefit the entire planet. "Normally a human being has one responsibility only—and that is to join the Oneness. The world is a secondary responsibility," she said. "But nowadays, because the world is in such pain, it has become more important for spiritual seekers to help." She paused, then reflected, "And while we do these things, we have to watch ourselves carefully to make sure that only purity is flowing through us, that we are not giving any hurt in any way to anybody. We've got to be aware and alert and clear because the world is very sick, and it can only be healed through love. We must care for ourselves, and we must care for each other—that is caring for the Earth."

Nanima looked at us gently and observed, "Purity lives inside us, and as we come to know that purity, then that reality spreads, and our caring also spreads. We must care more and more because the darkness is very strong at the moment. But goodness and love are also strong and are growing. It is wonderful and beautiful that you care, and I thank you from so deep inside that I cannot tell you."

Nanima told us about her personal relationship to the river Ganga-ji. "She is very much a living presence. You see, She is Shakti: She brings life on every level. Ganga-ji comes from the heart, not just in one stream but spreading out everywhere. When I was holding the vase, I felt the contents of peace and how the peace and the love in the vase were going to spread out everywhere, through every crack and through every vein of the Earth. It is very correct to put it somewhere near Ganga."

Nanima's words connected me to my growing sense that planting an Earth Treasure Vase at the source of the Ganges was important not just for India, but for the whole world. Nanima confirmed my feelings. "In the body, all limbs are important, but the heart has a special place," she said. "India is the heart of this world. And, you could say, the main artery is Ganga-ji. Ganga-ji is the nectarine flow from the heart to the world."

Then Shantum asked Nanima to comment on the Tehri Dam being built on the sacred Ganges. "The dam is terrible for Ganga-ji! My guru called it 'Mother's rape.' The divine flow is love and knowledge, and when our selfish desire stops this flow, it is both symbolic and actual. What Ganga-ji really brings is spiritual bounty. But we are strangling, raping, and forcing her to do what we want, so of course everything is going wrong," she said forcefully. "Humans as a whole, as a race, have gotten so far from the center, from divine understanding. Ganga-ji is water, but She is not just water, just as we are not just flesh and blood. There is a soul, a pure individual. Ganga-ji is pure Shakti, but her individuality is a devi. Now, can that devi live in water that is being contaminated and corrupted and cut off from its divine source? No. Baba-ji said we are driving away these spirits and devis and gods from the Earth. But he also said they will stay for their devotees; they will stay for those who relate to them. There are so many subtle realities!"

Shantum plucked a yellow flower growing next to the porch and presented it to Nanima to offer into the vase. We opened the vase, and she poured the flower out of her two hands held together in prayer in the same way she offers water from the Ganga each day. Then she told us it would be good if the vase went to the source of the Ganga at Gomukh, the glacier, but that could only happen in summer—not now, in spring. She told us the spiritual source of Ganga is in Gangotri, which we may or may not be able to reach now. Shantum mentioned that we needed to bury the vase in a place that will never be disturbed, an anonymous place. Nanima let us know that it would be impossible to find such a place in Gangotri, but that up on the sides of the mountain in the forest along the road, we would find a place.

Nanima took the vase in her hands once again, and then she passed it around our little circle. We each added our prayers to hers. When the vase returned to me, I wrapped it in a white khata and put it back in its traveling container. As the group prepared to leave, I told Nanima, "When I met the Tibetan lama who gave me the practice of the Earth Treasure Vases, he said, 'Even just one person practicing deeply will bring benefit to the whole area around where they are.' This is such a place and you are such a person."

The next morning, we returned to her ashram to pick up a shovel and trowel, and she told us she had dreamed about the vase and was certain, having lived on the glacier for so long, that the forest before the bridge was the place we should take the vase.

For our closing ceremony, we drove to where we could walk down to the white sand next to the river's edge and shared one final meditation, placing our last offerings into the little holy vessel before ritually sealing it for burial. Once the vase was ready, we made our way up the steep road cutting through the mountains, the glacier ice-melt running like blue milk in the gorge far below. Marveling at the beauty of Her waters, Shantum told us how the sailing ships of old would pay dearly for fresh water from the Ganges to store on board for the long haul across oceans, for it would stay fresh longer than any other water in the world.

As we approached mile marker 108, we found the spot to bury the vase in the forest of Jangala, just as Nanima had indicated. To avoid suspicion, we decided to divide up as a group, with three of us going to the bridge for a "picnic" and three hopping out into the forest to "explore" the area. I was sorry that we could not all share the final burial experience but grateful to our fellow pilgrims Marge, Carolyn, and Paul, who agreed to the plan and allowed the burial to happen without them—bodhisattvas all. And I was confident Shantum, Jagdish, and I had found the right place since Nanima had been so clear where the vase was to go.

Back at Nanima's the next morning, she greeted us warmly and was very happy to hear our story. She confirmed that it had been wise of us to send decoys to the bridge in the van while just a few of us buried the vase in the forest. She led us to the river to meditate next to Ganga one last time.

When it was time to go, Nanima and I walked toward the gate together, and when I asked her to pray for us, she looked me in the eyes and said yes. At the gate, all of us hugged her, and Jagdish touched her feet. As I started up the steps from the gate, the sun came out from over the mountains and touched our skin. The sky was the bluest of blue, clear and beautiful, and the fruit trees were flowering everywhere. She stood at the gate and watched us go. I turned back, with tears in my eyes, to see her standing there. When I looked again, she was gone.

The pilgrimage in India was a journey to the source—the source of the Buddha's teaching; the source of the Ganges, the Great Mother of Life; and the true source within our own hearts. We came to see the Buddha not as an idealized mythic figure but as a real person alive in you and in me. Looking at India, we saw not the romanticized postcard version, but the dammed and poisoned river and the ravaged wasteland, and were able to ask, Where am I poisoned, too? Where am I blocked, dammed, or damaged? And, Where is my beauty amid all the rubbish—my compost on its way to a rose, as Thich Nhat Hanh would say?

After such a pilgrimage, do we return home to the safety of our familiar life with self-assured answers and fabulous pictures to show, or do we walk the path home into all aspects of our life? Reentering our familiar lives, do we dare look at each experience with the eyes of new awareness, seeing things through a different lens gained from our journey? How do we share our experience for the benefit of all?

SECTION TWO

HEARING THE CRIES OF THE WORLD

CHAPTER SEVEN

PLANETARY ACUPUNCTURE

In the beginning, it was relatively easy to know where the vases should go in our own part of the world. But they needed to be spread around the whole planet. India was a good start.

I spun the globe on my altar, and let my gaze fall on places that seemed to call out. In my meditations, I would find myself contemplating certain parts of the world and how the suffering or beauty in those places affected the whole. The global situation seemed impossible to take in, and I would end up looking away. It was all too much. But my love simply would not let me turn away from the beautiful web of life, so in need of healing and protection. I realized I was going to have to go places I did not necessarily want to go and that this would not be easy.

Over time, the vases would go out in every direction; each one we planted, another point on the mandala. We were activating a kind of acupuncture for the planet to restore balance and bring harmony in every location. The vases, like acupuncture needles, literally grounded our intentions for healing in Gaia's body—on mountains and at rivers, in forests and in seas, in war zones and in sacred places, in urban jungles and in remote villages, embracing the whole Earth in our love.

My husband, Hugh, who is an acupuncturist—as well as a veterinarian specializing in protecting endangered species—counseled our sangha about the difference between strengthening positive energy and reducing negative energy in acupuncture treatments. He suggested that places where the Earth has been clear-cut, dammed, drilled, or degraded, and the vital energy is weak, need to be strengthened to facilitate the flow of energy. And in places ravaged by war, rape, violent storms, or terrible pollution, the congestion of negative energy needs to be reduced and released. When the treasure vases were brought into an area, it felt as if they naturally brought the needed balance to restore and regenerate the whole system.

The focus of our full moon meditations shifted from the local to the global, taking in the whole Earth, not just what was happening in our own backyard. In the process of filling each vase, we would form a direct relationship with the location where it was destined to go. As we focused our attention on different parts of the world, those places revealed themselves from afar. Clues would come in, guiding us to where the vase needed to go. Someone would call to make an unexpected introduction that would later prove to be a key in opening the way to going there. Something was guiding the process that was beyond my rational understanding. Later, no matter where we went or what culture or spiritual tradition we encountered, when we took the vases to receive offerings and prayers from local elders, activists, and community members, everyone recognized how Mother Earth was out of balance and renewal was needed. The vases became our ambassadors, opening doors and connecting us to communities in countries far away—and the offerings given to the vases activated all of our prayers.

I felt it was critically important for the vases to be kept open until the final burial so that the people in the region where the vase was to be placed could become full participants in the work of healing their own corner of the world. After all, the offerings arising from the local culture are always much more appropriate and meaningful than anything we might offer from somewhere else. And since the whole world was calling for healing and protection in very serious ways, I had to acknowledge that the medicines in Tibet may be unheard of in Africa, the outback of Australia, or the heartland of America. I imagine most Tibetans would be horrified to know someone once offered natural fertilizer (dung) into an Earth Treasure Vase, saying it was "black gold" for restoring the health of the soil. But what better offering could be made nowadays? Keeping the Earth Treasure Vases open to the planet's diversity has allowed the pots to embody something meaningful to everyone, everywhere.

As the vases were embedded in various regions, we began to sense the connections between them. I later learned the Aboriginal Australians call these connections in the land where the energy flows "songlines." Those who study geomancy refer to the Earth's ley lines. In our meditations, we would perceive the meridians carrying healing energy from one vase location to the next, from one bioregion to another.

The treasure vases were giving us a way to administer to the sickness of Mother Earth, feel her pulse, lay our hands on and place a healing remedy in key points of her body. An untapped potential of deep caring and compassion was arising within us like a wellspring, and cultivating this felt like a key to our planet's survival.

Every location to which I would take a vase would connect me to a wound in the body of Mother Earth—whether physical, mental, emotional, or spiritual—a wound that I would feel physically in my own body, or deeply in my heart and mind. Bringing along a little clay pot whose sole purpose was to inspire healing and protection would bring me into contact with difficult truths—in myself, in the land, and in others.

To heal wounds that have been carried for a long time, even lifetimes in the case of intergenerational trauma, as is the case in New Mexico where we still need to heal the wounds of colonization, it would be necessary to reenter those old wounds held in the land—and in ourselves. I would discover that reexperiencing those old wounds in the light of a sacred intention for collective healing makes transformation possible.

How could we be certain that this remedy would work? We couldn't. But in carrying it out, we were taken beyond ourselves to that field that the great Sufi poet Rumi talks about when he says, "Out beyond ideas of wrongdoing and rightdoing there is a field. I'll meet you there."[1] The more we were willing to open and be a vessel for healing for all the places calling for an Earth Treasure Vase, the more possibility there was for something new to happen, for healing to occur—something we could never predict with the limited views of our conceptual mind.

We didn't know how the healing would happen. But sometimes an individual wakes up, an entire community is catalyzed in a new direction, and we see clearly what we couldn't see before.

CHAPTER EIGHT

A THOUSAND ARMS

Burdened by the enormous assignment I had taken on, I often felt alone. Yet I was possessed by a sense of purpose I could not shake, and I knew that one way or another, I had to make it happen. With the state of the world breathing down my neck, I heroically muscled through even though under the surface I had terrible feelings of inadequacy.

The lamas in the Himalayas had told me to just "plant the vases in the ground and they'll do the work." But they gave me no guidance after I left Nepal and I was not authorized in the traditional way. I imagined there were others within the tradition who wondered, "Who does she think she is?" So I kept a low profile and felt my way, not really knowing what in the world to do or how to do it, only that I had to do it "right"—for the sake of all beings.

I was striving hard to do it all myself, heal the entire world, and bring all the broken places back into wholeness. That is naturally what women do, right? I accepted this task was mine to do and was happy and grateful I had something so meaningful to pour my heart into. But as the job became global in scope, there came a time when I realized I could not keep going without support. I was used to doing everything myself and did not know how to ask for help.

When others started offering to take vases, I was relieved. A creative response was being catalyzed in us as a group. It seemed like the locations where the vases were going embodied some of the most pressing issues to be healed today. We did not decide where the vases should go. We simply responded to the requests and suggestions that presented themselves when we met each full moon.

Then it all came to a screeching halt. I had a little money but not enough to take this global healing project where it needed to go. I had to learn to receive the generosity of others, and this humbled and remade me. Carrying on was only thanks to the generosity of those who recognized the worthiness of this work—and joined me in it. To keep going, I had to invite partners and collaborators. I had to learn to be supported by something larger than myself.

Like the thousand arms of Avalokiteshvara, the Bodhisattva of Compassion, a larger community formed around the treasure vases, with more and more of us answering the call. Our little sangha was quietly becoming a global healing community. Avalokiteshvara is known as "the one who hears the cries of the world and responds in countless ways." I was immensely relieved not to have to distribute the vases entirely on my own and grateful to those who stepped forward to help serve the mission.

About Avalokiteshvara, Buddhist scholar Vessantara writes in *Meeting the Buddhas: A Guide to Buddhas, Bodhisattvas, and Tantric Deities*, "Each of the arms is reaching out to help suffering beings, and from the palm of each hand a beautiful eye gazes down compassionately."[1] Vessantara sees Avalokiteshvara as a symbol for the spiritual community, with each person "reaching out in their own life to offer their talents and capabilities; yet they also work in concert, united by their common vision . . . a perfect symbol for the blending of unity and diversity."[2]

Master gardener and Zen teacher Wendy Johnson responded passionately to the practice of the Earth Treasure Vases and brought her capable hands to the process of planting the vases in the Earth. Realizing what a formidable task lay ahead, Wendy invited a large group of kindred spirits to Green Gulch Farm Zen Center in California to hear about the assignment.

After a meditation and prayer ceremony with the vases, a number of key allies came forward, offering to take vases to important locations around the world. One went to Hiroshima, Japan. Another to the former Yugoslavia. And yet another was taken to the headwaters of the Amazon River. I was encouraged to imagine that together we could realize our dreams for global peace and healing.

Wendy took up the practice of the treasure vases enthusiastically and engaged with a number of them directly. In 1998, she accepted one of the first vases to travel beyond New Mexico and took it to the Headwaters Forest Reserve in Northern California, to the frontlines of the "Redwood Nation" where forest activists had been protecting the last stand of old-growth coast redwoods. With a small group of intrepid activists, Wendy hiked into the deep forest for hours, skirting a raw, twenty-acre clear-cut to drop down into unmapped primeval forest. She wrote:

We disappeared hip-deep in drifts of decayed duff. The moist sloughed-off litter of the ancient forest. Sword ferns towered above our heads. Huckleberry and native salal grew thick in the snapped-off crowns of dead snags. On the floor of the forest, we could hardly move, so dense were the downed logs.

After a long time, we arrived at the Headwaters Grove. Exhausted, we sat down beneath three-hundred-foot-high trees, some with a ten-foot girth. Cold mist blew through the forest, dripping down twisted scarves of old-man's beard lichen that hung like pale shrouds from the prehistoric trees. This was the heart of the forest, and dark. We found a high ledge above the sweet water that is the source of the Elk River and agreed to plant the vase there, between a wild gap-toothed snag and a huge, healthy redwood giant. We bowed, lit candles, dedicated our work into prayer, and, with an invocation to the Shambhala Warriors, buried the vase well under the surface roots of the guardian redwood leaning over the convergence of two icy streams.[3]

Wendy also stewarded a vase to New York City, in response to the tragedy that struck the World Trade Center on September 11, 2001. While the dust was still settling, she brought a vase to sit on the Ancestors' Altar of the Village Zendo, two miles from Ground Zero. She and local sangha members contemplated where to find a home for the vase, and ultimately, the vase was shepherded one early morning to Inwood Hill Park at the end of the A line on the subway. There, the caretaker gave permission to bury the vase high above the Cloisters, overlooking the Hudson and Harlem Rivers, on beautiful land protected in perpetuity by the state. Digging by hand, they lined the deep hole with autumn leaves and, while chanting to Avalokiteshvara, passed the vase once more before placing it in the ground.

Wendy stepped forward a third time, and together, we delivered an Earth Treasure Vase to Ajahn Pasanno, co-abbot of Abhayagiri Monastery in Northern California, a Theravada Buddhist monastery in the Thai Forest Tradition of the late Ajahn Chah, whose disciples are strict renunciates and live very simply. Following the Buddha's example, they do a three-month retreat during the rainy season every year in the remote Dtao Dum Forest in Thailand near the border with Burma. This region is under constant threat from civil war and is prey to illegal drug trafficking. The pristine forest is also vulnerable to clear-cutting and development. Wendy and I journeyed to Mendocino County to meet the monks and nuns at Abhayagiri Monastery and present them with the vase that would be placed at Wat Pah Nanachat. After burying the vase, Ajahn Pasanno wrote, "The vase was planted in a powerful spot where the local devas live, overlooking the valley on a rise of land. Buddha relics and golden protection amulets were offered to the vase and as the hole was dug, everyone sprinkled flower petals on top of the vase as the monks chanted a victory blessing." To this day, the pristine land and wildlife found in Dtao Dum Forest is still protected.

• • •

Abigail Alling and Mark Van Thillo were founding members of the team behind Biosphere 2, an architectural wonder built in the Arizona desert to contain all the ecosystems of Earth's biosphere inside a structure that would model a living, breathing, life-enhancing support system of the whole Earth—a laboratory for the study of global ecology. They helped construct Biosphere 2, lived inside it, and demonstrated how our world is a delicate living system, needing care. Their work and that of the other Biospherians was misunderstood, and in 1994, two years into the experiment, they were forcibly evacuated, suffering greatly over the loss and violent takeover of their visionary adventure in sustainability that was years ahead of its time. In 2002, still coming to terms with what happened, they asked if we could take an Earth Treasure Vase there to symbolize the healing so needed for the entire biosphere.[4]

"We were filled with intention as we eagerly climbed the path into the hills," Abigail reflected. "Giant saguaros stood like sentinels along the path. Hawks soared above, circling a location ahead. We breathed the crisp morning air and knew the spot lay before us. We buried the vase below an old saguaro standing among the boulders overlooking the stream. When the deed was done, our hearts leapt into the morning air, and we bounded back down the path, convinced a new story had been initiated as two white-tailed deer scampered along with us."

Indeed, something new *had* been initiated. Abigail, a marine biologist, and Mark, a crafty engineer, had learned a lot about our planet during their time inside of Biosphere 2. The coral reefs in the "ocean" they designed were the first ecosystem to let them know their enormous replica of the web of life was going out of balance. After they left their experiment in Arizona, they sailed the seas to bring awareness and protection to the world's coral reefs. They requested another Earth Treasure Vase for the South Pacific Ocean, which traveled onboard their research vessel where scientists, environmental activists, and young interns sailing around Papua New Guinea and Southeast Asia gathered with communities on remote islands to honor the intention of the vase with prayers and offerings.

In 2007, Hugh and I joined the expedition. The final ceremony with the vase took place in the magnificent setting of Isala Island at dawn on board the ship, with many members of the island joining us. We lit candles and floated tropical flowers in giant seashells for our altar, and everyone made offerings into the vase—including haunting island songs the women sang in perfect harmony. When the chief held the vase, he prayed for their ocean community that was slowly disappearing under the rising waters and wept.

We set sail for Egum Atoll, which has a vertical reef wall on its outer rim. Dolphins gathered at the surface, close to the narrow entrance into the deep lagoon. The vase had been sealed into an underwater camera housing unit. A small group donned scuba gear and dove ninety-three feet down to find a perfect little crevasse to secure the vase while gentle reef sharks patrolled all around. The group made an underwater circle and held hands briefly to celebrate the moment just as an enormous manta ray appeared, fanning the turquoise waters as they swam back to the surface—mission accomplished!

Together we had succeeded in adding two more treasure vases encompassing the entire biosphere and the oceans of this water planet, and they were now beaming their prayers out from these unforgettable locations.

• • •

In 2011, Brad Laughlin and Leslie Temple Thurston, the cofounders of a spiritual and humanitarian school called Corelight, assisted us with the burial of another two Earth Treasure Vases—this time to strengthen the energy coursing through the Nilotic Meridian from South Africa to Egypt. The Nilotic Meridian is one of the Earth's major ley lines, starting at the Great Pyramids and the River Nile and stretching all the way to the tip of South Africa. This is the spine of Africa, the axis mundi of the Earth, where life began.

We started our South Africa Earth Treasure Vase pilgrimage in the Kalahari Desert to meet the Khoisan elders and ask for their blessings for the vase. The Khoisan culture is one of the oldest on Earth, and these elders should be held in the greatest regard. Instead, the remaining members of this peaceful tribe live in poverty and desperation. We knew we must honor them and were grateful they received us warmly. At a sacred cave, we met with the old grandmothers, only one of whom still spoke the language. It was here that we brought out the Earth Treasure Vase for a special ceremony to offer our prayers for their well-being and to receive theirs into the vase.

Continuing on our pilgrimage, the vase was then taken to the Global White Lion Protection Trust in the Greater Timbavati region. Established by our friend Linda Tucker, this home for the prophesied white lions offers protection to these noble creatures. We arrived at the refuge at sundown, and in the fading light went out for a game drive in open-roofed Land Rovers to meet the white lions. I will never forget the breathtaking sight of the lioness, Zirah, dozing with her offspring in a dry riverbed after a big feed. Hardly breathing so as not to wake her, we watched and waited as she eventually roused herself to sit up in a regal pose. She gazed at us just as the full moon broke through the treetops and cast its brilliant light on her white fur. I lingered in this timeless moment; I have almost never seen anything more beautiful in all my life. Her three juvenile cubs woke from their nap, too, and played around her as she held court in the lap of Mother Earth, granting us a transmission rivaling that of any great spiritual teacher.

That night, tucked in bed, we were awakened by a strange sound. The lions had come to where we slept in our protected corral and roared the whole night long. Linda was sure they were there in response to our sacred mission, and in our ceremony the next day, the vase was opened to receive their roars!

We buried the vase near a thirty-thousand-year-old stone altar at the rim of the Blyde River Canyon. This ancient altar had been identified by the renowned Zulu sangoma and elder Credo Mutwa. The night of the burial, Brad received permission for us to stay in the park to meditate after closing. As night fell, we planted the vase deep down in the rock. When the vase was lowered into the Earth, we all felt a powerful vibration traveling up the Nilotic Meridian as if our prayers had entered a planetary communication channel like a current of intentional healing energy for Gaia being carried all the way up to the pyramids. With this, we knew we had to anchor our prayers for the Earth with another vase in Egypt.

Six months later, Brad and Leslie took a vase to the Giza Plateau with a group and planted it near the Great Pyramid to connect north to south on the African continent. They gathered at the pyramids on 11/11/11, a date foreseen by some spiritual leaders as significant. But rumors of terrorism shut everything down at the pyramids that day. Luckily for the group, there was nobody there, which made it much easier to bury the vase. Brad noted:

In Egypt, the spiritual energy is so powerful—amplified by the Great Pyramid with its vortex of energy that heightens one's intentions and whatever is going on. With the treasure vase, we experienced being held in a protected bubble with everything conspiring to support us in fulfilling our mission. Even though the Giza Plateau had been shut down, we were allowed to go incognito to a power place we had foreseen as the burial location adjacent to the Great Pyramid. There were barricades and soldiers all over the place and we could not bring attention to ourselves in any way—which was hard to do with a group of twenty-one. But we snuck out in the dark on camels with the vase wrapped, sealed, and packed like a precious royal mummy in her little tomb.

Just five hundred meters from the pyramid, the group circled up, and, remarkably, were given privacy, singing songs and ringing bells to hide the sound of the shovel clanging against the rocks in the sand.

Brad concluded by saying:

Finally the vase in her little casket was placed deep in the ground, and everyone covered her with sand, until, at last, she was fully entombed. Once the burial was complete, we laid down on the ground with our heads together to take in the moment. Gazing at the full moon and stars, we prayed for protection for the vase. It was a heavenly evening, blessed and holy. It felt like with the placement of the two Earth Treasure Vases along the Nilotic Meridian, we had "turned up the dial" on the energy that was already flowing and the natural spiritual power of the vases was enhanced and amplified.

By the end of that November, a hundred thousand people were protesting in Cairo's Tahrir Square, calling for an end to military rule in what came to be called Arab Spring. We innocently imagined the vase might have played a part in bringing change. It may be that with the little holy vessel planted next to one of the most powerful sacred sites on Earth, our prayers will one day be answered. For now, I feel the vase working every full moon when we invoke all the treasure vase locations and a palpable energy from Egypt radiates out from the Giza Plateau as if it is feeding the whole global mandala with ancient wisdom and vast knowledge beyond time and space.

• • •

My mother would have probably been one of those people who scoffed at a little clay pot filled with prayers and offerings as a form of activism to bring about social or environmental change. She never went to church a day in her life—she was more about rolling up her sleeves and getting to work in her community.

So I was surprised when, without having intentionally set out to do so, one of the vases ended up being buried in my hometown of Oakland, California. My friend Claire Greensfelder, a dedicated activist who directed the Martin Luther King Jr. Freedom Center in Oakland at that time, worked with young people in the African American community to empower them as rising leaders. The Center, located on the shores of San Francisco Bay, was part of a regional park started by African American elders in the community and dedicated to Dr. Martin Luther King Jr. The Freedom Center's cofounder, an elder named Charlie Mae Davis, spoke to me about her experience traveling in the back of the bus during the struggle for integration. She hand-sewed a little quilt to wrap around the Earth Treasure Vase when it was buried, and she held high hopes for its impact.

Much to my surprise, when Claire took me to the Freedom Center, on a brick wall with the names of local patrons engraved on each brick, I discovered my mother's name on not one but *two* bricks! Florence L. Jurs was a long-time member of many of Oakland's community organizations. She was an innovator in public school programs and founded Oakland Potluck to distribute leftover food to feed the hungry. When I saw her name on that wall, I knew we had found our spot.

My mother had died six years earlier, but I felt her spirit caring for Oakland and the social justice issues that the park and the Freedom Center represented. I recalled how she imbued in me the activist's heart. So when we made our final offerings into the vase, I placed some of my mother's ashes into that little clay pot. I also offered some of my father's—for he grew up in Oakland and loved that land, too. Gene was a businessman and woodworker, who also served on Oakland's agencies and boards. He had once mapped every inch of that town himself to earn a merit badge as an Eagle Scout. I think he knew every road and neighborhood like the back of his hand. Although my parents would not have called it "sacred activism," they were certainly engaged in a path of service in their home community, the place they loved.

• • •

Going to meet the elders in South Africa, witnessing the Arab Spring after the vases were planted along the Nilotic Meridian, and burying a vase in Oakland activated my awareness of civil rights and the pressing issues of social justice around the globe that I knew we had to address if we wanted to bring healing to the Earth. The vases were calling me to go more deeply into action, and I felt the hand of fate directing me to go from Oakland to Liberia, a place whose history as a nation—founded by freed American slaves—would be the next step on the path. The plot was thickening, the interconnection between the vases and their locations were being revealed, and there were some deep core wounds calling out around the world.

I came to realize that part of the global healing called for is rethinking the belief in the West that we must do everything individually. Systemic change will require a massive movement not unlike the Arab Spring, only bigger. I was personally moving away from the old destructive patriarchal worldview to finding solidarity with others. My time of solo striving was giving way to a collective responsiveness unlike anything I had ever seen or experienced before.

I saw that the Bodhisattva of Compassion needs a thousand arms to accomplish the great task of alleviating suffering in every direction. And so does Gaia. In order to accomplish the task of global healing in these dire times, we simply must unite in our efforts. Gaia was asking for a collective awakening. Thich Nhat Hanh had pointed to this one memorable day during a retreat at Plum Village in 1993, when he told us in no uncertain terms: "It is possible that the next Buddha will not take the form of an individual. The next Buddha may take the form of a sangha—a community practicing understanding and love, a community practicing mindful living. This may be the most important thing we can do for the survival of the Earth."[5]

As his words rippled out into the group gathered there, you could hear a pin drop. It felt prophetic. He was recognizing the path of awakening for our times. We were going to need to wake up *together*.

CHAPTER NINE

TWENTY-ONE TARAS

I was starting to get the message: the only way to accomplish the work of global healing was in community. But in concentrating so hard on the task "out there," I was ignoring the subtle messages coming from within. I was overriding my own needs to keep doing the more "important" work of healing the Earth, taking on more and more to "save the world." Finding balance between the inner and outer was not easy.

I had been deeply programmed by conventional expectations in my family and conditioned by our culture to serve the patriarchy by being a pretty sexual object. To prove I was more than just my appearance, I sacrificed myself to the work, doing as much as I could to respond to the cries of the Earth, plunging blindly into unknown territory with no one to guide me. I encountered judgment and jealousy, often from other women who were trained to compete to get ahead, and was often met with dismissal. Although I could not admit it, I needed healing myself and desperately longed for a healthy model of the sacred feminine to serve as a spiritual guide.

Then Tara arrived. She had actually been there all along, repeatedly knocking at the door of my heart. But I had not been capable of receiving her.

• • •

It is said Tara was born from the tears of Avalokiteshvara, the Bodhisattva of Great Compassion, when he beheld the suffering of the world and became so overwhelmed that he broke down weeping. According to legend, Tara had been a spiritually devoted noblewoman in her lifetime who was told by the male adepts that she should pray to be reborn as a man so that she might attain enlightenment. She dismissed them all and vowed that until the end of cyclic existence, she would only ever take birth as a woman and ceaselessly devote herself to benefiting beings who are suffering, confused, lost, or afraid. She would be known as Tara, the Savioress.

"The goddess Tara, green in her primary and most popular forms, appears to blossom, delicate as a flower petal, amid her aureole of leaves and lotuses," writes Miranda Shaw in her book *Buddhist Goddesses of India.* "Her persona is redolent with the richness of the earth as she sits on a lotus throne in a lush, harmonious landscape, the very image of the benevolent face of mother nature. Tara encompasses the starry heavens, the teeming oceans, the flowering planet. As the Star Lady, she shines in the firmament as a guiding light. As Savioress, she guides her devotees across the perilous seas of life. As the lotus-bearing goddess, she tends the universe as if it were her garden, nurturing beings from the budding of aspiration to the full bloom of enlightenment."[1]

My first connection to Tara formed shortly after I began to practice meditation in the 1980s, when I decided to do a solitary retreat. I had been drawn to learning more about Tibetan Buddhism and visited the local spiritual bookstore to equip myself for a deeper understanding. As I stood before the Buddhist section, a recently published book called *Women of Wisdom* by Tsultrim Allione fell off the shelf. I purchased the book and drove to the foothills of the Sierras in Northern California to a place our family called the Ranch—a refuge built by my grandparents and maintained by my aunts and uncles. The quiet of the place would be good medicine.

Arriving at the Ranch, I walked the rolling, golden, grass-covered California hills and found a knoll overlooking a lake. I constructed a circle of rocks, and within that circle, I meditated. That night, I arranged a bed next to the fireplace and read *Women of Wisdom*. Tsultrim described her search for women teachers as role models inside the patriarchy of old Tibet. I soaked up her translations of the biographies of the extraordinary women practitioners whose stories we so rarely hear. The next day, an experience of the sacred feminine began to awaken in me. Sitting in meditation outside, within my protective stone circle, I saw a Tibetan-style deity rising from out of my heart into the space in front of me—on a lotus!

She was beautiful and captivating, but being new to Vajrayana Buddhism and with no prior teachings or training in this kind of visualization, I was not familiar with this imagery—or so I thought. But there she was, nonetheless. The female figure that appeared in the space in front of me was fully formed and life-sized. As I sat absorbed in this vision, she faded, and another similar goddess rose up out of my heart on a lotus into the space in front of me. One by one, different images of the goddess appeared. Each was vivid and real, and each had distinguishing characteristics. Time and again, day after day, I saw her appearing before me, in what seemed like countless forms, "resplendent as a thousand constellations,"[2] as one of the texts says—very real and yet insubstantial, like a rainbow. When this happened not only during my waking hours in meditation but also in my dreams, I really began to wonder!

When I returned home, I signed up for a retreat Tsultrim Allione was holding nearby. We became spiritual friends, and through her, the Vajrayana path opened up for me. She invited me to travel to Tibet with her on a pilgrimage to Mt. Kailash with her teacher, Namkhai Norbu Rinpoche, and soon he became my teacher, too. I assisted Tsultrim with her early retreats on the Mandala of the Five Buddha Families and learned so much from her. She went on to found Tara Mandala, a retreat center in southern Colorado, and was later recognized as the reincarnation of Machig Labdron, a great female teacher of the eleventh century.

About Tara, Lama Tsultrim Allione writes: "Green Tara is very appropriate for this moment in time because she is a contemplative activist . . . She has one foot in and one foot out of meditation. The foot in meditation is in nirvana, and the foot that is out is in samsara and active in the world. She is able to keep her meditative awareness as she steps out to confront suffering. And she is green—she has her own Green Party!"

Tara embodies active compassion and is said to always come when called. She is also known to provide protection from fears and helps us to overcome obstacles. Tsultrim points out that Tara's feminine wisdom and compassion are much needed now to bring balance back to the Earth. "The reemergence of Tara's energy, her feminine wisdom and her compassion are essential for the Earth and all people right now. We are out of balance and feminine wisdom is lacking. . . . For those who know this, but are not sure how to access this feminine wisdom and bring it into the world, entering a practice like Green Tara creates a template for the development of that wisdom. . . . It begins to help you access the wisdom of the feminine through the process of identification."[3]

After that first solo retreat when Tara appeared to me, I organized the Peaceful Cultures Council, and a few months later, traveled to Asia for the first time. In Bhutan, searching for peaceful cultures, I met the lama who became my first guru. Rinpoche welcomed us warmly to his monastery and invited us to stay. He spoke no English and had yet to travel outside of this remote region of the world. We formed a heart connection, and, in spite of the language difference, we understood each other. I managed to tell him about my experience of this female deity appearing in meditation and dreams during my retreat. Excitedly, he took me down to the sprawling old temple courtyard and introduced me to Tara and her twenty-one emanations, which were depicted in paintings behind the prayer wheels that encircled the main temple. Could this be her? Yes! It most certainly was exactly what I'd seen! Rinpoche smiled knowingly and took me back inside, where, through his translator, he told me more about Tara and gave me her mantra.

Reciting Tara's mantra and visualizing her in meditation became my practice throughout my travels in Asia. Over the decades of my evolving dharma study and practice, I was aware that even if she wasn't the main focus, Tara was always nearby.

Then, in 2009, the other Lama Tsultrim came back into my life. I could hardly believe it had been nineteen years since Lama Ngawang Tsultrim Zangpo had guided me to meet Charok Rinpoche, and I had received the Earth Treasure Vases. We had maintained a friendly relationship over the years and witnessed each other grow and change. He would disappear for years at a time, and so would I. Then we would come back to pick up right where we left off. He always responded warmly with his characteristic kind heart and quiet, sensitive demeanor.

When I shared with him the way the Earth Treasure Vases had become such a powerful practice for me over the years, he was pleased. Then he brought out another practice that he said would greatly support our work with the Earth Treasure Vases—the practice of the Twenty-One Taras, in which one visualizes the goddess in all her different forms and prays for her help.

One morning, after several public events with Lama Tsultrim to reconsecrate the remaining vases and give teachings, I joined him in front of the altar in the round room at home where we practice. He sat preparing offerings for the vases, joking with me and sipping his tea. Setting his work aside, he suggested we do the practice of the Twenty-One Taras together. As we recited the liturgy, I felt my long-held connection to Tara and search for the sacred feminine being reawakened. I also felt Lama Tsultrim's companionship. He had been a true friend whose simple way of being invited me to relax and open to receive Tara's spiritual support. I realized I had become stretched thin in my efforts to carry out the Earth Treasure Vases in recent years. I was about to go to Africa and I needed her more than I cared to admit.

It had been a long journey to meet Tara again, and as I sat with Lama Tsultrim, I wept to feel her presence and reconnect. As a woman, I deeply needed a compassionate, feminine guide to put my faith in, whose commitment to all beings is, as it says in the teachings, "like a mother to her only child."

From then on, I took Tara with me everywhere I traveled with the vases, and as I did, I felt as if each of those twenty-one aspects of this feminine embodiment of Buddha Nature was like a different personification of the Earth herself. She had so many forms—each one a response to a given situation, all attempting to bring balance and be helpful, even if at times she was wrathful or destructive. Sometimes she seemed beautiful, peaceful, and calm, like a quiet pool or a gentle, flowing river. At other times, she appeared fierce or tempestuous, like a hurricane or volcano. She was an old-growth forest, a vast desert, a mountain massif, a forest fire, a gentle rain.

Tara became my constant companion, my protector, my guide, my spiritual friend, and my ally. Whenever my journey with the Earth Treasure Vases was particularly demanding, she showed me the way to open, trust, and act. As I set off for Africa, she accompanied me. I knew she would help me see the final treasure vase burials to completion. I had finally found the sacred feminine guide I had been looking for. Tara was showing me how to take care of myself. And I knew that if I was to succeed on the path of healing, both personally and globally, I needed her with me.

CHAPTER TEN

THE SOUND OF THE BELL IN AFRICA

In 2008, I received an invitation from activist-healer and author Deena Metzger to consider taking an Earth Treasure Vase to Liberia. Deena was working with a group called *everyday gandhis,* co-founded by an American, Cynthia Travis (Cyndie), and a Liberian, Bill Saa, to help bring peace back to the land after a terrible civil war. Together, they developed programs with women peacemakers, tribal elders, traditional healers, ex-combatants, and former child soldiers to tell their stories, mourn the dead, and build peace. I had no idea where Liberia was or anything about its history, but I knew I had to go.

The fourteen-year Liberian Civil War ended after Christian and Muslim women joined forces to start a peace movement of nonviolent resistance. The conviction and courage of these women united people across tribal and religious differences to stop the atrocities. The women took to the streets dressed in white. They fasted and prayed, stopped cooking and doing laundry for their men, and refused them sex. Demanding peace, in 2003 they *ended* the war and showed the world collective nonviolent action works, and that women can lead the way.[1] Although prayer was their mainstay, these women were in no way passive. Through their relentless and powerful presence, they found the strength to change Liberia and model how women could stand for life everywhere. After the war ended, Liberia's women united again to elect Ellen Johnson Sirleaf, the first woman president of any country in Africa, who, along with the founder of the women's peace movement, Leymah Gbowee, shared the 2011 Nobel Peace Prize.[2]

"Mama Deena," as she was affectionately called by the Liberians, invited me to conduct an Earth Treasure Vase ceremony at a gathering of a large group of American and Liberian peacebuilders hosted by *everyday gandhis* in California. I felt some trepidation entering their circle, not knowing how the vase would be received, but I unwrapped the little clay pot, set it before us, rang the bell, and hoped for the best. After the meditation, we passed the vase around the circle, and I witnessed, one by one, the most powerful prayers and offerings for peace I had ever heard—prayers from those who had survived the horrors of war. At the end of that ceremony, I knew for certain that the vase had to get to Liberia, to Lofa County, which borders Guinea and Sierra Leone in the north—where the worst fighting had taken place, and where *everyday gandhis* had done most of their work.

One of the people in the circle that day was Christian Wolo Bethelson, a former commander of the rebel forces in the region. Known as General Leopard, Bethelson had a long military career and was, by all accounts, a powerful leader. But like so many other ex-combatants after the war ended, he was disgraced, alienated, ashamed, and out of work. Without help from the government, he had no way to put rice on his family's table. The only thing he knew to do was to offer his services as a mercenary in the nearest war, so in 2005, he headed for Ivory Coast.

The dirt roads in Liberia are notoriously rough, especially during the rainy season, and on his way, Bethelson's car got stuck in the mud. As luck would have it, this was the very same place the *everyday gandhis'* vehicle was stuck in the mud, too. Overhearing their conversations about peacebuilding, he introduced himself to the group, which included Mama Deena, Ma Cyndie, and Bill Saa. Much to his surprise, Bethelson was invited to join their peacebuilding team—and said yes.

After the Earth Treasure Vase ceremony in California, Christian Bethelson approached me and, with his engaging laughter and slightly aggressive persona, questioned me about the practice. I did not think he was serious when he asked me to teach him to meditate. Then, a year later, when I flew to Monrovia with the vase, he was waiting for me as part of *everyday gandhis'* team that brought me to Lofa County.

It was a sweaty twelve-hour drive to Voinjama, the county seat of Lofa, on the famous muddy road that in the dry season transforms into a fine red dust. The deep ruts made the going rough, but when we arrived, close to midnight, the community welcomed me and asked to hear my story and that of the Earth Treasure Vase they had heard so much about. There was singing and dancing and I was honored with traditional gifts (a white chicken, a woven sleeping mat, and a bowl cut from a large gourd containing a bundle of the original Liberian money—long sticks of twisted black iron with flared ends—wrapped in a new white handkerchief). The vase was regarded with interest. I settled in for the night.

Bringing the vase as a gesture of peacebuilding opened the door for meetings with Christian and Muslim elders of various tribes, city and county leaders, women's groups, and former child soldiers with whom *everyday gandhis* had worked for so many years. In order to determine if the vase should be accepted, it was decided that a group of women led by a magnificent healer and diviner named Mahwen, who had assisted *everyday gandhis* with ceremonies they hosted in the community after the war to mourn the dead, would call upon the Ancestors to ask for their guidance and permission. A few days after I arrived, the drums came out at sunset, and Mahwen and the other women, wearing white bras and long skirts of colorful ribbons, began to dance. I sat on the edge of my seat, not knowing what would happen next.

After what felt like a long time, during which I wondered what I would do if they said no, the women entered a trance, and one of the women heard a voice speaking through her. It was the local paramount chief, recently deceased, who let us know that the vase would be a very good thing for the community and that the people should accept it. I breathed a sigh of relief, and the elders sitting around me nodded in agreement. Everyone was very happy, and permission was granted. The community leaders consulted with each other the next day and determined that the vase should be buried in the village of that same paramount chief. His village on the outskirts of Voinjama was where the community had once planned to build a cultural center honoring all the tribes of the region. But the war ended that dream. Now the elders concluded that the vase could serve to reignite that impulse and bring people together.

The community embraced the Earth Treasure Vase. A local carpenter in the market was commissioned to make a box for the vase to be buried in. Some of the former child soldiers got involved, decorating the box with their drawings. Invitations were sent to government officials and to respected elders representing Liberia, Guinea, and Sierra Leone, which share a common border and were equally affected by the war. This was going to be an important ceremony for everyone.

A few days later, the dignitaries arrived dressed in their finest hats, cloaks, and dresses, and assembled in *everyday gandhis'* courtyard ready to pray together before the final ceremony with the vase. A white sheep had been procured for the customary sacrifice at the start of such an important occasion, and from this, a meal would be prepared to eat together. As the speeches began, another member of *everyday gandhis* arrived. He was called Master General, and had also been a rebel commander in that region. I was impressed by his gentle presence as he took it upon himself to enter the large circle and tenderly hold the sheep that was to be sacrificed. He sat with it for several hours stroking its ears and talking to it in a soothing voice, while one by one the prayers and speeches were made.

That afternoon we gathered in Voinjama's city hall for the final ceremony with the Earth Treasure Vase. Hundreds of people came from three countries—all of whom took their seats in an enormous circle underneath red, white, and blue crepe paper streamers, and respectfully listened as I led the guided meditation. This was slow going as it was translated into three languages. After the meditation, the vase was opened and passed around the circle to receive everyone's prayers and offerings. Master General appeared again, and recognizing the treasure vase was fragile, came forward to accompany it around the entire circle—taking it carefully in his hands and passing it to the next person when needed, making sure it would not drop.

The ceremony took hours. Every single person there wanted to hold the vase and make their offering, and all listened attentively as each person blessed the vase and poured their prayers for peace into it. After making their prayers and offerings, some people went outside to talk among themselves, but they did not leave. This was a community who had lost everything during the war, and the vessel of peace represented life to them. Most had little to nothing of value to give. For many, a coin or Liberian dollar bill was an extremely precious offering—and giving it, a big sacrifice. But they gave all they had and did so sincerely. In addition to money, many placed a kola nut into the vase, as these are considered a gift of honor and respect to the traditional elders. I could not believe how much that little pot could hold!

At the end, Bethelson came forward to help me drape the silks over the vase, tie them in place, and seal the vase forever. We lowered the little pot wrapped in white scarves into the wooden box. With Mahwen by my side, I opened my bags of dried flowers, medicinal herbs, rice, and grains. The women in her group rushed forward to take handfuls and toss them in over the vase, filling the box and packing it protectively. The box was secured with a little luggage lock, and closing the lid, I handed Mahwen the tiny key to lock it for good, which she pocketed. I like to imagine it can now be found in her collection of divination bones.

Excitement filled the air as drumming and dancing commenced. *Everyday gandhis'* cultural troupe took to the floor, followed by Bethelson putting on a show, and finally everyone was on their feet celebrating. Master General scooped up the box and marched it around the hall surrounded by Mahwen and her women, city leaders, and elders, including one gentleman brandishing a sword, who was wrapped in a long tunic with the large image of a lion on it. Everyone was singing as we followed the box outside to the van where a small group of elder men were waiting to take the vase to Tellewoyan Village to be buried. I insisted there needed to be more women in our group and invited Mahwen to come with me. She took charge of the vase and cradled the box on her lap for the drive. When we arrived, she walked tall, carrying the box on her head into the village.

Nestled on the edge of the forest, Tellewoyan Village is an assembly of thatched-roof huts made of bamboo and wood for the extended family of the late Paramount Chief Baysah Tellewoyan, about twenty kilometers outside of Voinjama on a dirt road. Gathering with the family upon our arrival, the elders decided the vase should be buried at the base of a kola tree in the center of the village. The young men grabbed picks and shovels and dug into the hardened dirt. The sun was setting just as the hole was finished.

As the box was lowered into the ground, who should arrive but Master General on his motorbike! He immediately determined that the front of the box with the lock should be turned to face east and the rising sun—exactly as the Tibetans would advise. The box was turned and carefully set down into the hole. Everyone tossed handfuls of dirt over the box until it was covered and well buried. The children of the village joined us, and, holding hands in a circle, we shared a final blessing. Everyone agreed that something extraordinary had happened.

A seed had been planted and the Earth Treasure Vase had become an anchor for the possibility of peace in this volatile region. The elders turned to me then and said, "Now what? This was important. We want to remember our prayers!" It was Christian Wolo Bethelson who reminded the community of their long-held hope for a cultural center there and suggested we build a Palava Hut in Tellewoyan Village as a place to gather and keep the peace.

A Palava Hut, or Peace Hut, is a round, open-walled structure that has traditionally served as a place where people in a community can go to resolve conflict, meet with elders, welcome visitors, hold ceremonies, and be together in peace. In old Liberia, one of these round huts could be found in every village. But during the war, the fabric of traditional life was all but destroyed.

When Ellen Johnson Sirleaf became president, she recognized the importance of this grassroots justice system, and as part of the Liberian Truth and Reconciliation Commission, she recommended the "Palava Hut Peacebuilding Mechanism" as a way forward to "foster national healing and reconciliation at the community and grass root levels creating the opportunity for dialogue and peacebuilding."[3] *Palava* means "to discuss or to argue," so these were places where disputes were settled and issues were discussed until they were resolved. Under President Ellen, the name was officially changed from Palava Hut to Peace Hut.[4]

The idea to build a Peace Hut struck a chord and was met with much enthusiasm on the part of the community. Our organization, Alliance for the Earth, raised the money to build the hut, and Christian, along with several other friends in the area, oversaw its construction, taking on a new kind of leadership from his heart. A year later, I returned for the dedication ceremony. I was given the honor of cutting the ribbon, after which everyone spilled into the Peace Hut and danced. I had brought Certificates of Appreciation for all who worked on the project, and there were many honorary speeches and important ceremonial dances. At the end of the day, I sat down under the kola tree to eat a communal meal with members of the paramount chief's family. They waited for the right moment to quietly thank me for burying the Earth Treasure Vase under the tree where we sat and expressed their appreciation for the Peace Hut. But, they revealed, what they really needed was water, explaining that the women had to walk long distances every day to fetch water for the village, and people got sick year after year from dirty water. They asked us to help them dig a well and install a hand pump.

Not long after I returned home, Bethelson and his *everyday gandhis'* colleague William Jacobs (affectionately called Uncle Jake), came to New Mexico to study mindfulness meditation with me and help raise the funds for the well. It is an understatement to say I was challenged to work with Christian Bethelson. But in doing so, I discovered in myself a fierce clarity born of tough love I had not known was there.

Bethelson grew up the first of twelve children. His father had nine wives. The family worked in the fields and lived in a simple hut in a poor region. At eighteen, Bethelson was told if he joined the army he could go to college—his biggest dream. But the military provided the only education he ever had. Under President Samuel Doe, he worked his way up the ranks until he became one of President Doe's personal bodyguards. He was sent to receive special training in Libya, Romania, and Israel.

Christian had served in the Liberian army for twenty years when Charles Taylor's former rebel ally Prince Johnson formed his own party and advanced on the presidential palace to overthrow Doe. The president and his men were cornered and lived for three months in the palace. Deprived of food, Christian shared with me that they survived by eating cats and mice. Finally, they were tricked into believing that Prince Johnson was willing to negotiate and came out, only to be ambushed. Doe was assassinated and many men were killed.[5] Bethelson was injured, but he escaped and eventually ended up in a refugee camp in northern Sierra Leone. From there, he crossed the border into Liberia and joined the rebel forces in Lofa County where he commanded many troops and became known as General Leopard.

He had been, in his own words, "a man with no conscience." But after getting to know him, I saw how deeply he wanted to taste the calm equipoise of mindfulness, and I was moved to accept his request to teach him meditation.

We started at the beginning, with how to breathe in and out, deep and slow, and come back over and over to the present moment with mindful awareness. Listening to the sound of the bell became an invitation to stop, return to the here and now, and take another breath. From this basic act of conscious breathing, repeated over and over, Christian was able to touch seeds of peace within and begin the transformation and healing he yearned for.

Although he had been training as a peacebuilder, Bethelson still applied his leadership skills forcefully, and every time he would get triggered, which in the beginning was often, his anger would get in the way and chaos would ensue. He lived his life from one drama to the next and consistently fell back on the learned behavior he was familiar with—making threatening demands to get his way.

Christian reflects now on that time, taking a deep breath and chuckling in amazement at his turnaround: "When I first met

Cynthia, I would describe myself then as desperate. Very temperamental. On the edge. Grasping. Uneasy. I was like a terrible person trying to grab someone else to survive. Full of PTSD, I was loaded with trauma I kept perpetuating. My human dignity was lost. Something overshadowed me that I couldn't get over because of fear."

He continues, "I was a man of no vision. No sense of direction. A man who had lost his consciousness. I was just living, a man without purpose. I was only living for myself. Living by the will of the gun, the AK-47."

Bethelson was a force to reckon with. But in spite of his history, inside was a man determined to become someone else. He gave me his trust and we slowly worked together to facilitate his transformation. We met each other in a place neither of us had ever been before.

Bethelson's innate compassion for others had been buried for a long time, but it surfaced more and more as he learned to listen to a still, quiet voice rather than the incessant shouts of his inner commander. Christian took to the practice of mindfulness like a fish to water, as if he had always known the wisdom of the sages. Together we raised the money to dig the well, and, once again, Bethelson went back to Lofa County where he had caused much death and destruction as General Leopard. This time he stayed in Tellewoyan Village and helped dig the well. He took a bell of mindfulness that I had given him and practiced walking meditation in the bush around the village. He invited the community to breathe with him under the Peace Hut and enjoy the sound of the bell. When fresh, cool water began to flow from the well, he knew his process of healing had truly begun and life was returning back to the land.

The following year, Christian and Jake returned to the US for another mindfulness retreat, this time with Thich Nhat Hanh at his Deer Park Monastery. Thay and his long-time colleague, a nun named Sister Chân Không, who is very dear to me, embraced the Liberians warmly and offered Bethelson a scholarship to spend three months at Plum Village, Thich Nhat Hanh's retreat center in France.

Meanwhile, other conflict-prone communities in Liberia expressed interest in having a Peace Hut, too. Uncle Jake oversaw the building of a second Peace Hut in Ganta, the most populous city in Nimba County, near the Guinean border where much violence took place during the war. Ganta is still a hotbed of unrest, and on my next trip back to Liberia, we met with local peacebuilders there. To begin the meeting, I invited the bell to sound and suggested we take a few deep breaths and sit quietly before speaking.[6] When we opened up the circle for sharing, with no prompting from me, my new friends said:

"When I heard the sound of the bell, I felt so calm."

"As I breathed in and out, I felt like I came back to my true self. Back to the present moment."

"Stopping to be quiet, it was so much easier to hear what everyone was saying."

The language they spontaneously used to describe their experience could have been lifted straight from the writings of Thich Nhat Hanh! Clearly, these simple tools of mindfulness were finding fertile ground in Liberia.

Accompanying us as a filmmaker on our trips around Liberia was a quiet man named Harper Momolu Karmon. It turned out he was a specialist in trauma healing and conflict resolution and had actively worked with the women's peace movement to stop the war.

Harper was continuing his filmmaking education with *everyday gandhis* and was with the group when Bethelson introduced himself on that muddy road.

Harper arranged for us to visit a large refugee camp on the border of Ivory Coast where he was working at the time. I recognized him as a skilled organizer and asked him if he would help to build our third Peace Hut in Wainsue, an area he knew well. Through Harper we met Annie Nushann, a powerful leader in the Women in Peacebuilding Network and expert on the traditional justice system of the Peace Huts. With Harper and Annie's help, our third Peace Hut was built. Regular programs with women and ex-combatants were now taking place under each of the Peace Huts. A vision to build one Peace Hut in each of the fifteen counties in Liberia was born, and the Peace Hut Alliance for Conflict Transformation (PHACT) was incorporated as an NGO operating in Liberia, and Harper has been running it ever since.

Learning the practice of mindfulness slowly transformed Christian. After his first three-month visit to Plum Village, he returned a number of times over the course of the next three years to stay for long periods. It was not always easy, but it was just the refuge he needed to heal from his violent past. Harper joined him there for a winter retreat and returned the next winter with Annie. The three Liberians forged a deep connection with Sister Chân Không, who respected their peacebuilding work, so akin to the peace work she had dedicated her life to in Vietnam. She gave them her generous support as they continued building Peace Huts and digging wells. In the peace and quiet found at Plum Village, Annie, Harper, and

Christian received teachings, guidance, and recognition from Thich Nhat Hanh, Sister Chân Không, and their large monastic and lay community. Being held in this kind and gentle container catalyzed the transformation Christian, in particular, had been seeking all along. He was lucky to receive Thay's teachings before a paralyzing stroke in 2014 prevented Thay from speaking. Many traumatic memories held inside Christian began to surface, but listening to Thay, meeting with him in person, and practicing deeply every day brought a healing that changed his life forever.

He describes the struggle:

> *I was like a man in a theater watching himself; it was like a movie I couldn't comprehend. The old life kept perpetuating in myself. I caused everyone suffering because I didn't know how to manage my emotions. There was a serious battle in me I couldn't deal with. I was running and running and running—even when no one was running after me anymore. The trauma and PTSD pursued me into my new life, and I dealt with the struggle through the practice of mindful breathing. Gradually, gradually, as I went deeper into practice, the PTSD had no power over mindful breathing.*

One day, after hearing Thay's dharma talk at Plum Village, Christian realized he had to forgive the man who had killed five members of his family during the war and whom he had vowed to kill in revenge. He knew he must reconcile with this man, Harry Weeks (whom General Leopard knew as "Greene" during the war). From Plum Village, Christian called Greene's wife back in Monrovia to let her know that her husband, who was living in self-imposed exile in Sierra Leone to escape Christian's vow of revenge, was free to return home. He invited Greene to meet with him inside one of the Peace Huts in order to let go of the past and move on.

Returning to Liberia from Plum Village, Bethelson anticipated meeting his old enemy. But when he landed in Monrovia, he was arrested for questioning and put in jail. His travels to the US and France had alerted the authorities, and the government was suspicious about the activities of this former general. They wanted to know where he had gotten his funding and why he was meeting with other ex-combatants in Liberia. Drawing strongly on his mindfulness practice, he calmed his reactive emotions and explained that he was a reformed man who had been training in meditation in the US and France. He was now working for peace and stability in his country and teaching peacebuilding to other former combatants like himself.

Bethelson shared, "I told them that I am a different person now and that there is no need to be afraid, that Christian Wolo Bethelson"—the Black Monk of Liberia, as he called himself— "no longer thinks of anything that will cause suffering to anyone. I told them that the energy of mindfulness helps us to recognize our pain and embrace it tenderly like a mother whose baby is crying."

After four days, his captors released him with an apology. He reintroduced himself to the public by going on the radio:

"I went to the local radio station to clear some doubts about me that were raised by the State Security. I said it is time that we forget about dualistic ways of thinking and practice deep listening and loving speech to restore communication, because once communication is restored anything is possible—including peace. I told people that it is about time we calm our fearful minds and embrace reconciliation."

Christian assured his fellow Liberians he had retired his role as General Leopard and was now working with other former fighters to transform as well. Calls of gratitude poured in. It was shortly after this that Christian was finally able to reconcile with Greene. Harper had recently finished overseeing construction of the Wainsue Peace Hut and facilitated the session with Annie Nushann. He told me, "Bethelson began by teaching everyone gathered in the hut to ring the bell. He described the bell as a friend whose sound can calm your body and mind, bringing a smile, happiness, and relief."

Harper continued: "Bethelson acknowledged that it was time to initiate the process of reconciliation, so he and Greene could be free to live life without fear, feeling threatened, or thoughts of revenge. Greene explained how he was forced by his commander to kill anyone found in the area where Bethelson's relatives were, and how, after the war ended, knowing that Bethelson wanted to kill him, he had fled to safety in exile, leaving his family vulnerable and without support for a very long time."

Harper went on to say that when Greene received Bethelson's call for reconciliation, he decided to return, although he was still suspicious. "Bethelson came to Greene's home," Harper reported, "and reassured him, saying, 'We need to move forward.' Because of Bethelson's decision to forgive him, he also decided to forgive Bethelson. Greene thanked Bethelson, asked for his forgiveness, and expressed the desire for them to move forward. Bethelson thanked Greene, giving him a huge hug." Harper concluded by sharing, "One of the other ex-combatants who witnessed this event was a man who had been brutally beaten during the war and paralyzed. He came forward to express his own wish to forgive his perpetrator. Many tears were shed, and it is expected that others will also give their stories now and ask forgiveness from those they have offended."

The region where the Wainsue Peace Hut was built is in the same region in which Christian, as General Leopard, had been camped in the bush with thousands of men planning an attack that would likely kill twenty thousand women and children. To try to stop him, Annie Nushann led one hundred women on a long march to find him and implore him to reconsider. When they arrived at Bethelson's camp, they begged him to choose peace. But Bethelson just laughed at the women. So, the women started singing. One of the songs was in his native language, and it awakened a long-distant childhood memory that touched his heart. He began to cry and commanded his men to lay down their weapons. Annie and the women washed the feet of the many men who were ready to surrender, gave them clean shirts, and walked them home. Harper witnessed this event, and when he took me to meet Annie for the first time at her Peace Hut with many of these same women, she gasped when she saw Christian traveling with me, hardly recognizing the man who had once carried guns across his chest. It took Annie time to fully trust him, but they came to work together for peace in Liberia.

Beginning in 2013, the worst Ebola outbreak in world history shut down the country, creating chaos and igniting new fears in the population. With Ebola came military-imposed curfews and quarantines. The same women who stopped the war took to the streets again to pray for a peaceful resolution to this latest crisis. Christian and Harper were unable to travel upcountry to meet with Annie and the Peace Hut communities. People were rapidly dying, so Christian and Harper also took to the streets to teach people how to stop the spread of disease. Mindful awareness became a critical tool in helping the public understand how to effectively meet the moment. They started a national radio program, inviting listeners to join them for *Conversations Under the Peace Hut* where they rang the bell of mindfulness every week and taught ways to respond calmly and safely to this deadly threat.

In spite of the tremendous challenges of life in Liberia, Christian tells me: "I am more able to maintain my equanimity and not react violently or blindly like I used to. I just take another breath and calm down. I used to think only of myself. My selfishness and anger ruled my life. But now I have a different life altogether. A life of careful existence. I know that I must help my family and community—the whole world—we must all help each other." General Leopard is no longer calling the shots in Christian Wolo Bethelson; the seeds of his true nature, which have been there all along, are ripening. He told me, "When people I work with—former child soldiers and ex-combatants—hear the bell, it gives them a moment of mercy, a moment of freedom from the mental and emotional anguish they are living with."

Witnessing the Liberians return to their traditional ways inside the Peace Huts and adopt the practice of mindfulness feels like a miracle. Holding an earthen vessel to their hearts, filling it with their most sacred offerings for healing and protection, and asking the Earth to help hold their intentions as they are planted in the soil and watered with mindful awareness has brought healing and transformation in ways I could never have imagined. Many conflicts are being resolved now without police intervention in communities trained under the Peace Huts by Annie, Harper, and Christian. It is my hope that someday the traditional ways of Liberian peacebuilding could also serve to reduce conflict in communities here in the US.

Times are hard again in Liberia, though. Violence is on the increase, prices are skyrocketing, and people are going hungry. Christian, Harper, and everyone they know deal with life and death issues on a regular basis. Harper has been sick many times with recurring malaria. When he is not sick, he is all too often attending the funerals of his colleagues or family members. Annie was diagnosed with cancer. She fought valiantly thanks to the medical treatments Sister Chân Không secured for her. Annie, who was loved and respected by all who knew her, tragically passed away in 2022. Christian almost died when his blood pressure spiked and blood spewed from his nose and ears. Harper rushed him to the hospital unconscious, and he was admitted by none other than Harry Weeks (aka Greene), who worked there as a nurse. Recognizing his dire circumstances, Harry paid for and personally administered the transfusions and medicine that saved Christian's life.

When he was well again, Christian and Harper got back to work to complete the fourth Peace Hut in Margibi County, and, with this, a second Earth Treasure Vase, dedicated at Plum Village, was buried. The women brought a kola tree to plant, and the vase was placed at its roots. Christian excitedly shared, "The hut is already being used day and night, and after the burial, the community was so surprised to discover a herd of deer, including little fawns, grazing there! This is an extremely rare sight because deer are usually killed by hungry

Liberians for their meat. But the people celebrated their presence as a sign of peace and agreed to let them be."

Bethelson knows now there is a larger purpose to his life. He dreamed that he was at the United Nations, and the late Colin Powell was on the stage speaking to a huge international gathering of war veterans. General Powell singled Christian out of the crowd and invited him to come forward where he could address the gathering of former combatants like himself.

Christian is firm in his vows to practice nonviolence and not to kill. He says he will not take sides and can never pick up a gun again. He cannot be pressured to change the direction of his life now. Harper has stood by his friend, witness to what some might consider an unbelievable transformation. But there is no going back for Christian or his children. In recent years, thanks again to the generosity of Sister Chân Không and the Thich Nhat Hanh Foundation, along with *everyday gandhis*, all of Christian, Harper, and Annie's children have been able to continue receiving an education. Christian's oldest daughter is the first in his family to graduate college.

Christian continues his practice of mindfulness and when he can, he studies English so he can become a better communicator and fulfill his dream of reaching other veterans around the world with his message of peace. If conflict and disease can cross borders, so can peace and reconciliation. Like the women of Liberia who prayed to end the war and succeeded, the Peace Huts are a tangible manifestation of the power of prayer. It is our ongoing work in Liberia that reminds me without a doubt how a humble little clay pot filled with prayers and offerings can inspire creative solutions to the most overwhelming problems. I am certain that if the former rebel commander General

Leopard can put down his AK-47 and pick up a bell to become a passionate peacebuilder, anything is possible. I have never been more grateful to work with anyone than I am to work with Christian Wolo Bethelson—a man who has given his life to become a vessel of peace.

He may say I am his teacher, but the truth is, he is mine.

CHAPTER ELEVEN

DO NOT CLOSE YOUR EYES BEFORE SUFFERING

Every time I hold an Earth Treasure Vase in my two hands, I wonder how I can hold both the suffering *and* the beauty of this life on Earth. Is it possible to find peace within this profoundly inspiring and awfully disappointing world?

Looking deeply, I realize my ability to hold the suffering in my heart and not turn away is strengthened every time I bathe in the beauty around me and let it in. The fragrance of the rose and the pink sky at sunrise fills me with overwhelming love for this world. And yet, the awareness of thousands of people dying in the pandemic or current wars who will never see another sunrise or be able to appreciate the beauty of the rose is heartbreaking.

The great poet Jelaluddin Rumi wrote, "Let the beauty we love be what we do. There are hundreds of ways to kneel and kiss the ground."[1] Letting in the beauty and getting in touch with what I love fills me with renewed energy to face the difficulties and roll up my sleeves, while the loss of life on Earth makes me appreciate the beauty all the more. One of Thich Nhat Hanh's mindfulness verses, called "gathas," reminds us, "Exquisite the rose on her way to the compost, fertile the compost on its way to rose. Wheeling my barrow of dung, impermanence greets me in beauty."[2] Remembering the impermanent nature of all things is helpful in learning to accept this very challenging and paradoxical life.

Thich Nhat Hanh's Fourteen Precepts of the Order of Interbeing ("Mindfulness Trainings") have been showing me the way ever since I first heard them in 1985. When I joined the Order of Interbeing that year, I took them as vows and promised to practice them.

The fourth precept in particular became a guiding principle for my life and for working with the Earth Treasure Vases: "Do not avoid contact with suffering or close your eyes before suffering. Do not lose awareness of the existence of suffering in the life of the world. Find ways to be with those who are suffering, including personal contact and visits, images, and sounds. By such means, awaken yourself and others to the reality of suffering in the world."[3]

Bearing witness to the suffering in the world opens my heart and connects me with the places calling for an Earth Treasure Vase. Whether it is war and rape, toxic pollution and epic storms, disease, exploitation, or oppression and injustice, every region of the world is suffering in some way and in need of healing. The places we care about and what we love—the ecosystems, animals, bioregions, cultures, and communities—this is where, as vessels of healing, we need to pour our love.

As I face the realities we live with, my heart breaks again and again. I am raw in the brokenness. I weep for my sisters in the Congo who bear unspeakable sexual abuse. For the coral reefs bleaching beyond recognition, for the polar bears standing on melting ice, for the tar sands' sickening spread visible from outer space, and for the endless wars.

Do not close your eyes before suffering.

Consider the sea turtles, the largest of whom is the leatherback—almost gone. Creation stories tell us that the turtle holds the whole Earth on its back. Without the sea turtle holding up the Earth, who will?

And the whales, commuting through the depths of the world's oceans, connecting north, south, east, and west on this water planet. What will be left for them when the shipping lanes leave them no place to go and sound pollution destroys their sonar? How will we ever go on without the dolphin's contagious joy and great intelligence?

I recall the sound of elephants as they walk through the bush, softly going their way so tenderly upon this Earth. I imagine the way elephants walk upon the land as a kind of vibrational balancing for the Earth as they migrate across vast spans of geography. What happens to the body of Mother Earth when the elephants are gone?

Do not close your eyes before suffering.

I grieve the losses and the sacrifices of whole cultures, landscapes, forests, and species. I mourn the way the Earth has become so small, so known, so tame, and so polluted.

In the mountains of Colombia, the Elder Brothers in the Heart of the World see that life is out of balance and call out to us "youngers" to listen to their message. The same message is coming from the Arctic, where the Gwich'in—the Caribou People who make their home in the Sacred Place Where Life Begins—live next door to the Trans-Alaska Pipeline. Here, oil is pumped from the

Arctic Ocean, of all places, while the glaciers melt before their very eyes. Meanwhile, the oceans are rising, the tsunamis increasing, the hurricanes gathering momentum, feeding upon the warm seas and moving ashore to destroy cities, flattening low-income neighborhoods and communities.

The winds of change are howling outside my door. I hear the voices of denial and the sound of pretending that these things don't affect us. This is the shadow we live with on every corner and continent—a centuries-old dissociation from Earth.

Do not close your eyes before suffering.

Joanna Macy has defined this as the age of The Great Turning, when we have the opportunity to restore the life force draining out of Mother Earth. We, who have been born now, are alive to do this sacred work. That the animals may migrate freely and roam wild, that the last remaining undeveloped land may be protected. That Indigenous cultures, our planet's elders, may be honored for their wisdom. And that human greed may be the commodity we sacrifice now to ensure the survival of the great diversity of planet Earth.

• • •

I wanted to close my eyes and turn away from my own heart screaming in anguish. I yearned for the vases to fulfill their promise and make things right in the world. My privilege allowed me to retreat into a protected bubble under the clear blue skies of northern New Mexico where I often succumbed to despair. I could not avoid suffering. Wherever I was, it was there, too. The pain of the world only brought me closer in touch with my own pain. I had no choice but to let it all in.

I had to let it out, too. But I often felt as if I were shouting, calling upon deaf ears. I mourned our ability to turn a blind eye and go on as if nothing is wrong—as if there is no elephant in the living room or bomb in our backyards.

My heart was broken, my soul exhausted, weary with humanity's lack of response to the state of the world. What was it going to take? Why aren't more people, more leaders, bringing about a course correction to turn this spaceship Earth around? What are we doing? Why aren't we evolving?

It seemed like many of us didn't care. We didn't want to know. Or we were too busy trying to survive to even think about it. I sometimes pretended, too, and told myself a story about the beauty of life, clinging to happily ever after. Anything to avoid the ugliness.

There had been a part of me that wanted so very much to tidy it all up—plant those vases, and all will be fine. We will overcome. But that was clearly not happening. Trying so hard to get through, to be heard, to make a difference, my faith was wavering and I felt as if I were slowly killing myself. How could a little clay pot make a difference anyway? People would say, "Really? You're still doing *that*?"

But the vases staring down at me from my altar did not go away. They let me know I could no longer ignore the cries of the world within.

CHAPTER TWELVE

RECKONING

It might have looked on the outside like I was firmly on the path—on a mythic journey, burying the vases with the help of community and friends around the world and carrying out a powerful practice of global healing—but inside, I was experiencing a deep struggle.

Like millions of women, my core wound is sexual. The wound of sexual abuse is shared by one in three women worldwide, and, as we know too well, this kind of abuse springs from the same mind of domination that has oppressed Indigenous peoples and people of color, clear-cut old-growth forests, leveled mountaintops, slaughtered animals to extinction, extracted minerals from deep in the recesses of the ground, and poured toxic pollution into the waters of life. The heartless mind that rapes women also chronically abuses Mother Earth.

My own history of abuse was kept firmly hidden until, one day during my meditation practice, I got in touch with a deep-seated anger I had not realized was there. As I breathed into the strong feelings that were arising, I identified this anger in connection to a family member who had seduced and raped me when I was fifteen and told me never to say a word. This came just a few years after being molested by another family member. I kept these things to myself and pretended they never happened. It was not safe to talk about, so I lived with the shame inside. But when the true feelings associated with the memory finally surfaced, I realized that if I was to have any hope of experiencing something remotely resembling liberation, I would have to deal with this secret darkness inside of my family.

Buddhist teacher Thanissara reminds us that "The awakening process brings old wounds to light, which gets us in touch with places in ourselves that need healing."[1] I could not avoid these memories any longer, and I was going to need to let my family know what had happened. To my regret, I did not do this skillfully. Our family had a lot invested in maintaining a perfect image, and my revelations were not well received. Thankfully, one of these two family members apologized. But the other one told himself and others that I had wanted it, and refused to take responsibility for his actions or say he was sorry. Instead, I was blamed by my family, with one notable exception. Like the crowded campsite in Iran where everyone ignored my screams, my family did not want to hear about my experience.

It was unbearably painful to lose my family, but I had to walk away. I took solace in the wisdom of the great Tibetan saint, Milarepa, who knew that to be liberated, you must leave your family behind. Maybe this was metaphoric, but in order to transform the unconscious conditioning and intergenerational patterns of abuse in my extended family, I had to let them go. Anyway, being on the receiving end of their blame was too painful. I had to break free of my family system.

Soon after, I learned that one of my root teachers was procuring fifteen-year-old girls against their will in his home country of Bhutan.

The cultural backdrop for this—in the country, ironically, known for its commitment to Gross National Happiness—is called "night hunting." Occasionally it is consensual, but most often in this "sport," a boy picks out a girl, stakes out her house, breaks into her room, and rapes her.

I had encouraged some of my closest friends to attend a retreat in Bhutan with my beloved lama in order to receive the highest Dzogchen teachings from him. But the stories they brought back were not about the Great Perfection. They told me things I did not want to hear about my teacher's activities and about a girl who got away. When I confronted him later, his response was that I just wished it had been me. And because I questioned him, I was shunned by his community.

Inside this spiritual system, one is not allowed to suggest that the guru's behavior is in any way questionable. One is supposed to look upon one's guru as omniscient and maintain a "pure view." If you see him as a regular human being with faults, you are breaking your vows, and if you bring this out into the open, it is said you will go to "Vajra hell," poisoning the sangha on the way! It was completely unacceptable to question the lama's integrity—just as it is unacceptable to reveal abuse inside a family system.

Devotion and love are the very foundation of one's relationship with the guru. I was shattered by this loss. I loved my family, too. But I could no longer live with my secret shame and cover up such harmful misconduct. With these situations colliding in my life, the requirements of Guru Yoga became intolerable; to pretend that my guru was perfect, when I knew very well that he was not, was an impossible task. And to be blamed for inciting "wrong views" in the sangha, by talking openly about the abuse that was taking place, was incredibly painful—in both my families.

I have a lot of compassion for Rinpoche as a human being—a man caught in an old feudal system, living inside an ancient fortress in remote Bhutan. I was his first Western student. In the beginning, when he traveled to the United States he stayed in my home until he became known as a teacher in the US. Once he shared with me how much he wished he could take off his robes, put on a pair of pants and be a regular guy. My heart went out to him as a fallible man caught inside that old system—and it still does.

I received the very best teachings from Rinpoche and was devastated to lose our relationship. There is an exquisite beauty to the teacher-student relationship that is beyond words. But the codependency between a spiritual teacher and a devoted student in a relationship of faith, if not handled with skill, can create an immature situation that does not support the true recognition of one's own awakened Buddha Nature. And the misuse of power and subordination of the feminine to uphold a system that keeps the high lamas in their seat is shameful in this day and age. When the sincere faith and trust of students is irresponsibly and selfishly abused, there is something wrong with the system. Thanissara, in her book *Time to Stand Up*, says it clearly: "We cannot rely on the powers of government, or corporations, or entrenched religious hierarchies, to show our path forward. Unless they undergo radical change, they are part of the crisis and not part of the solution. So we are on our own."[2]

In the patriarchal system of the Vajrayana tradition, the feminine is encountered mostly in idealized images of youthful female consorts through whom it is said one can realize the blissful nondual state of awareness. Or we are taught to contemplate the beautiful, motherly figure of Tara (who is nevertheless depicted as youthful). Delving deeper, one can find powerful female deities like the fierce Vajrayogini or the lion-headed Simhamukha, who dances naked on a corpse amidst flames of wisdom, representing having overcome the ego. It was in forming a connection to these wild dakinis ("sky-goers") that I finally found a truly liberating personification of a feminine form of Buddha Nature to work with. I needed support as a woman to stand up to wrongdoing, shed my shame, and find compassion for myself.

There was also the troubling issue that some of the lamas I studied with did not seem to care about the Earth. From them, I understood that to be preoccupied with the Earth was an irrelevant and misguided attachment compared with the teachings on the Nature of the Mind. While the Earth Treasure Vase practice was an activity that was carried out by the various lineages, it was considered a side issue, not a practice that could provide the basis for personal liberation. I came to feel there was something wrong with me for the depth of my caring for the Earth. But the deeper I went with the Earth Treasure Vases, the more I felt I was connecting with a potential source of liberation for our times.

The Buddhist lineages I studied and practiced within had become overgrown by the patriarchal and hierarchical power structures that held them in place. These institutions seemed now to be dying of old age, the true teachings of love and selflessness stifled within the rich temples fraught with abuse. Although I knew there were realized female teachers within that tradition, the system did not authentically model the respect for the feminine I was seeking.

Heartbroken, angry, and alone, with no safe ground to stand on and no one to show me the way, I knew it was a long, dark, and painful process to reckon with the deepest threads of my life unraveling in every direction, with the relationships I most depended on no longer safe and loving. Shunned by all my relations for speaking my truth, I did not know what to do or where to go next.

I yearned to stay in the imagined safety of a devotional relationship to my lamas—and my family. But the dependency on an external authority that the system required prevented me from claiming my own true spiritual calling. I was reluctant to leave behind the tradition I loved, but somewhere deep inside, Gaia was calling.

• • •

Slowly I began to realize that the vases were forcing me to stop looking out *there* and turn instead to what most needed healing in *here*. My core wound was mirroring the same brokenness in the world. Aware of the connection between the body of the Earth and my own body, I attended to my own healing with the awareness that the Earth and I dwell in a relationship of interbeing. And as I healed, I could only trust that I was contributing to the healing of the Earth at the same time.

Unavoidably, I saw that the place I needed to go to next was the Democratic Republic of the Congo (DRC), formerly known as Zaire.

I did not want to go there. But I would gaze at the map of the world and ask, Where is an Earth Treasure Vase needed? Inevitably, I would find myself looking at the center of Africa and wonder, What country is this? I would read "Congo" and quickly tell myself, Oh, no! I don't want to go there! Surely there is another place for a vase? A few months would go by and I would look at the map again and the same thing would happen.

Then, I heard Dr. Denis Mukwege speak. The founder of Panzi Hospital in Bukavu, in eastern DRC, Dr. Mukwege has devoted his life to repairing the fistulas in women who have been brutally raped in the ongoing war in DRC that no one talks about. No one except the writer and activist V (formerly Eve Ensler), that is. Her passion for the liberation of women and the healing of women's bodies inspired me, first through her groundbreaking play *The Vagina Monologues*, and then through the movements of V-Day and One Billion Rising that she launched. She went to the DRC, where she witnessed the work of Dr. Mukwege and brought his message to the rest of the world; I heard him speak at one of her large events.

Congo is a war zone played out on the bodies of women—all for the rich natural resources of that beautiful land. From my own experiences, I knew about women's bodies being objectified, used, and abused. But what I learned about Congo was beyond the worst I could imagine. Women are raped so hard they are ripped from front to back, vagina to anus. Then it all spills out, the shame and the stench. They are raped not just by men's penises but by the gun barrels of the men who hold them. Women are raped in front of their husbands and their children. Husbands are killed slowly in front of their wives and children. Young men and boys are ordered to rape their own mothers or sisters at gunpoint. Babies are cut out of pregnant bellies—and cooked.[3] All of this is for power. Old women. Young girls. Child soldiers. Men with guns.

When Dr. Mukwege spoke about his work to surgically repair the fistulas in women's bodies, I learned that there are so many women in need of this operation that he built an entire hospital dedicated to performing this surgery. V spoke powerfully about how violence against women in the DRC has reached epidemic proportions, with an estimated over 420,000 women brutally raped *every year*.[4] A 2021 report by RAINN (Rape, Abuse, & Incest National Network) underscores how in the DRC, "rape is more than just a crime or cultural issue, it is a method of war."[5] In the heart of Africa, a *gendercide* is taking place.[6]

I suddenly knew why I kept being drawn to Congo. No, I did not *want* to go there, but I *had* to go there. I wanted to address this core wound in the body of the Earth. Going to the "rape capital of the world" was a necessary step in my own healing. Although their experiences were vastly different and so much worse than what I experienced within my own family and earlier with Jack, going to Congo with an Earth Treasure Vase would allow me to find solidarity with other women.

I needed to find my sisters.

CHAPTER THIRTEEN

THE HEART OF … DARKNESS?

Ever since the author Joseph Conrad wrote his book in 1899, Congo has been labeled the "heart of darkness."[1] Certainly, the unthinkable atrocities inflicted on the Congolese people and the rape of that resource-rich land by the Belgian King Leopold II in his desperate quest to plunder and colonize Congo—carried out by his surrogate, the heartless American "explorer" Henry Stanley—brought a terrifying darkness to the Congo.

But in truth, as my Congolese sister Neema Namadamu says, Congo is an Eden—beautiful and abundant—one of the richest lands on Earth. Sadly, because of the dark history of torture and exploitation embedded there by colonizers, systematic sexual violence, human rights abuses, and the unchecked exploitation of natural resources continue to this day.

We, as a global community, have mostly turned our gaze away from what is happening in the Democratic Republic of Congo. Congo is home to endless wars, mining of natural resources, rapid loss of rainforest, and the epidemic rape of women. This land embodies our collective shadow in the very heart of the abused body of Earth Herself. I was compelled to focus my attention and the power of our Earth Treasure Vase prayers there. It seemed to me that the issues that we must face, heal, and transform are being played out nowhere on Earth as graphically as they are in the DRC.

But I was terrified by the horror stories of armed militias and the genocide in Rwanda that had gone underground in the DRC. How could I venture into such a place? Would an Earth Treasure Vase be received? Yet, deep down I knew I had to bring an Earth Treasure Vase to Congo as an offering for healing and protection and stand with the women to do my small part. I needed to make the connection in my own body between the rape of women and the rape of the Earth. And so, after twenty-six locations and fourteen countries, in 2012 I packed up another Earth Treasure Vase and went.

Since the Rwandan genocide in 1994 when armed militias fled across the border to hide in the DRC's forests, the country has been victim to a succession of armed conflicts involving at least six other countries. These wars have profoundly impacted the DRC socially, economically, and environmentally, and created a humanitarian crisis leaving close to *six million* Congolese dead. Militarized rebel groups continue to plunder and exploit Congo for her natural resources, and UN Peacekeepers have little to no power to stop them. In fact, some believe they are sometimes complicit in these violations.[2] The most valuable of minerals these groups are after these days is columbite-tantalite, or coltan, which is needed for the manufacture of electronics, including our ever-present smartphones and laptops. Congolese militia groups armed with big guns have raided, hacked, killed, and raped to gain access to the coltan, terrorizing local communities throughout eastern DRC, clear-cutting the rainforest, and mining the minerals that are then illegally sold to the companies that make our communication technology.

Besides having the world's largest deposits of coltan, Congo has a mineral wealth that is unmatched by any other nation on the globe, with vast reserves of diamonds, gold, cobalt, cassiterite, copper, and much, much more. The World Bank estimates that the Congo possesses $24 trillion in untapped deposits of raw minerals.[3] The global coltan market alone is expected to be valued at 933.92 million by the end of 2026.[4] My Congolese friend Bitshilualua Bashala, who founded a permaculture center there, wrote a powerful piece I heard her deliver in person that describes how Congo "is the only country on Earth that houses all elements found on the periodic table—and enough hydropower potential to power most of Africa. Yet, its people live in poverty, without electricity or potable water, and international laws have yet to be enacted to govern the global trade of Congo's minerals or how they are mined."

The Congo Basin is such a fertile land that it supports the world's second largest expanse of tropical rainforest, after the Amazon rainforest. The oxygen generated for the entire planet by the lush forests and mighty rivers of Congo is a resource few remember, much less protect. There is enormous pressure on Congo's biodiverse and resource-rich forests. The deforestation rate in the region was estimated at around 1.2 million acres per year in 2020 by Global Forest Watch.[5] Needless to say, Congo desperately needs a constitution implementing the Rights of Nature,[6] which recognize and honor the inherent rights of ecosystems—extending fundamental human rights to rivers, forests, and mountains, and challenging twentieth-century laws that frame nature as a resource to be owned and extracted.

The Indigenous inhabitants of the forests of eastern DRC are the Batwa Pygmy people. One of the oldest cultures on the planet, the Batwa have endured a long history of oppression, and the fighting in the DRC has had a devastating effect on the forests that are their traditional home. These gentle hunter-gatherers carry priceless wisdom about living in right relationship with the forest. But they have been killed, forced into slavery, and even cannibalized by armed factions who believe that eating Pygmies will give them supernatural powers. Forced out of their forests, they must now learn to farm, but this does not come naturally. The Batwa communities in eastern DRC are struggling for survival along with the forests they once inhabited, in kinship with elephants, gorillas, bonobos, and countless other animal and precious plant species, too many to name. The Batwa are being decimated, their magnificent forests clear-cut, and the animals, minerals, plants, and great rivers of Congo threatened to extinction.

• • •

I didn't know how to get to Congo and I needed help. Then I learned about an organization called World Pulse that is dedicated to connecting women from the most remote corners of the world to share their stories of empowerment online. Neema Namadamu was a correspondent with World Pulse in Bukavu, South Kivu Province, eastern DRC. I read her articles and was deeply moved. She wrote, "I'm no longer interested in making a little noise—I'm looking to CHANGE THE PARADIGM! I'm no longer interested in playing politics, in pushing against the status quo . . . We're going to create a new culture, a new environment, A NEW WORLD!"[7]

I contacted Neema and inquired if she might help me bring a little clay pot filled with prayers as an offering to the women of that land and the Indigenous people of the forest. Unhesitatingly she said, "Yes, my sister, come. I will help you." We began to plan the trip. In Neema (pronounced "NAY-ma," meaning "grace") I met an unstoppable and enthusiastic force to be reckoned with. Her articles gave me a sense of a woman with tremendous love, great caring, and a highly developed spiritual awareness. Neema was also a skilled organizer and social entrepreneur. We seemed to understand each other, and she gave me her full support. But I had many sleepless nights as I weighed placing my life in the hands of a woman I had never met in the most dangerous place in the world to be a woman. Yet, something told me she could be trusted and I would be safe. The deal was sealed when I got a request to bring Neema's husband, Danny, some green chile from New Mexico and learned that, incredibly, he was from Albuquerque!

For many months, I prepared to go to Congo. Every full moon, our sangha poured our hearts into the vase. I raised the money and invited a young filmmaker, Raji Mandelkorn, to go with me. The women of Open Way Sangha crafted a beautiful handwoven basket for me to carry the Earth Treasure Vase in, and the women's peacebuilding group in Liberia sent a video message of solidarity.

World Pulse asked if I would help them in their work to uplift women. Neema suggested we provide trainings in citizen journalism to women activists and promote their grassroots efforts to link Congolese women to the world through the Internet. We designed three trainings on media for social change, focusing on empowering women to tell their stories and stand up for a new Congo. I was grateful for this added sense of purpose to highlight the voices of women through social media and documentary filmmaking, and to bring global attention to what is taking place in the DRC. Even though the Earth Treasure Vase had not been planted in Congo yet, it seemed it was already doing its job.

Neema Namadamu is a dynamic and strikingly beautiful woman who lights up the room when she enters. I loved her from the moment we met. Disabled from contracting polio at age two, she is one of the most relentlessly capable women I have ever known. Neema grew up in a remote village with seven brothers and five sisters living in a small hut on the edge of the forest in the Hauts Plateaux region of South Kivu Province, eastern DRC. The Banyamulenge Tutsis she descends from are a minority who have suffered much discrimination for their presence in the DRC. Her family was rich—they had fifty cows. Since she could not walk, her mother frequently carried her on her back so she could go to school. Neema became the first woman from her village to graduate from college—twice. Never mind that she had great difficulty getting around: it was not until she was thirty-seven that she got crutches. She crawled or vaulted herself along with one pole until then.

In the spring of 2012, we arrived in Kigali, the capital of Rwanda, near the border of the DRC, on the eve of the memorial anniversary of the 1994 Rwandan genocide. Visiting the Genocide Museum, which was preparing to receive the nation's dignitaries for a formal remembrance ceremony, I confronted the unspeakable horror of those hundred days when neighbors turned on neighbors and *one million people* were brutally slaughtered. Rwanda's genocide was a tragedy we must never forget.

At the end of our first day, we sat outside in the dusk interviewing a woman who survived the frenzied killing by hiding in the engine of an abandoned truck, while her entire family and everyone around her were murdered. We sat with her as the light faded from the sky and day turned to night. We huddled close to keep warm and give her our love. We listened until there was no more for her to say, and still we stayed. The darkness crept in, the camera shut off, and we held her and each other until all that was left was silence.

The next day, we interviewed a young Congolese woman I will call Sophie (her name has been changed to protect her), who had traveled to Kigali from a refugee camp in Kenya to tell us her story.

Sophie was shy but slowly opened up, especially with Raji, who at age twenty-five was just a few years older than she. Sophie told us how she had been held captive after her brother's murder but managed to escape her rapists and flee to Bukavu where she told her story to the press. This angered the military leader and his men who pursued her with the intention of killing her, so she kept running—over the border to Kigali in Rwanda. But they followed her there, too. She finally ended up in a refugee camp where she has been ever since. To this day Sophie is still trying to get out of that camp and seek asylum in the US, one of thousands who are hoping to find a better life.

Leaving Rwanda, we drove through the countryside toward Bukavu, and found people gathered to commemorate the genocide in every town we passed. It was a haunted time, chilling and sobering. Our driver told us his own stories as we passed through places where there had been tragic massacres in churches, schools, homes, and fields. As the hours wore on, we were glad to see children playing on the road, running and laughing.

Once in Bukavu, the media training workshops for women (and a few enthusiastic men) got started. We had brought video cameras, donated by friends back home, and art supplies. Neema was hoping to inspire a movement. Raji taught the group to operate a camera, conduct an interview, and become comfortable on both sides of the lens. Eventually, members of the group teamed up and bravely went out on the streets (an activity not legally permitted by the government) to gather their own interviews and stories, learning on the go. Neema introduced them to the online platform of World Pulse. I rang the bell and taught them the practice of mindfulness as a way to heal from trauma. We visited the local TV station (and were interviewed) and met with journalists who were trying their best to be a voice for democracy.

One night, a warm-hearted woman named Faida and her husband, Pastor Samuel Mutula, of the Peace and Conflict Resolution Project, came to meet us. They were looking for partners to bring assistance to the women and children in their community. Faida pleaded eloquently to our camera, asking the world to recognize Congo as the heart of Africa. She spoke about how the heart is breaking, and, without the heart, the body dies. Faida attended our workshops, and, through her, Raji was able to interview other women in her community whose lives had been shattered by rape, murder, and AIDS. Faida and Samuel's loving kindness and care were a great inspiration.

We witnessed so many lives lived with so little hope, so many people holding on by a thread. But there were just as many enthusiastic, engaged young people wanting to make a difference. My life was forever changed to witness the women of Congo through Neema, whose own suffering and that of other women with disabilities whom she introduced us to was hard to fathom. Often treated like animals, these women are used, abused, rejected, and relegated to the dark alleys and shadows, barely able to survive. But with Neema's leadership, they are working together to change their circumstances now. Neema's disability never stopped her, and the love in her heart and the light in her eyes pours out to everyone equally.

"Love for one another has opened our eyes and built us up with a profound strength," Neema wrote. "Love for each other has caused us to respect each other's community. Love and respect for each other's community has bound us together in hope, in possibility. Love and respect for each other's community has given us a passion for our country, and a vision for its people."[8] The truth she spoke from the heart of Africa lit a flame in me and in everyone who came in contact with her. With her help, we carried the little Earth Treasure Vase to group after group, offering it with the prayer that the women of Congo would be affirmed and have a chance to be heard in their call for change. Every night back in my room, I would wipe my tears around its rim and ask for the courage to stand with Neema as we took the next day in stride.

Neema organized a large ceremony for the Earth Treasure Vase in a hall on the hill in the center of Bukavu. Then-president Kabila was in town, and outside the hall where we gathered, the tanks rolled in in a great show of force. There was tension in the air, but workshop participants, community leaders, and Neema's many friends attended anyway. It was a powerful gesture to bring the little clay pot into that hall full of people and invite their prayers for peace and healing, while men with guns sat outside on their tanks. Congo is highly Christian, and the Earth Treasure Vase was hard for people to understand. Many seemed uncomfortable with such an unfamiliar spiritual practice, but I learned from Neema and Danny that if I simply added the words "In the name of Jesus Christ, amen" at the end of our meditations and prayers, everyone could relax and feel safer in participating, and more open to what we were doing.

We were planning to take the vase to the Itombwe Forest and present it to the Pygmy community of Mwenga, but before we left, we met two other passionate activists doing important work in eastern DRC on behalf of women, children, and the Pygmy people.

Amani Matabaro is the founder of Action Kivu, which he created after losing much of his family in the conflict and seeing the desperate situation of women and children. He set up a microcredit loan program, started vocational training for women, and provided education for children. We drove to his home village where he showed us the covered marketplace he had built and then brought us to meet a group of mostly women and some men who had assembled to hear about the Earth Treasure Vase and share their voices for change in Congo. The vase did its job well, serving as the vehicle for everyone to open up and offer their most heartfelt hopes and prayers, clearly and directly. Peace in Congo, the end of violence against women, life without fear, no more rape: we heard the same messages over and over.

After we completed the ceremony, we visited a sewing cooperative to meet some of the younger women. Neema invited them one by one to stand and share their vision for Congo. They bravely spoke into the camera about what they wanted to change. Both Amani and Neema were quite surprised to hear such strong words coming out of these shy young women who had never expressed anything like it out loud in a group before.

Amani's friend Dominique Bikaba invited us to meet his beloved Pygmy community near the Kahuzi-Biega National Park, a forest where the endangered eastern lowland gorilla has been given protection. Dominique began his career working with the gorillas, and then became a specialist in ecosystem conservation, rural development, and environmental studies before founding Strong Roots Congo, a community-based organization dedicated to sustainable development and conservation. With only 250 gorillas left in Kahuzi-Biega today,[9] he hopes the gorillas will have a better chance of survival with a corridor of community-managed forests between the Kahuzi-Biega and Itombwe Forests. Dominique kindly arranged for us to hike into the forest to see the gorillas in the wild. Our guides led us deep into the thickly overgrown canopy, where we came upon a large group of gorillas with many females and children and one large silverback male. The gorillas allowed us to come quite close, and in their presence we opened the Earth Treasure Vase, prayed for their protection—and invited their powerful energy into the vase.

After decades of conflict, the Indigenous Pygmy people of eastern DRC live in extreme poverty, having been displaced from their forest home and suffering terrible discrimination, with virtually no rights. The Pygmy village of Buyungule, near Kahuzi-Biega, is where Dominique's adopted family is trying to make a life from nothing. Here, inside their simple church, we conducted another Earth Treasure Vase ceremony. I rang the bell, led a meditation, and invited the community to share their hopes and prayers into the vase, which, we explained, would soon be taken into the forest. Although the people of Buyungule were clearly hungry, they welcomed us warmly and, after the ceremony, led us outside where they joyfully danced to the music of their drums.

Finally, it was time to deliver the vase filled with prayers to the Itombwe Forest in Mwenga. Neema's associate Patrick Namatomwa was excited for us to visit his homeland and had made all the arrangements for us to meet the Pygmy community he calls family. But it was a long drive, and many people we met in Congo told us that the roads were not safe for us to go. Neema assured me the region was safe—her relatives and the government officials she knew along the way checked the situation regularly and reported to her that there was no danger at this time. Neema and Danny said, "Cynthia, if you don't want to go, we'll go and take the vase ourselves." But if they were not afraid to go, neither was I. I knew that if there was one person divinely guided in this life, it is Neema Namadamu. What happens around her is a testament to her capacity to put everything into the hands of "The Coordinator," as she puts it.

A palpable joy descended on us as the vehicle became more and more crowded. Charles Uwiragiye, a respected Pygmy leader we had met in Rwanda, arrived with his wife from Kigali to join us, and Neema's friend Collette Mikila, a minister in the local government representing the Pygmy people, also climbed on board. It took many hours of driving on dirt roads through that wild and beautiful Eden to reach our destination.

We were welcomed at the village by Patrick and his entire tribe. The women stood at the entrance to the village singing, and the "King" of the Pygmies, Chief Mwami Walumba, came down to greet us by the car. He carried a staff and wore a grass skirt and a hat with beads hanging over his eyes. Kindness flowed from his heart, and he smiled widely. He led us toward the women, and together we danced our way through the village to a large, rough-hewn hall. There we were seated at a small table where we were presented with baskets of the most delicious food, all gathered from the forest, prepared especially for us and served on palm leaves. Charles, our beloved Pygmy elder from Rwanda, exclaimed, "Now *this* is *real* food!" Chief Walumba recognized Charles and presented him with his ceremonial staff. I was given a large basket to be worn on my back for harvesting, a wand made from wild-harvested sap that becomes a natural torch when lit on fire, and a woven sleeping mat. The use of the mat was demonstrated by the King himself, which brought gales of endless laughter to the crowd, and from then on, he became known as my "husband."

The next day we met with the mayor of the village in his office and toured the area, visiting a site called Kasika. This was the site of one of the worst recorded massacres of women that occurred during the civil war, when women were targeted with rape and sexual violence and more than a thousand civilians were killed—some burned alive, others tortured and mutilated with machetes.

Still overcome with emotion from learning about the tragedy of Kasika, we continued toward the Pygmy village with the Earth Treasure Vase. Mourning the community's unrelieved pain at the loss of life and the abuse the women had suffered, I began to pray for healing once again. I was sitting in the front seat of the Jeep with Danny driving and Neema in the middle when, suddenly, Neema and I looked at each other, simultaneously realizing that we were going to bury the vase—now. This was it. There would be no going back. We gave each other a nod of understanding and felt ourselves align with the moment. When I turned to look out of the windshield again, there, flying directly in front of the car just a few feet in front of us, was a white dove leading the way, the sunlight brightly illuminating its wings. The Holy Spirit was with us! I breathed a sigh of relief and relaxed a little, receiving this miraculous sign from the Universe that we were being guided, and all was well. The Coordinator was at work, leading us on to fulfill our purpose.

With the white dove accompanying us, we followed the dirt track about ten kilometers into the bush to the edge of the forest, where a large group was waiting. In the grassy field where they had gathered, a theater troupe of youth activists donned large wooden masks behind a makeshift curtain set up between two trees. They gave a powerful presentation that exposed the poverty and oppression they were struggling with. Then it was time for the Earth Treasure Vase to be brought forward into the circle of chiefs, elders, community leaders, men, women, and children, all of whom drew in closely with curiosity to see it.

I unfurled a flag of the Earth—my traveling altar cloth—under the big trees where we made our crowded circle. Pointing to the DRC on the flag, I spoke about the importance of Congo's forests to the whole Earth and explained how rainforests are called the lungs of the planet for their role in absorbing carbon dioxide and producing oxygen. Then I pointed to the other side of the planet on my flag and told them that the forests of Congo provide fresh air for people around the world to breathe, including us in America. I explained as best I could how we all depend on rainforests for our survival. I shared that hundreds of people had poured their prayers into the

Earth Treasure Vase that I was now offering to them. I honored them for the knowledge and wisdom they have carried for so many generations. I hoped they understood how much we could learn from them about living in harmony with the forest. And I wanted them to know how important their culture is to the Earth and how their forests, if protected, will stabilize the entire global climate system, producing nourishing rainfall and fresh air around the planet.

Charles Uwiragiye, who is a worldly social-change agent dedicated to representing the Indigenous Pygmies, was a great help in interpreting the Earth Treasure Vase practice so that everyone could understand. The vase had been filled with so much intention, from so many friends, over such a long time, and it held the awareness that this land, this forest, and this very place was critically important to us all. This was our most precious and heartfelt spiritual gift, and Charles skillfully translated this for me. I wanted the people to know they were not alone in caring for the special place where they live. At the end of our prayers and meditations, Charles invoked the magic words "In the name of Jesus Christ, amen," and all was well.

Several chiefs then came forward and, along with a few women leaders, offered their prayers into the vase. The women and children gathered around, eager to know what was inside that little clay pot, and as it passed around the ever-widening circle, they peered inside to see what kind of treasure was there. When they understood there was nothing inherently valuable in it but only spiritually meaningful or symbolic offerings, there was a stirring of excitement in the group. One person offered some cassava, saying it is the food of life; another offered a small but precious wild red fruit; still another offered earth from right where we stood for the protection of their land. As the vase was passed through everyone's hands around the circle, we prayed for the violence to end and the forest to be protected. At the end of the ceremony, after the vase was sealed, the chiefs (including my "husband") came forward to hold the Earth Treasure Vase together as one, and solemnly vow that once buried in the ground, the vase would never be disturbed but protected for all time.

We made a long procession walking single file on narrow paths through the fields out past the village, with the vase being carried in its special basket by one of the chiefs at the front. Chief Mwami Walumba chatted with Charles, and I followed behind. We proceeded over a stream, past water lilies and a fishpond, through a cassava farm, to a clearing in the forest. Here, Patrick was waiting for us. He had already dug a deep hole for the vase. The site was a sacred place to the community, and there was a great eagerness in the air. We lowered the vase in its colorful basket into the Earth. Then everyone filled in the hole with handfuls of dirt until the vase was well covered and laid to rest.

I wanted to linger after everyone left to absorb the feeling in the forest. I yearned to know more about these wonderful people and their culture. From Patrick, I had heard about a "rock of initiation" high above the village. He told me about a "miracle lake" that was some days' walk away. And he revealed that an ancient "world tree," towering and expansive, was hidden deep in the forest. How I wished to see these special sites, but it was too dangerous, so no one went there now. I prayed for their protection. An army officer Neema had discharged to watch over me hovered in the shadows, and, concerned for my safety, finally said we needed to go—now. Reluctantly, I turned and walked back with him. Later, as we were driving away, I learned that just three days before we arrived, the community fought off rebels who had attacked and tried to take their village. The community managed to fend them off successfully, but it had been tense.

• • •

Like all true odysseys, it took time to unwind the many strands of what I experienced in the heart of Africa. I am certain we were guided and protected by The Coordinator's unseen forces and the accompanying field of prayers provided by our global Earth Treasure Vase community. The collective intention we generated was palpable and continues to ripple out from Congo. I know that in some small way, our presence there, and the little vase buried in the fertile soil of that great forest, contributed to the movement that Neema envisions. Our citizen-journalism trainings catalyzed Neema to open an Internet café soon after we left. Women came from all over to join the Maman Shujaa Center ("Hero Women" in Swahili) and learn how to tell a new story—their story. It was exciting to witness the blossoming of Neema's leadership on behalf of the women in the DRC. Not long after our time together in Congo, she came to the US for the first time, as one of three World Pulse correspondents selected as "Voices of the Future." She was invited to speak at the United Nations, CNN, the State Department, and the Clinton Global Initiative. I hosted her in preparation for the tour, and Alliance for the Earth served as her fiscal sponsor until she founded her own US nonprofit, Hero Women Rising, a few years later.

But the Earth Treasure Vase in the Itombwe Forest was still talking to me, and I knew there was more to do. After I came home, Neema returned to the Pygmy community we had visited in the Itombwe Forest to meet with the women. "One of the women spoke with such astonishment," Neema wrote, "saying she had no idea that their forest was cleaning America's air and creating its oxygen. She was shocked, but this new perspective gave her such a sense of responsibility!" She added, "I wish for the people of the forest to receive the necessary education so that they can, with all comprehension, learn to keep their forest and manage it so that they not only receive the inherent benefit to so many aspects of their wellbeing, but also receive worthy recognition and just compensation for their stewardship." I introduced Neema to Osprey Orielle Lake, the founder of the Women's Earth and Climate Action Network (WECAN), who is dedicated to supporting Indigenous women as leaders for climate change. Osprey joined Neema's online community and informed the Maman Shujaa about the Rights of Nature movement and the pressing issues of climate change, identifying Congo as one of three key locations in the world to focus WECAN's protection efforts.

Most of the world has thrown up its hands and said Congo is a lost cause. But I believe that Congo is presenting humanity with an unprecedented opportunity to turn around a situation that is an embodiment of our collective shadow.

After going to the DRC, I came to see that for my own healing, the only way to wholeness would be to forgive those who have wronged and abused me. This seemed like an impossible task, but Neema has shown me that love is the only answer to restore life out of balance.

The year after I was there, Neema's daughter was beaten by soldiers, and at first Neema wanted revenge. But she understood that revenge would only bring about more violence, and in order for her daughter to heal, she knew she had to let go of her anger. "When I did, the most amazing thing happened. Love filled my heart," she said. She went and met with the soldiers who had harmed her daughter. "I told them I was their mom, and I expected better of them. They asked me for forgiveness and begged me to come visit them often. I realized that love is the most powerful weapon of all, especially coming out of the heart of a mother."[10]

I am humbled to have met a true holy vessel in Neema Namadamu, whose life is dedicated to helping the women of Congo recover their dignity and become a unified voice for real change. Neema is way ahead of the rest of us. She has already moved into the new paradigm and is acting from there. Thanks to her, being able to deliver an Earth Treasure Vase to the people of the forest and plant that vessel of protection and healing in one of the most vitally important ecosystems in the world has contributed more to fulfilling the promise of the Earth Treasure Vases than I could have imagined. And in bringing the awareness of how important their forests are for the whole planet to the people I met, I feel my life has been worthwhile.

I doubt I will ever understand why Congo has had to endure all it has, nor will I ever be able to transmute the grief, loss, oppression, and injustice enacted upon that land and the bodies of its women. But for me, going to Congo was a journey of a lifetime to take my stand as a woman along with my sisters and begin my own work of healing and repair.

There is an expression I learned from the women of Congo: *"Umoja Ni Nguvu."* It means "Together we are strong." And so it is—another call for our collective awakening. We simply cannot transform our world alone.

CHAPTER FOURTEEN

POISON INTO WISDOM

Speaking up about abuse in our families where we should be safe, or in our spiritual communities where the teachings of wisdom and compassion should be guiding us to higher ground, is confusing and scary. I did not want to upset the family system I was born into or confront my spiritual teacher with accusations of sexual misconduct. Being blamed and scapegoated took years to recover from, not to mention healing from the original trauma of abuse.

Eventually though, I strengthened my relationship with the sacred feminine through a direct relationship to the Earth. The freedom that came from letting go of a spiritual system and a family system filled with denial, judgment, and blame allowed me to find a new path.

Going to Congo, I discovered a hidden treasure that connected me to other women the world over, and my calling to serve the healing and protection of the Earth took on much greater meaning. I had grieved enough. In Congo, I met women who get up and dance to tell a new story. I wasn't dancing yet, but I could hear the music.

• • •

Women embody the rhythms of nature in our cells. The life force flows in us, grows in us, and gives us an instinctual access to a source of knowing that is intimately aligned with Mother Earth. We know about opening to receive through the deepest bones and muscles of our body, and we know about birthing new life and nourishing it. We don't need anyone to tell us this. We are born with it. Our feelings, our bodies, and our intuitions are the very source of our deepest knowing, where our power comes from. We are instinctually programmed to care about life. Valuing this inner knowing, listening to the voices in us that have been silenced for too long, and integrating what they say restores balance to our world. Our wisdom is needed.

But when we are abused, our natural wisdom becomes dissociated from the truth we know it is our purpose to fulfill. I was silenced, so I doubted myself and pretended for years that nothing was wrong. It was not until I stopped keeping up appearances that the liberating truth could emerge. Owning the validity of my own experience, I came back into my body and felt my feet on the path for real.

The key that unlocked my healing process was the Mandala of the Five Buddha Families.[1] This is a Tibetan Buddhist teaching that provides a basic framework to integrate our emotional wisdom and not push it away or reject it. The Mandala of the Five Buddha Families gives us a map for the process of transformation.

According to the dharma teachings, there are five poisons. These manifest as anger or hatred, desire or greed, pride, jealousy, and ignorance. These poisons operate insidiously in the ways we put each other down, backbite, and compete in our desire for power, recognition, and success. Painful feelings of jealousy plague us. We rage at others or at the system, and it turns back on ourselves, festering like a wound. The unconscious ego is like a dictator who inflicts poison into the places we live and work. This poison then seeps into all kinds of unexpected territory. This unhealthy inner and outer environment has conditioned us to be fearful and angry. When we quietly ignore it, things never change, and the five poisons continue to play out over many generations in this world of cyclic existence.

Yet, when we can experience these poisons as energies, we discover that each one contributes something profound to understanding our true nature. Within the poison, wisdom is found. And the path to wisdom is through the elemental energies associated with each of the five poisons—fire, water, air, earth, and space—that are the very building blocks of our embodied life on Earth.

In Tibetan Buddhism, these elemental energies are personified as dakinis—semi-wrathful, liberated aspects of Buddha Nature in a feminine form. In each of the directions of the Mandala of the Five Buddha Families—east, west, north, south, and center—the dakinis represent the elemental energies of phenomenal existence.

These wild and free feminine aspects of our awakened nature offer us a way to embody our fierce truth in these times. The dakinis are often imagined dancing naked on top of a corpse to symbolize having overcome ego-clinging, with hair flying and fangs bared. Their wisdom is so powerful that it flares out like the flames of holy fire they dance within. This multifaceted model of the awakened feminine is not exactly the idealized version of feminine goodness we might expect. A dakini cannot be contained or even defined. She is a shapeshifter, riding the waves of birth and death. Her wisdom is unpredictable.

If we see the dakinis as embodiments of the elemental energies of our own nature—the water element in us, the air element, the fire, earth, and space elements—then each of these elemental energies together comprises the whole of us. Like us, the Earth is dependent upon the flow and function of these elemental energies in a balanced relationship. We live within a symbolic representation of this wholeness—the mandala—where the elemental energies flow through the meridians of our bodies and through every ecosystem on the planet. When these elemental energies are blocked or out of balance in us, they become reactive, expressing themselves emotionally.

The dharma teachings invite us to understand how the reactive emotions (i.e., poisons) actually take root in our lives. When we identify with the energies of ignorance (space), anger (water), desire (fire), jealousy (air), and pride (earth), they manifest or take root as emotional patterns. But if we can witness them operating and experience them as energies, these five reactive emotions are set free and their inherent wisdom can shine. With this comes liberation.

Through meditation, visualization, and contemplation, we learn to dissolve our conceptual and emotional fixations and habitual tendencies in order to become more and more free. As we do this, many of our reactive emotional patterns will release all on their own—like a snake untying its own knot. The ones that don't release stand out as the places we need to transform. Our habitual grasping at or identifying with a sense of self out of fear and ignorance limits our experience to only what is familiar. But as we learn to rest in the state of awareness in meditation, the "poisons" can be experienced for what they are, and gradually we become free from those patterns. If we live in a state of habitual distraction due to our dualistic fixation on self and other, we will never recognize the primordial wisdom that is the nature of all that is. The teachings say that our nonrecognition results from ignorance—and from ignorance we react with anger, pride, desire, and jealousy—and thus, the emotional body is born.

When we visualize the dakinis within the Mandala of the Five Families, we are training to recognize the wisdom within each emotion. We see each dakini appearing in a color that expresses that emotion, dwelling in one of the directions of the mandala, and recall their elemental energies. Then we invite the five poisons associated with each of these to be present in our awareness. Finally, through a process of transformation, we come to recognize the presence of the five primordial wisdoms.

• • •

Just outside my door in New Mexico is a path that leads up the flanks of the mountain. I walk this path most days, marveling at the many-colored stones that can be found on the land. For years I have picked up stones in the colors of the Five Buddha Families—red, yellow, green, white, and blue-black—carefully placing them in distinct arrangements, each one with a prayer. This little ritual has been a simple yet powerful way to connect with the teachings of the dakinis of the mandala, and is my way of remembering to balance the reactive emotions arising from the neglected elemental energies within me and invite more wisdom into my daily life. Like the Earth Treasure Vases, every stone becomes an offering and a reminder to walk in mindfulness and restore balance when I am not in harmony.

I sometimes see the ordinary rocks at my feet as multicolored jewels. Walking the path, I encounter rubies, topaz, and jade. There are pearls, shimmering crystals, and lapis lazuli. I climb a mountain path that shines with vital energy and is a wealth of offerings to the dakinis and to Mother Earth. When I offer stones of five colors in the five locations along the path, I dedicate each stone to that particular dakini, forming the intention that the associated elemental energy may empower the transformation of poison into wisdom in myself—and in the wider world. After making these offerings, eventually I arrive at the top of the hill where I step into a stone circle, face each of the four directions, and stand in the center of the mandala.

Facing east, I invoke the blue-black Vajra dakini, and, as I imagine, gazing at her is like looking into a deep, still pool. She is the element of water, clear-seeing and powerful. The poison of anger she embodies, when transformed through awareness, can sometimes feel sharp and cold, but her Mirror-like Wisdom clearly reflects what is true. My ego may react to her truth, but at my core I am grateful for her incisive directness. I see her appearing with black skin and long dreadlocks falling down her back. The skirt around her bare belly is indigo-dyed, her muscular body is strong, and her black eyes hold a steady, unflinching gaze. I bow to her in the east and to the energy of anger in me. And I pray for her help in transforming that poison into Mirror-like Wisdom.

Next, I turn to the south and invoke the golden Ratna dakini, resplendent in jewels that decorate her enriching presence. She is the earth element, nourishing, nurturing, and solid. I feel her support as I gaze into her eyes, which reflect a bright golden light, and see her golden hair falling over ample brown shoulders. She is utterly comfortable in her full, round body. I bow to the south. She shows me the way of transforming the poison of pride into the Wisdom of Equanimity. She is poised in her capacity to balance all that comes to her in a nurturing embrace, embodying a solid, trustworthy wisdom that invites a much greater understanding beyond selfish pride.

I turn to the west and face the red Padma dakini, who dances with fire. Flames of wisdom burn brightly around her, illuminating her passionate nature. She holds a lotus in her hand. The fiery red dakini is seductive in her beauty, with thick auburn hair flying and a rosy blush that flushes her cheeks as she dances in front of me. I ask her to give me the capacity to choose life and to serve love, not selfish desire. This discernment is her wisdom. From where I stand facing west, I see the Los Alamos National Laboratory—the ultimate repository of the "poison fire." I bow to the Padma dakini's presence and pray for the transformation of the poison of desire and greed into the Wisdom of Discerning Awareness. May we humans know better than to use weapons of mass destruction, and may the minds that created them turn to new tasks now: cleaning up the mess we have made, guarding radioactive waste into the future, and restoring the land and waters.

Again I turn, this time to the north to face the Karma dakini. Her body is a fertile, lush green in color, and her green eyes flash with a unique capacity to effortlessly accomplish whatever is next. Her hair is tied up out of the way in a practical knot on her head. Because she has realized she is empty of a separate self, she is able to transform competitive jealousy through awakened activity. Like Green Tara, who is a member of this family, she is ready to leap into action the moment she is called. I invoke her a lot—and what a help she has been! She embodies the air element, quick and full of movement. A breath, a breeze, or a tornado—whatever is needed, she will get the job done through her embodiment of All-Accomplishing Wisdom. I bow deeply to the destructive energies of jealousy and envy. She helps me realize that we are in this together and that I may serve all beings in my actions.

Once more I turn, this time to step into the center of the mandala in the hills above my home. I face the Buddha dakini who embodies the dimension of All-Encompassing Spaciousness—a selflessness completely open and able to relax into all that comes to her. She shows me how to face life directly, without ignoring or becoming overwhelmed, when I would rather turn away. Looking up into the vast element of space above and around me in the clear blue sky, I feel at peace. I am grateful for the vision of this naked, white-haired, open-hearted dakini dancing in space, and I go empty—I receive her blessing at the center of the mandala. Here, I can fully sense the transformation of ignorance into the Wisdom of Spaciousness.

Every day that I walk this path, I imagine the dakinis surrounding me, pouring forth their wisdom. I ask for their support in fulfilling my purpose in my lifelong dedication to the sacred mandala of life on Earth. I take refuge inside this circle of wholeness and am grateful for the wild and untamed forces of nature that cannot be grasped. Though the dakinis are as insubstantial as rainbows, they appear in mysterious ways when invoked. On most days, I simply sense their presence on the wind and in the waters, the fire of the sun, the earth beneath my feet, or the space all around. Sometimes they appear to take form: I have heard one must always be alert and pay attention so as not to miss the striking young woman or wizened old hag waiting on the corner to impart a lesson—unexpected aspects of the Buddha's feminine nature in the flesh, come to call.

Some of us may identify more with the Karma dakini, working our way competitively through life. Some of us may struggle with anger, and it is the Vajra dakini who operates most strongly in us. Maybe we get caught over and over by our desires and the seductive nature of the Padma dakini. Perhaps it is our pride, like that of the Ratna dakini, that elevates our egos over anything else. Or, if it is all just too much, we space out, overwhelmed, and ignore what the Buddha dakini is trying to teach us. Our human nature operates out of these reactive patterns, poisoning the world around us and all of our relations. By facing these parts of ourselves within the mandala and experiencing our habitual emotional reactions completely, we can transform. In this way, we liberate ourselves from the cycles of endless suffering and come to embody our true nature, our Buddha Nature, whole and complete—empowered to stand up and speak truth to power.

• • •

As the Earth Treasure Vase Mandala took root in the body of the Earth, my own healing process deepened. Transforming a lifetime of dissociation into an embodied experience of being true to myself and not avoiding pain and suffering is a life's work. But thankfully, the wild dakini nature does not require me to be nice. Fierce compassion is a gateway to liberation. That much I know.

I also know that forgiving abuse is not easy. Sexual abuse happens in the very core of our being where creation begins. It is only after a lifetime that—along with the gathering storm clouds looming dark gray over the mountains, thunder rumbling in the distance, the clouds mirroring my own internal state—I see these horrors clearly, and the sorrow and pain I feel releases.

Yet, the truth still hurts when I admit that the system that is at war with life, at war with the planet, is the same system that has oppressed women, burned them at the stake, colonized the Indigenous, and enslaved Black lives that matter. The heartless mind that clings desperately to the last drops of water, the last gasp of oil, and the power of guns and terror, that starves entire populations, poisons whole towns, imprisons people of color, locks children up in cages, and would even consider dropping a nuclear bomb on an enemy is the mind of a maniac. But this attitude is changing as women, and the men who respect them, stand up together to bring balance and harmony back to the world on behalf of Mother Earth.

Forgiveness is hard. But holding on to the hurt does not help. It only festers. I know that my family members are in me. Jack is in me, too, along with the rapists, the dictators, and the warlords. But the whale, the elephant, and sea turtle dwell in me, too, along with an old-growth forest, an ocean, and a vast night sky. In the story of interbeing, we are not separate within the mandala.

SECTION THREE

BECOMING A HOLY VESSEL

CHAPTER FIFTEEN

TAKING REFUGE IN THE EARTH

In the early 2000s, after many years of dedicated dharma practice, I had become quite disillusioned. But I didn't want to throw the baby out with the bathwater. I had received many valuable Buddhist teachings and would forever be inspired by the wisdom of the lineage masters. But my heart ached, especially as I struggled to come to terms with the patriarchal structure of Guru Yoga, which is practiced in the Vajrayana. So, I focused on the Earth Treasure Vases. As they continued to go out around the planet, I was increasingly listening to the Earth to know where to take the little clay pots. It began to dawn on me that the Three Jewels are actually embodied in the Earth as a living being, and I sensed an invitation to awaken to this sacred relationship.

In Buddhism, we talk about three sources of refuge: namely, the Buddha, the one who shows us the way in this life; the Dharma, the teachings of understanding and love; and the Sangha, the community that practices harmony and awareness. The Buddha, Dharma, and Sangha are called jewels because they are considered the ultimate and most precious source of protection, guidance, inspiration, and wisdom. At the beginning of any dharma practice, these Three Jewels are invoked as a way to give ourselves over to something larger than ourselves and put our practice in this context. And when the path calls us seriously, we participate in a ceremony to formally "Take Refuge" in these Three Jewels.

The teachings and practices of the historical Buddha have served to enlighten many on the path he illuminated. And the sacred community of practitioners provides precious witnessing and spiritual support for us as we walk the often difficult path of liberation, individually and together. The teacher, the teachings, and the community truly are jewels beyond compare, for they serve to bring us to the most important thing in this life—the relief from suffering and the realization of enlightenment.

Yet, in spite of the advances of the last 2,600 years since the Buddha's awakening, most Buddhist schools have neglected to include the precious jewel that is the Earth in their practices. But as I looked deeply into the planet's miraculous capacities and beautiful living systems, I wondered, how could the Earth *not* be considered a Great Awakened Being?

Thich Nhat Hanh was one Buddhist teacher who did recognize the Earth as a bodhisattva. He powerfully included Gaia in a new version of the chant "Invoking the Bodhisattvas' Names" and invited us to touch the Earth with our awareness in every step of our walking meditation. In his book *Love Letter to the Earth*, published in 2013, he makes it clear: "When you are able to see the Earth for the bodhisattva that she is, you will want to bow down and touch the Earth with reverence and respect. Then love and care will be born in your heart. This awakening is enlightenment. Don't look for enlightenment elsewhere. This awakening, this enlightenment, will bring a great transformation in you, and you'll have more happiness, more love, and more understanding than from any other practice."[1]

But most of us have forgotten our interdependence with Earth, the One who supports and witnesses us all. We have taken advantage of Her, sacrificed Her, and neglected to protect the web of life of which we are each a part. Over the centuries, our Ancestors, Indigenous elders, and a few awakened masters have tried to remind us that we need to listen to Her. But trapped in our self-importance and blinded by our greed, we have lost the Way.

For many of us, the need to connect with nature in order to heal ourselves is paramount. But the desperation we feel as the web of life unravels around us is devastating. Humanity's greatest source of refuge has been desecrated beyond recognition. In my own desperation, when encountering aspects of the Buddhist tradition that I could no longer uphold, I found myself taking a leap of faith into the arms of a refuge I could trust: Mother Earth.

In nature, we observe the myriad living systems of the Earth working together, informing each other, feeding each other, and supporting each other. We see the teachings of interdependence, present in the web of life, and the Dharma is revealed—the teachings of selflessness, cooperation, wisdom, and compassion. Here, the way of understanding and love and the path to enlightenment become clear.

The web of life comes alive when we sit at the base of a tree in the forest, gaze at the sunset over the ocean, or listen to the sound of the crickets at night under the stars. We feel profoundly connected to All That Is and the great diversity of life on Earth is revealed—a living relationship of interbeing. We recognize a vast community of harmony and awareness in every direction and understand our place in the great awakened Sangha, here and now.

Like a multifaceted jewel in space, Mother Earth gives birth to all life and supports us with Her whole being. The Earth is truly a living, breathing, complete expression of the whole, of which we are each an inextricable part. And Gaia's dharma lessons can be found in every direction. To look deeply into the nature of Earth is to see our own infinite nature reflected back to us. Our Buddha Nature!

For me, forming this relationship with Earth, with Gaia, was like encountering an enlightened master, or perhaps the Beloved. Exciting, humbling, and magnificent—empowering and awe-inspiring. This is what I was looking for as a source of refuge: something, someone, so much larger than myself, beyond my capacity to figure out, who embodies innate natural wisdom and compassion and expresses it selflessly and generously in exactly the way I need to hear, see, and feel so that I may learn, grow, and be nourished.

As I took refuge in the whole Earth and made this the basis of my dharma practice, the Three Jewels came to life, not as an abstract idea but as a living, breathing reality. Within the Earth, I found a truly reliable source of refuge and could let go of my dependency on a fallible human religious system or godlike spiritual being. I came to honor Her as my greatest teacher and respected elder—my beloved.

As this process unfolded, the suffering of cyclic existence also became clear. As the Buddha taught, it is our suffering that points the way to our awakening. To think we can pursue our own individual isolated course of action any longer and get away with it is to deceive ourselves. The world we live in has become far too small. The suffering of our friends across the ocean, even our neighbors down the street, is truly our own suffering, as I was discovering with every Earth Treasure Vase I planted. There is no escaping the relationship of interbeing we find ourselves in with each other and planet Earth.

But what an opportunity we have in this evolutionary moment of life on Earth to take up the bodhisattva's task! The great vow of the bodhisattva, or spiritual hero, is to dedicate ourselves to the liberation of *all* beings. In recognizing our interbeing, the bodhisattva realizes that individual enlightenment is an illusion because we are all connected. Every single sentient being counts. We will not become personally free from suffering until we are *all* free from suffering. Bodhisattvas set aside their own personal enlightenment to join the ranks working for the enlightenment of others, for the whole planet.

As human beings, compassion is our special gift. The moment we understand our interdependence, we understand that we truly *can* help one other. And when we do, we see that the causes and conditions that brought us to this moment are completely interwoven. I see that my happiness is dependent upon your happiness, just as my survival is dependent on your survival. Breathing this air, the by-product of strong trees with deep roots in forests the world round, and seeing mountains reaching into the clouds, their rivers flowing down and out to meet the sea, we small humans—rushing around on this vast ocean planet in space—are poised to realize that every gesture we make affects every other living being.

As I witness the web of life unraveling right before my very eyes, the Earth has become my teacher—whether I like it or not. The Earth has become the teacher of us all.

Thich Nhat Hanh once again writes, "For us to survive, both as individuals and as a species, we need a revolution in consciousness. It can start with our collective awakening. Looking deeply, with mindfulness and concentration, we can see that we are the Earth and, with this insight, love and understanding will be born."[2]

The moment for waking up from the slumber of ignorance as a species has arrived. The sorrow of losing our own little corner of the woods, the wild places where the deer sequesters herself quietly, the great savannah where the elephants roam, the fresh air and clean water that nourishes us—these losses serve as catalysts for finding the path of collective awakening as a globally connected body inseparable from Mother Earth.

Our Mother Gaia has reached the limit of what she can tolerate and is speaking to us more and more loudly. Many of us are listening now to a long-silenced voice trying to get our attention. We have seen that our irresponsible growth and development has occurred at the expense of the planet's living systems, and the vast, seemingly endless supply of resources within the web of life are threatened and dangerously out of balance. It is now a matter of life and death for us all.

As my relationship to the traditional views of Buddhism relaxed and my relationship with the Earth came more into focus, I became curious about the story of the Buddha's awakening. The story goes that when the Buddha was on the verge of enlightenment, he was sitting under a tree (the Bodhi Tree) and reached down to "summon the Earth" as his witness.

Who exactly is the witness Buddha invoked? Early Indian texts refer to Mother Earth as Prithvi and describe her as "The Vast One," "The Stable One," "The One Who Nourishes Life." In Buddha's time she was perceived as a goddess whose body is the Earth, and her lap or womb was considered the seat of awakening. "When Mara, the king of demons, challenged Siddhartha to provide a witness to his worthiness to attain enlightenment," writes Miranda Shaw in *Buddhist Goddesses of India*, "the Bodhisattva stretched forth his golden hand and touched the Earth, invoking the one who observes and remembers every event that transpires on her vast body. Responding to his summons, the earth goddess rendered her testimony in world-shaking tones and personally dispersed Mara's armies. In so doing, she created the environment of peace necessary for the Buddha-to-be to enter the subtlest spheres of meditation and attain full spiritual awakening."[3]

Of all the possible witnesses that the Buddha could have summoned, that it was the Earth tells us there is no greater witness, no better source of support to dispel the negative forces that Mara represents. Mother Earth is here for us.

Furthermore, the Earth Goddess provided the very throne upon which the Buddha achieved liberation. "[Prithvi] implicitly supports his right to attain enlightenment by allowing him to occupy the powerful spot at the center of creation, the center of her power," writes Shaw.[4] "Thus, the earth goddess not only authenticated the Buddha's worthiness of enlightenment but also accepted him as the legitimate claimant to her throne, which she reserves for a 'righteous king' (dharma-raja) who has acted in accordance with the universal order, lived in harmony with all creatures, selflessly served others, and above all, demonstrated the generosity that is the primary qualification of a virtuous ruler."[5]

I was stunned to realize the role Prithvi had played in the Buddha's awakening and wondered . . . Had Buddha taken refuge in the Earth, too?

Then, one day, to better express the sense of refuge I was seeking, I had a moment of sudden inspiration and adapted Thich Nhat Hanh's Verses of Refuge that were so familiar to me into a new version of that prayer that could be recited at the beginning of any formal practice. [6]

Perfection of Wisdom; Mother of Buddhas, bodhisattvas, and all beings; nourishing, holding, and healing all; Great Mother Earth, precious jewel of the cosmos, to you we bow in gratitude.

We take refuge in the Earth as our teacher, the one who shows us the Way in this life.

We take refuge in the Earth as an expression of the dharma, the teachings of interbeing, understanding, and love.

We take refuge in the Earth as an embodiment of the sangha, the vast interdependent community of life in balance and harmony.

Living within the web of life on Earth, we dedicate ourselves to embodying awakened awareness on the path of healing in service to all beings. We dedicate our lives to realizing our oneness with Gaia.

The Earth Treasure Vase (ETV) Journey in Photos

The cave at Charok in 1990. Behind the structures built out in front is the opening of the cave.

His Eminence Kushok Mangdon, Charok Rinpoche, 1990. *Photos by Cynthia Jurs.*

After preparing the ETV for burial with the Gyumed Monks and Tewa elder, Vickie Downey. *Photo by Vickie Downey.*

The Guymed monks performing the ETV ceremony above Los Alamos, New Mexico. *Photo by Louise Baum.*

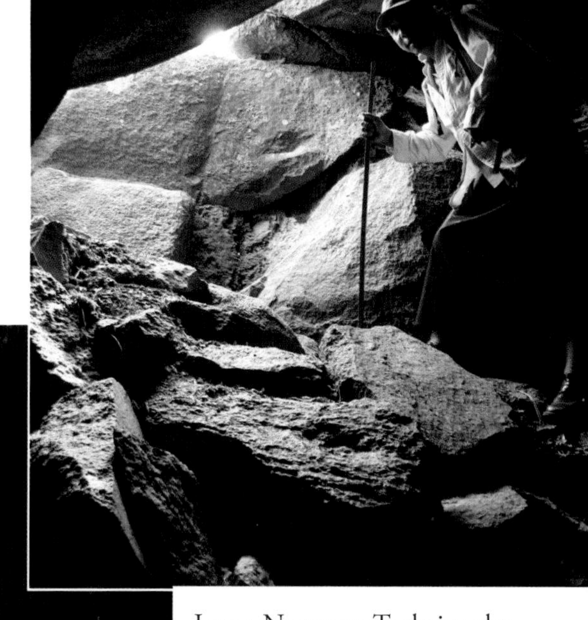

Lama Ngawang Tsultrim also visited the Center of the Mandala. *Photo by Cynthia Jurs.*

Shantum Seth and pilgrimage group with the ETV under the Bodhi Tree at Bodhgaya.

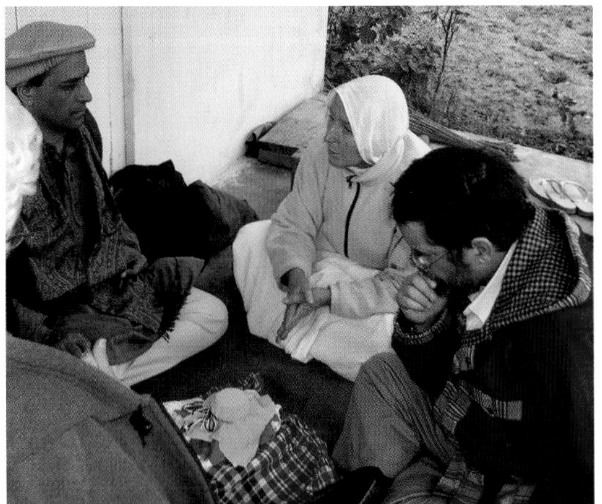

With Nani-ma who blessed the vase and directed us to the source of the Ganges, India.

Left and below: Guimolo Dolo, Elder and diviner of the Dogon tribe in Mali, who received the first ETV for Africa and blessed it.

All photos courtesy Cynthia Jurs.

Prayers and offerings were made by hundreds of people from three countries into the ETV for Liberia. Many civic leaders and tribal elders celebrated the ETV in Voinjama. The vase was buried under a kola tree in Tellowoyan Village with Mahwen looking on. *Photos by Harper Karmon.*

Two years later, our first Peace Hut was dedicated where the ETV was buried. *Photo by Cynthia Jurs.*

Women's peace movement leader, Annie Nushann, stands next to me with her team at our second Peace Hut in Ganta. *Photo courtesy Cynthia Jurs.*

The activities under our third Peace Hut in Margibi are directed by women peacebuilders. *Photo by Harper Karmon.*

Former General Christian Bethelson practicing peace in the Buddha Garden at Plum Village. *Photo by Anthony Carlson.*

In Liberia, Bethelson taught mindfulness to young people, including former child soldiers. *Photo by Harper Karmon.*

At Plum Village in 2014 with Thich Nhat Hanh when Liberian peacebuilders were living there. *Photo by Anthony Carlson.*

Brother Phap Lai, Harper Karmon, Christian Bethelson, Sister Chân Không, Cynthia Jurs, Annie Nushann, and Sister Peace. *Photo by Cynthia Jurs.*

Christian, Harper, and Annie in front of the Peace Hall that Annie built and dedicated to Plum Village Sister Peace. *Photo by Wouter Verhoeven.*

With Asdrubal Torres, who stewarded an ETV to Kogi Elders in Colombia and another to his Arhuaco homeland.

ETV burial in the tall grass prairie of Kansas.

Above: With David Nicol and Leslie Meehan and the ETV for Kansas.
Left: With Joanna Macy who holds the ETV for Alaska.

All photos courtesy Cynthia Jurs.

Yupik Elder Rita Blumenstein, who offered the white eagle feathers from her fan for the ETVs in Alaska and the South Pacific. *Photo by Cynthia Jurs.*

Ceremony with the ETV on the banks of the Yukon River. *Photo by Linda Ward.*

The youngest chief of the Gwitch'in, Evon Peter, who received the ETV for Arctic Alaska.

Evon Peter's family joined forces with our pilgrimage group to bury the ETV. *Photos by Cynthia Jurs.*

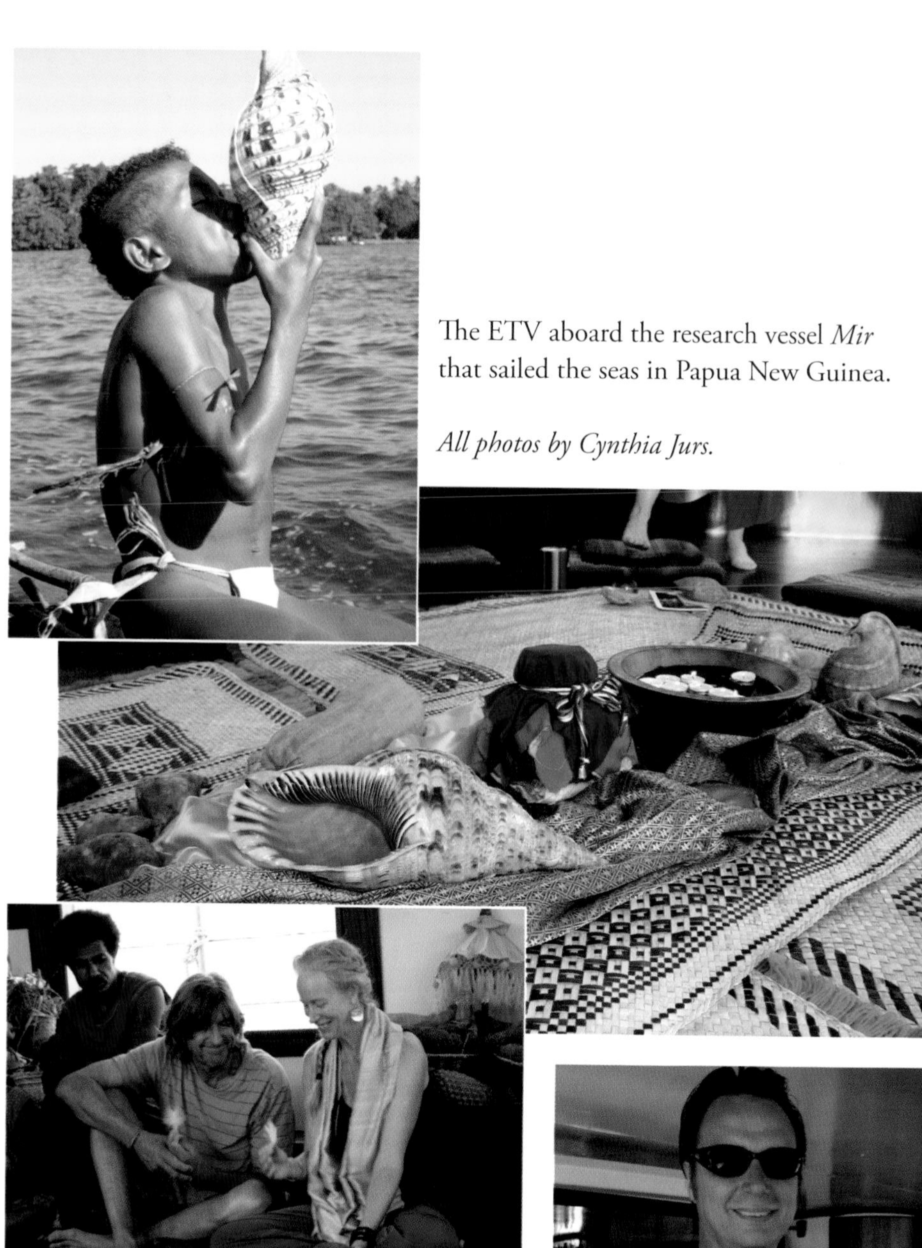

The ETV aboard the research vessel *Mir* that sailed the seas in Papua New Guinea.

All photos by Cynthia Jurs.

Above: Hugh and I offered the white eagle feathers from Grandma Rita Blumenstein into the vase. *Right:* The vase was packed into an underwater camera housing unit. Biosphere Foundation cofounder, Mark Van Thillo and friends dove 93 feet down to place the vase in an atoll for the protection of the South Pacific Ocean.

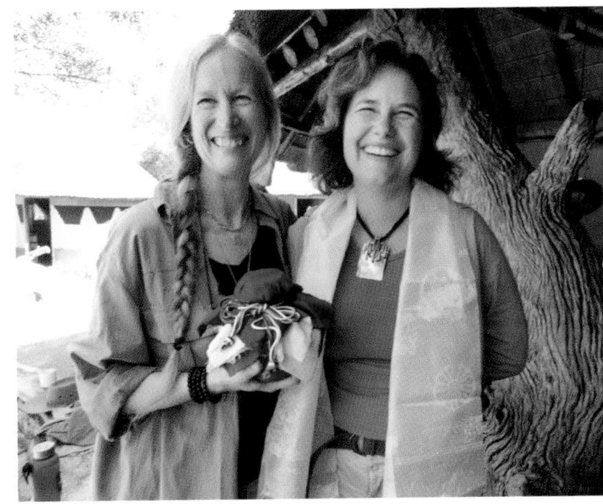

Left: In the Kalahari with Grandmothers of the San People, who blessed the ETV in their language. *Right:* With Linda Tucker who has dedicated her life to protecting the white lions in South Africa. *Photos by Cynthia Jurs.*

The vase was introduced to the white lions and elephants in the South African bush. *Lion photo by Brad Laughlin; elephant photo by Cynthia Jurs.*

Left: Hugh was happy to visit the animals he loves so much. *Right:* Offering the vase at the 30,000-year-old stone altar identified by Zulu Elder, the late Credo Mutwa, overlooking the Blyde River Canyon, Limpopo Province, South Africa. *Photos by Cynthia Jurs.*

WORLDWIDE MANDALA O

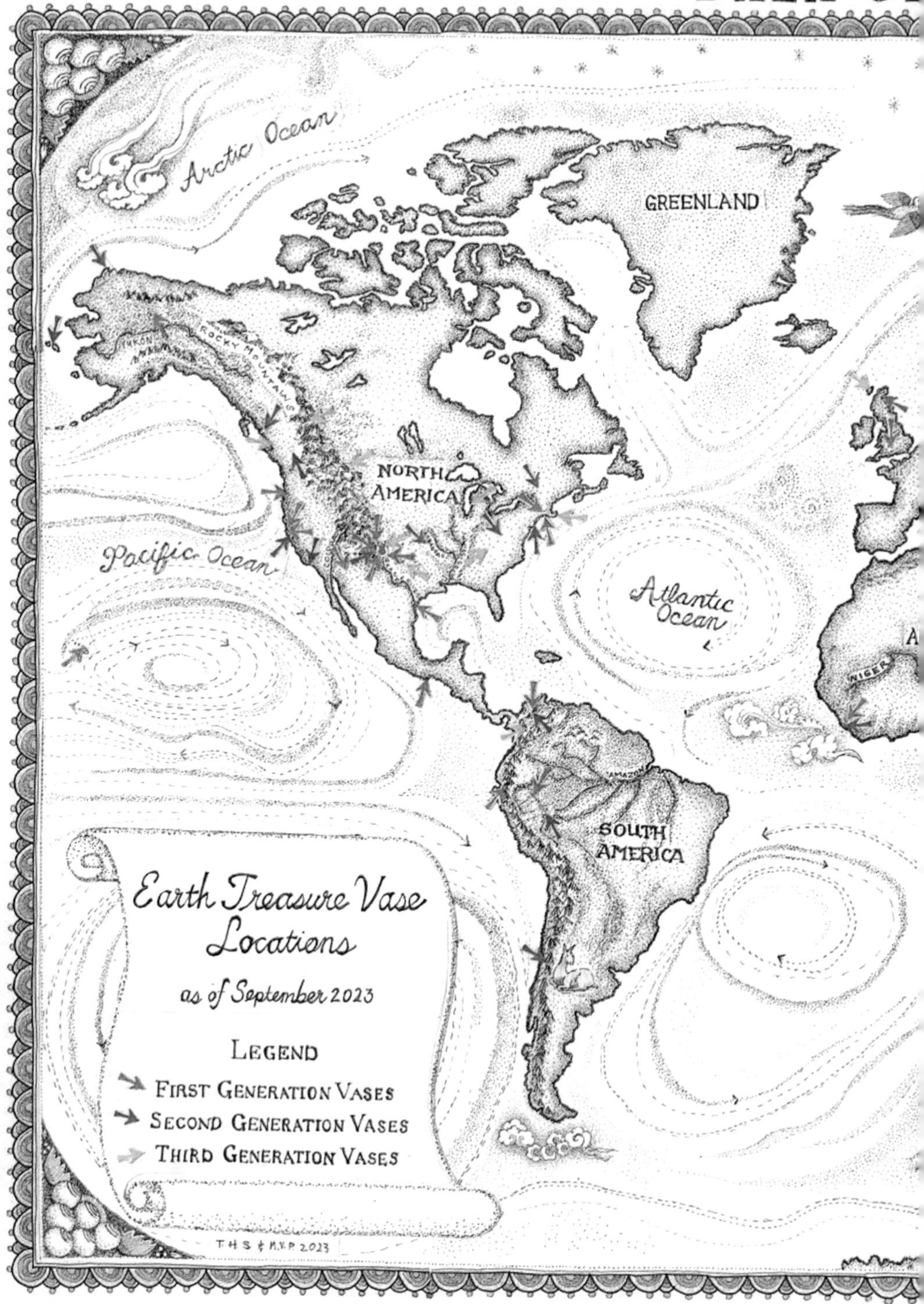

Arctic Ocean
GREENLAND
ROCKY MOUNTAINS
NORTH AMERICA
Pacific Ocean
Atlantic Ocean
NIGER
SOUTH AMERICA
Earth Treasure Vase Locations
as of September 2023
LEGEND
FIRST GENERATION VASES
SECOND GENERATION VASES
THIRD GENERATION VASES

ARTH TREASURE VASES

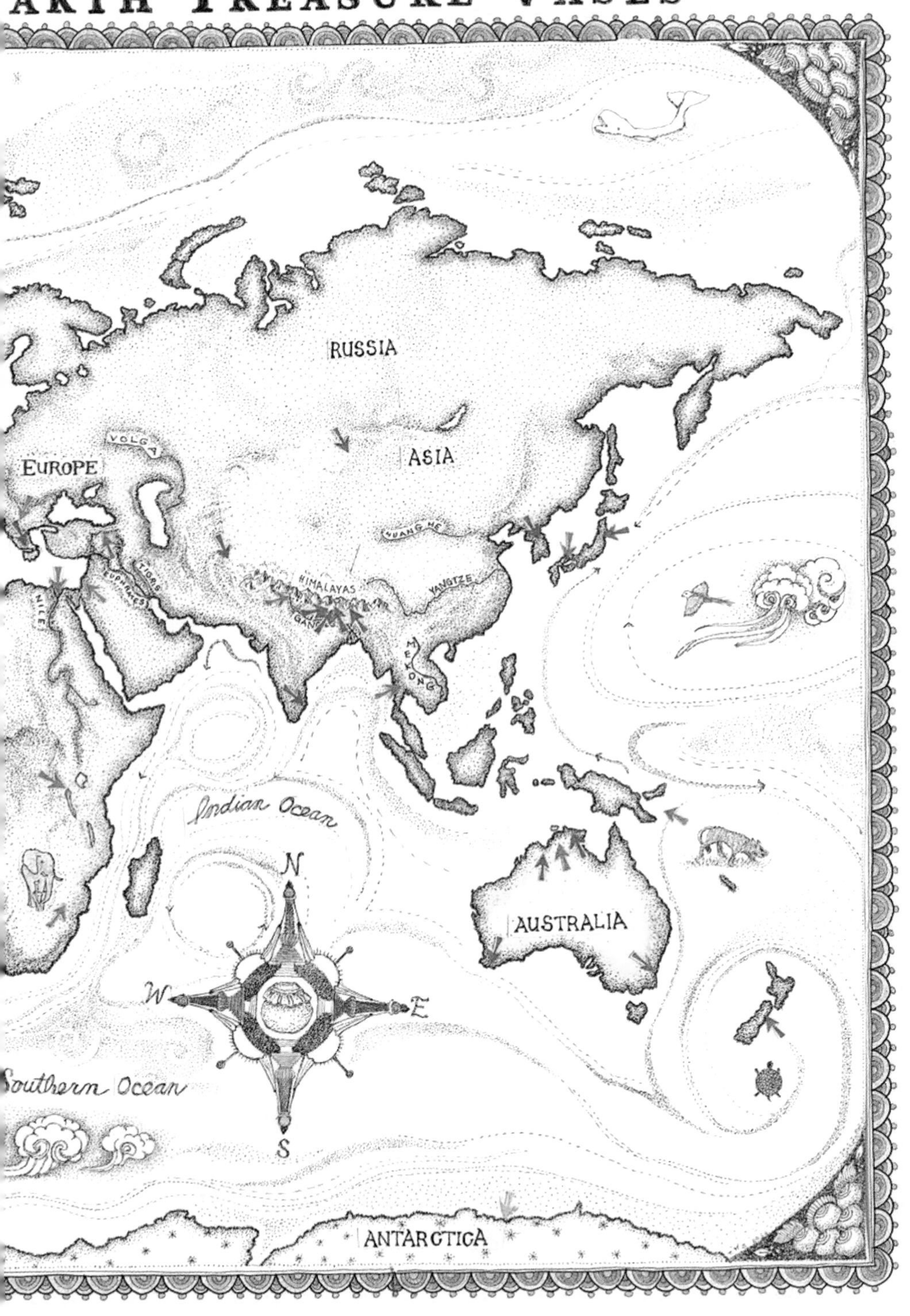

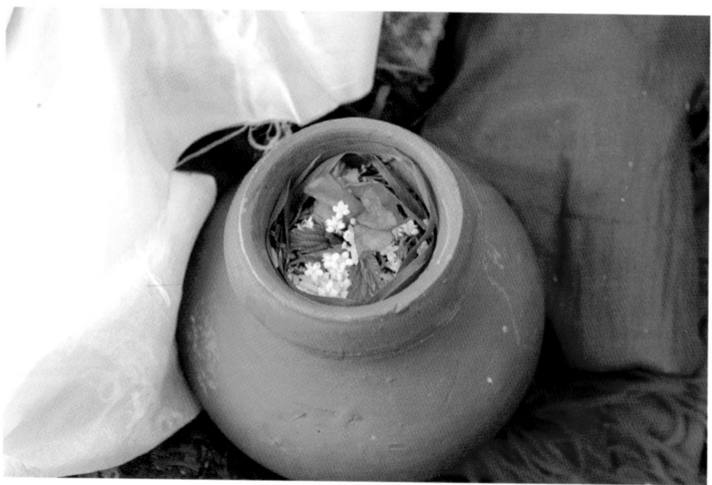

The beautiful vase that was buried near Avebury, Great Britain.
Photos by Rachel Bliven.

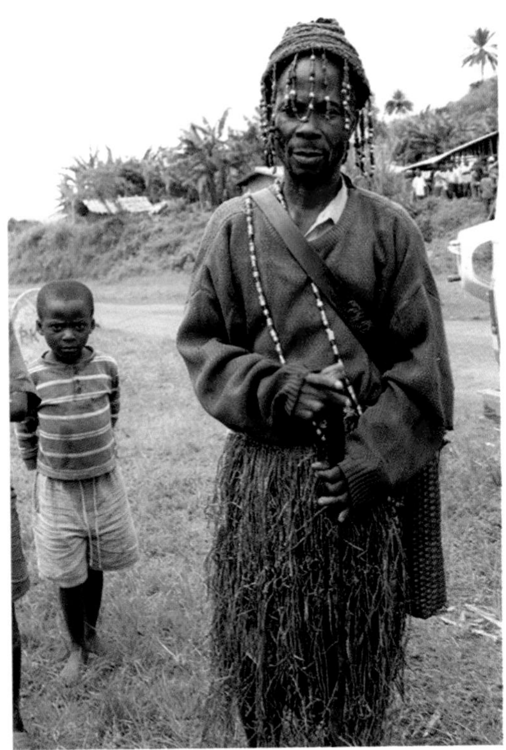

Above left: Neema Namadamu brought me in the Pygmy community to deliver the ETV in D.R. Congo. *Photo by Danny Walters.*

Above right: Chief Mwami Walumba greeted us when we arrived in Mwenga. *Photo by Cynthia Jurs.*

Members of the Mwenga community made offerings into the vase. *Photo by Cynthia Jurs.*

Collette's prayers were very heartfelt.

Charles Uwiragiye, Chief Mwami Walumba, and local leaders of Mwenga blessing the vase as Neema looks on. *Photos by Cynthia Jurs.*

In Australia, the ETV sat on the altar for Dalai Lama's teachings in Sydney. One morning his Holiness picked it up and blessed it! You can see the little vase on the altar to the right of the Dalai Lama's throne, above the heads of the second row of seated monks.

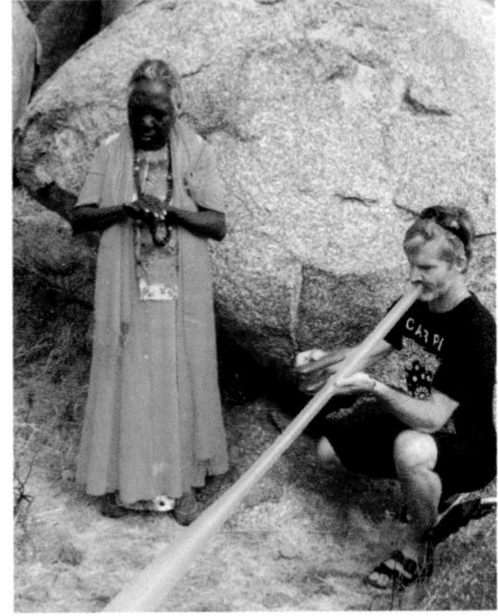

Left: His Holiness met Aunty Margaret Katherine at Uluru. *Right:* Aunty Margaret and didjeridu musician Julian Silburn came on three ETV pilgrimages in Australia. *Photos by Anthony Carlson.*

Praying with the vase at Kata Jutu.

Uncle Bob and Barbara Randall with the carved wooden ETV container painted by Aborignal artists at Uluru.

Custodial Elder of Uluru, Uncle Bob Randall with our group.
Photos courtesy Cynthia Jurs.

The vase traveled to Northern Territory, where it was welcomed by Aunty Margaret before being placed in her ancestral land.

Holding the vase before its placement in Australia was a deep fulfillment for me.
Photos courtesy Cynthia Jurs.

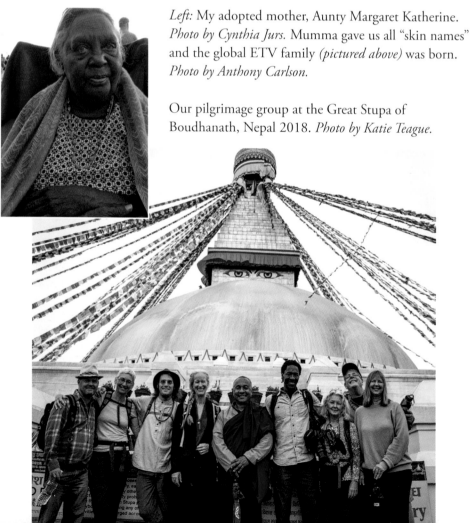

Left: My adopted mother, Aunty Margaret Katherine. *Photo by Cynthia Jurs.* Mumma gave us all "skin names" and the global ETV family *(pictured above)* was born. *Photo by Anthony Carlson.*

Our pilgrimage group at the Great Stupa of Boudhanath, Nepal 2018. *Photo by Katie Teague.*

The view of the Himalayas from Lama Tsultrim's seat, Tolu Tharling Monastery, where we took an ETV in 2018. *Photo by Katie Teague.*

With Lama Ngawang Tsultrim Rinpoche who bestowed on me the title of Honorary Lama at Tolu Tharling. *Photo by Andre Lambertson.*

Tolu Tharling Monastery after the earthquake. *Photo Katie Teague.*

Inside Tolu Tharling: two Earth Treasure Vases sit on the main altar. *Photo by Katie Teague.*

Lama Ngawang Tsultrim. *Photo by Cynthia Jurs.*

Full circle: returning to the cave at Charok, greeted by Ani Pema Chodron, daughter of Charok Rinpoche. *Left photo by Katie Teague. Right photo by Cynthia Jurs.*

Right: Teaching the Sublime Mother Gaia for the first time at Charok. *Photo by Katie Teague.*

Below: Nepal ETV pilgrimage group after the burial. Standing from left: Andre Lambertson, Tyler Hess, Cynthia Jurs, Lama Tenzin, Ani Pema Chodron, Lama Ngawang Tsultrim, a young sherpa friend from Tolu Tharling. Seated front: Ginny McGinn, David Nicol, Lama Tsultrim's daughter Sonam & Lenya Reese. *Photo by Katie Teague*

Meditating after the ETV burial. *Photo by Katie Teague.*

In 2021, a group gathered at Ghost Ranch on Native lands in New Mexico with Tewa elder Marian Naranjo, who guided us in crafting a third Generation of ETVs. *Photo by Kenna Klosterman.*

In 2023, we took an ETV to Delphi in Greece as an offering to Gaia, the original Oracle of Delphi.

Left: Temple of Athena Pronaia. *Photo by Glenyce Bean.*

Below: The Amphitheatre at Delphi. *Photo by Therese Hogan.*

CHAPTER SIXTEEN

SACRED TIME

While preparing to embark on my first trip to Africa with an Earth Treasure Vase for Liberia, I had to face the postwar reality there and was daunted. Then I had a vivid dream that got my attention and opened the way. The dream revealed that the pathway to peace in Liberia, and Africa in general, was through the Dogon tribe in Mali. I had heard of the Dogon—a mysterious ancient culture living on the edge of the Sahara Desert with magnificent wisdom linked to the star Sirius. I knew I had to go there with the vase and invite the blessings of that land and people. My guide was a dignified gentleman named Abdoulaye Diallo, with extensive knowledge of Dogon art and culture. Much to my surprise, when we arrived in Dogon Country, I discovered the name of the village was Sangha.

We settled into a simple yet lovely guest house and made our way down to a sweeping dry riverbed to meet a respected diviner, Guimolo Dolo. This striking elder was dressed in brown cloth the color of the land, and his bare feet looked like they had never worn a pair of shoes. He appeared to have always been there, his skin hardened by the elements, no different than the Earth he sat on.

I was invited to ask a question and gazed into the kindest eyes I have ever known. I told him about the Earth Treasure Vases. About my commitment to bring healing and protection to the Earth and my quest for peace in Liberia, in Africa, and in the world. I asked him if the task would ever be accomplished. He listened calmly and closely, then cleared and smoothed the dirt to do a divination. He laid out an arrangement of small sticks and pebbles to be left outside under the stars overnight. In the morning, he would return to read the footprints of the fox that was expected to come during the night. Its tracks through the sticks and stones would determine the answer to my question.

I watched as he carefully arranged the little pieces of wood and small pebbles in a pattern. The sections he set forth in the fine red dirt looked like some kind of hieroglyphics that only he could read. I stayed near him until the sun set low in the sky and the shadows grew long. We said goodbye, knowing we would return the next day to receive his divination. Sure enough, when we arrived in the morning, little footprints had traveled through the dirt, casting the pebbles and sticks this way and that. Pointing with a long pole in hand he told me not to worry, my mission would be successful, and all the remaining vases would find their rightful place throughout Africa and the world in just a few years' time. I saw the fox prints in the dirt as a pathway through my obstacles, a pathway to peace. Then he invited us to his home that afternoon where he would do a special blessing for the Earth Treasure Vase I would be taking on to Liberia.

We entered a courtyard contained by the mud walls of family rooms and made our way to a far corner covered by a thatched roof. We nestled in to be close to this quiet gentleman who squatted down next to a small, carved wooden door opening into a repository of sacred ceremonial objects. He asked to see the Earth Treasure Vase. I unwrapped the clay pot from out of my backpack and handed it to him. After holding it tenderly, he opened the little door and took out three sticks. These he gave to me, telling me to hold them and pray strongly into them. I was to concentrate with all my might on everything I wished for, for the vase and for myself, and to imbue these prayers into the sticks, including all that came before and all that would come after this moment. I did as I was told and after some time, handed the sticks back to him. He reached into his closet and carefully brought out a large, black, egg-shaped mass into which he inserted the sticks. This strange object, the size of a loaf of bread, was a "fetish" that contained all the magic that he carried, the prayers and wishes that he held for others, and the traces of all the sacrifices he had ever done to charge those requests with life-force energy and power. I was being connected to an unfamiliar system of belief, but the positive blessings I felt from him were palpable. He told me that whenever I had any doubts, I should think of this fetish, ask for help, and I would receive it. It was like an anchor to connect me to him and to the prayers I had placed into those sticks.

Then he asked me to open the vase. He took it gently into his own large hands and reached again into his little closet for a glass jar filled with a brown liquid. Dipping his finger into the jar, he wiped this medicine around the inside neck of the vase as his offering for protection and the realization of our prayers.

I struggled to find words. Finally, in a hushed tone, I spoke to him about the state of the world and the urgency that possessed me to take these little clay pots all over the planet to try to address the need for healing in the face of such devastating destruction and blindness. He looked at me silently for a long time. And then he said, "Urgency. We don't really have that here."

My mind stopped. Guimolo Dolo was unconditioned by the sense of urgency that most of us Westerners live with every day of our lives. Here was a man who truly resides in the present moment. As his statement slowly penetrated my awareness, I realized that living in reaction to a constant sense of desperate urgency does not help in any way but only contributes to more desperation and anxiety.

We spent the next few days wandering in the Dogon villages and absorbing that timeless culture. The morning of our last day, we drove down to say goodbye to Guimolo Dolo where he sat in his divining ground. As he gazed at me one last time, I felt a heart-to-heart transmission. He radiated an incomparably deep love and kindness directly into my soul. As tears fell from my eyes, I noticed the way the folds of his brown robes melted into the Earth around him, the skin of his bare feet and legs inseparable from the land. I was reminded of Charok Rinpoche's red robes merging into the cushion he sat on as his physical body became more and more insubstantial. This elder of the Dogon, Guimolo Dolo, took my two hands in his and, turning my palms upwards, spat into them as a farewell blessing.

Guimolo Dolo's words forced me to come to terms with my sense of urgency. Facing life and death issues in every direction around the planet brought pressure and concern that I was not doing enough. But slowing down long enough to sit with elders like this humble wise man in Mali taught me to surrender my ideas of what to do and the pushy, self-important attitude that does not know how to listen. I had to learn that it does not help to fearfully strive to accomplish the task. Instead, I had to learn to relax, open, and trust that the big change has already begun—and I am part of it.

As this experience sank in, I realized that the solutions to the planet's problems are not dependent on time as we know it. Our identification with time greatly limits our capacities to bring real healing and transformation and keeps us locked in an old story.

"When the time of our ordinary mind stops, we enter into the time of Spirit, the sacred time, the time when everything is possible," writes Arkan Lushwala in *The Time of the Black Jaguar: An Offering of Indigenous Wisdom for the Continuity of Life on Earth.* "The reward for our efforts comes when time is over—when the future is no longer a consequence of our past but a new reality, born from the Cosmic Mother who became pregnant with our prayers, dreams and visions."[1]

During a burial ceremony or ritual meditation with the Earth Treasure Vases, I often cannot tell whether we've been there for thirty minutes or three hours. It is then that I know we are in sacred time. We have entered a state of being where miracles are taking place right then and there, here and now. Living in a conscious relationship to the rhythms of the sun and moon, the solstices and the equinoxes, is one way to connect with sacred time. Perhaps this is really just natural time, which unfolds in a rhythm that is in harmony with nature—not a rhythm dictated by our schedules and sped-up lives. When we live in relationship with the sun and moon and seasons, we slow down to a pace that allows us to notice things that are, in fact, miraculous.

Sacred time is almost always at work when we bury an Earth Treasure Vase—like the time we buried the vase at Punta Cometa on the coast of Oaxaca, on the spring equinox of 1997. That vase had been offered to curanderos, healers, and activists in Oaxaca City who initiated it in prayer and ceremony—singing, playing the flute into it, offering healing herbs—on the winter solstice. It was taken to the mountains for a sweat lodge, or in the language of Mexico, a temazcal. After this powerful ceremony the vase was brought to the Pacific Coast. Hurricane Rick had wiped the land clean of enormous old-growth trees as the eye of the storm passed directly over the region for miles and miles, flattening the many small Indigenous communities and sea-turtle nesting beaches that are a special feature of that region. Birds had fallen from the sky, and the beaches were covered with enormous hardwood trees that had washed down from the mountains in engorged rivers, preventing the turtles from coming ashore to lay their eggs.

A local sanctuary for many generations, Punta Cometa is the westernmost point of land protruding into the Pacific Ocean in the state of Oaxaca and has been held as a sacred place for as long as anyone can remember. We prepared the vase in a final ceremony, and, burning copal with its fragrant smoke, we sealed it. Then, at dawn, we made our way silently to the *punta* with our offering.

The land was still recovering from Hurricane Rick, and the old saguaros and shrubs were flattened, along with most of the old-growth trees in the forest. Focusing our minds on mantras, we walked high above the ocean, winding our way along the dirt path overlooking whirlpools, crashing waves, and hidden beaches where local fishermen go. Three of us picked our way over the rocks until we could go no farther. Not finding anywhere to dig in that rock, we stopped and sat down on the huge oceanside boulders looking the waves right in the eye. I pulled the vase out of my pack and rang the bell. Holding the vase up to the sky, with our hearts full of prayers, we asked for guidance from the spirits of that place. Immediately, a pelican flew past us very close and following it with our eyes, just off the point only yards from where we sat, a humpback whale breeched! Its spray fell on the vase and on us, and then another whale, a little further out, breeched, too!

At that moment I recalled a spot we had hiked through, and I knew the vase's home was there. After receiving that wet, miraculous blessing, we packed up and turned back. My friends, Mario and Marion, walked ahead as I moved slowly in an altered state; fully immersed in sacred time, I felt as if the vase were pulling me to the place it belonged. As I climbed up the rock to the land above, instantly my eyes fell on the sight of a huge saguaro, its arms reaching up and out, still standing strong. From where I stood, across the dry dirt and sparse shrubs to that majestic guardian, a shining path of light revealed itself to me so clearly there was no question this was the spot. As I stepped onto that shimmering ground, my friends turned around and saw it, too. We converged at the tall saguaro and asked permission from the local protector spirits to dig. With our small shovel and trowels, we exerted much force, expecting the Earth to be hard as rock, only to have the ground open up like butter. We dug down three feet like a sea turtle would, and gently laid our treasure into the soft lap of Mother Earth. We covered our tracks and left, confident the vase would be well protected by the saguaro guardian overlooking cliffs, ocean at his feet.

I still see that shining path clearly and will never forget the blessing of the whales. It was five years before we were able to return to that place. Hugh and I hiked out in the late afternoon and found the guardian saguaro once again. Sunset was approaching, and we were settling ourselves for a meditation when much to our surprise, small groups of more and more people arrived, quietly and respectfully, making their way out to that very spot to witness the sunset as a kind of ritual. Silence fell on everyone as the red sun lowered into the western sky and slid into the endless ocean. We were all joined in hushed contemplation and reverence within close proximity to the Earth Treasure Vase. She had done her job, creating "a new reality, born from the Cosmic Mother," as Arkan Lushwala had written.[2]

These sunset meditations have become a public ritual that continues to this day as the beaches nearby have drawn more and more visitors to enjoy the area. The sacred land of Punta Cometa is a vital refuge, now with the Earth Treasure Vase radiating out its blessings for all.

"A miracle is an invitation to a larger reality," suggests Charles Eisenstein in his book *The More Beautiful World Our Hearts Know Is Possible*. "A miracle is the name we give to the light that shines through from a larger, more radiant world. . . . To the extent we ourselves are living in the realization of interbeing, we too are able to become miracle-workers."[3]

When we go for a slow walk in nature, breathing mindfully with each step and looking up on occasion to notice the blue sky or the clouds gathering; when we suddenly hear the animal calls, the birdsong, or the wind rustling in the trees at just the right moment; these can seem like little miracles signaling the presence of spirit moving between us, inviting us to be aware of something so much larger than ourselves—a relationship of interbeing. These are the moments when an opening to another world is revealed, and if we stop to catch our breath, we may glimpse the light.

So many of us are constantly rushing through our lives. Trying hard to get somewhere. Keeping up. Loading our plates so full, we feel we are in a constant state of overwhelm, as if we might collapse.

Collectively, we have a deep need to find a natural rhythm and slow down, releasing ourselves from the pressure that we live with day in and day out. It seems there is no stopping—but there is. To actually take time out from our pressured, fast-paced, demanding lifestyle and stop—this is a real miracle. To rest, relax, and retreat is part of our own natural rhythm. We need this like we need a drink of water. We can't live on caffeine. When we take a weekend or even a day—sometimes just an hour will do—we become aware that our need for instant gratification, quick results, or the immediate answer is just another habit we have assumed from the collective nightmare that tells us we must live like this.

Walking slowly is a radical act. When Thich Nhat Hanh was at the airport on his way to the gate to catch his flight, do you think he was rushing? No. He was practicing walking meditation every step of the way, breathing in and breathing out. And ripples of peace and calm were emanating from him. It was he who said, "The miracle is not to walk on water. The miracle is to walk on the green Earth in the present moment, to appreciate the peace and beauty that are available now."[4]

• • •

The year 2012 had been declared in Mayan prophecies as the ending of one long cycle of time and the beginning of another.[5] It was the year I was compelled to travel more than ever. It was then that I made the Earth Treasure Vase pilgrimage to Congo, returned to Liberia for the third time for our peacebuilding program, and embarked on an unforgettable journey to the magical region of standing stones around Avebury in England—a true portal into sacred time if there ever was one.

The Avebury pilgrimage began in Wiltshire, England, at the ancient circle of around three hundred standing stones that encompasses twenty-eight acres. Some mystics regard the area as the umbilicus of Mother Earth. Important ley lines run through the landscape connecting Avebury to sacred sites all over the planet—and to the cosmos.

The late Burke Denman, a dear friend and Open Way Sangha member, who loved that land with all his heart, had a strong sense of stewardship for this Earth Treasure Vase and a clear sense of where it might go. He met me there with another friend, Felicity Broennan, who had spent much time in the British Isles. Burke introduced us to a number of sacred sites and took us into the crop circles that appeared in the wheat fields while we were there. Crop circles are created by unknown sources who flatten crops into large geometric patterns that appear overnight in fields. These were another key indication of the magical nature of this region. We continuously asked for guidance and invited the local spirits to bless and accept the vase as an offering for the Earth. It seemed they were listening closely every step of the way.

Soon we were joined by several more vase pilgrims: Rachel Bliven, Margita Kobler, and Susan Buchholz, who had all enrolled in a program Wisdom University (now called Ubiquity) was hosting. I had been invited to share the Earth Treasure Vase practice with their students, and when the group converged, we meditated daily in and around Avebury as we explored, intuited, and absorbed the energies of that sacred landscape and scouted locations for the vase.

Local crop-circle expert Karen Alexander and her husband, Steve Alexander, who photographs crop circles from the air, were drawn to the Earth Treasure Vase. Early one morning, Karen directed us to a location Burke had suggested, and I intuitively felt that it was right. We were grateful for Karen's confirmation about this beautiful spot. She and Steve became our local allies, keeping our prayers alive to this day as they fly over the location to photograph the land from above during crop-circle season.

The burial took place on one of those days in the history of the world that will never be forgotten. A sense of great perfection accompanied us every step of the way as all the little details fell into place and synchronicities seemed to arise in every direction. With a cloak of invisibility firmly surrounding us, we made our way to the place that called the vase home.

There were five of us present for the final ceremony, where, inside an ancient, long barrow, we lit candles and meditated before sealing the vase. Slowly, we made a silent procession out past the standing stones that guard the entrance to the long barrow and into the sweeping grassy meadows covered with knee-high wildflowers that led to a beautiful spring below.

It was the summer solstice and the area around the spring had been decorated with flowers, ribbons, and an arbor of willow branches. Above this sacred shrine there were low-lying shrubs. It was in this thicket, well hidden from view, that Burke dug a hole. But this was no ordinary hole. With the small shovel he carried under his cloak, he dug a hole in the shape of a six-pointed star. Two interlaced triangles were carefully cut to preserve a mossy covering, then through the dark black topsoil he continued to dig two interlaced triangles out of the rich Earth. Much to our surprise, just under the dark surface layer, we encountered the pure white dirt one sees exposed in the large white horses carved into the hills around Wiltshire County. Three feet down, the entire hole was still white, radiating light in all six directions—the perfect union of above and below, masculine and feminine. We were stunned by the beauty. Laying wildflowers all around the little tomb, with tears falling like an auspicious rain, we held hands and then covered her up, replacing the mossy surface so that no one would ever know what was there.

We departed skipping and dancing, with the sensation of floating in a timeless bubble, carried by the awakened spirits of that enchanted English countryside.

As nightfall enveloped us, we lit a fire in the cottage, prepared a nourishing meal, and toasted our success. Burke checked online to see if any crop circles had manifested during our time together—and sure enough, one had. I gasped when I saw it—taken by surprise to find it was not a circle as is usually the case, but appeared to precisely mirror the "shape" of our experience. This was the image that appeared at the very time of our vase burial:

Photo by Steve Alexander / Temporary Temples

The mystical Margita shared her impressions with us:

> *There were five chambers in the cave where we sealed the vase. There were five standing stones outside and five of us. The little steeples on top of the chambers show an influx of cosmic energy channeled through the five chambers into the Earth. The star above symbolizes the connection to the cosmos—perhaps the star Sirius, which was in the sky at the time. The star can also be seen as the vase held aloft as an offering by the central figure. The five thin lines going downward look like us five, walking down to the spring. The five white drops seem an obvious reference to the waters that flow within the Earth to the spring at the base of the hill.*

Over the following days and weeks, we watched in amazement as this crop "circle" grew. By mid-July, this is what emerged:

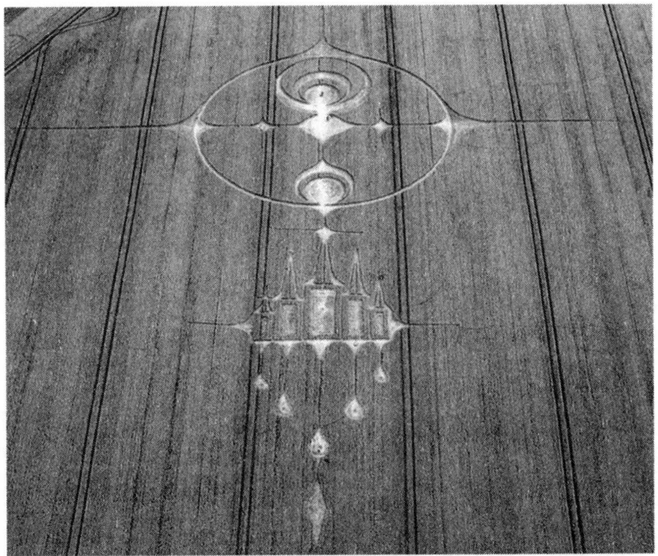

Photo by Steve Alexander / Temporary Temples

"The amazing addition," Margita excitedly wrote to me, "looks like the star Sirius revealing itself in its full glory! I take the addition as a confirmation from the crop-circle makers, showing that just like the small star is in truth a gigantic star system, this one Earth Treasure Vase is part of a larger system of vases doing their powerful work."

Our treasure vase burial in Avebury and the crop circle that appeared lingered in my awareness as a miraculous expression of beauty and cosmic power. These mysterious creations that cannot be easily explained entered my psyche, affecting me deeply. Like the impermanent sand mandalas depicting palaces of deities in Tibetan Buddhism, these present-day "temporary temples" also remind us of a wondrous world beyond ordinary reality. A world where miracles happen. It is from here that the treasure vases are doing their work, subtly but powerfully.

My experience has shown me that Mother Nature mirrors our own true nature. What we need to see and hear and know is reflected in the bird squawking overhead, the wind that picks up at that very moment, the whale that breeched right when the vase was held up to the ocean on the Punta Cometa, and the crop circle that appeared that day—all spiritual commentary pointing us in the right direction.

It was Marianne Williamson who wrote "Miracles are summoned by conviction."[6] When we are fully present and sacred time has made itself known, whatever we summon has the conviction of our hearts. We may not even be aware that we are summoning, or being summoned, but in sacred time, we are inviting a relationship with the divine. With nature and the stars. With a force so much larger than ourselves that is completely inaccessible if we rush blindly through our lives. When we live like this, we are no longer taking or using the precious gifts of life on Earth. When we live like this, we are *contributing to generating life* on Earth because we are restoring the sacred trust and unfurling our wings.

CHAPTER SEVENTEEN

OFFERINGS

During Buddha's time in ancient India, the treasure vessel was recognized for having a direct relationship to Mother Earth. The Earth Goddess Prithvi was depicted holding a vessel in her hands as the upper part of her torso emerged from the ground. "This full vessel or 'vase of plenty,'" writes Miranda Shaw in *Buddhist Goddesses of India*, "is implicitly understood to be overflowing with treasure—whether water, nectar, plant sap, lotus buds or jewels[;] . . . flowers, gems or pearl garlands . . . This accords with the Atharva Veda praise of mother earth as "she who bears her treasure stored up in many a place."[1]

Everywhere I go, I gather treasures as offerings for the vases. Behind my altar at home are pouches and bags, baskets, and bundles of earth from all the locations I have been with the Earth Treasure Vases, and from other places, too, whose medicine is a worthy contribution to a holy vessel. There are healing herbs and seeds from my own garden (I love the combination of rose, lavender, and chamomile) and from other gardens and growers as well. There are wild medicinal herbs like sage and juniper, grains like Native American blue corn, nourishing millet from Dogon Country in Mali, rice from my Tibetan Buddhist mandala-offering practice, ceremonial bread from Tewa elder Marian Naranjo, and the "three sisters"—corn, squash, and beans. I have lichen from mountains where the air is pure; feathers from eagle, owl, raven, flicker, hawk, peacock, parrot, and cockatoo; and South African elephant "tobacco." I have seeds of ancient redwoods, leaves from the two-thousand-year-old Árbol del Tule tree in Oaxaca, the Phoenix Tree in Hiroshima, and the Bodhi Tree in India under which the Buddha was enlightened, along with earth from all of the pilgrimage places of the Buddha's life. There are rolled mantras, prayers and poems, healing tinctures, homeopathic remedies, acupuncture needles, long-life medicines, and waters gathered from around the world. Precious stones of quartz, turquoise, coral, pearl, lapis, jade, and minerals like silver, copper, gold, and coltan from Congo. I have collected offerings of jewelry, coins, small stones and shells, and sands of all colors from around the world. (Someday I want to make a natural sand mandala from these locations.) And there are little rolls of red wool tied with ribbon to symbolize warm coverings and clothing.

Even more meaningful is that the very clay of the Earth Treasure Vases contains offerings—uniquely powerful ones. At the time of making the pots, Lama Tsultrim asked many lamas to contribute offerings and from them, he gathered hundreds of spiritual medicines, sacred substances, and relics to be mixed into the clay. When the vases were made, these offerings imbued the vases with a potent alchemical connection to great lineage masters, including Padmasambhava, Yeshe Tsogyal and Mandarava, Vairotsana, Vimalamitra, King Trisong Detsen, Longchenpa, Marpa, Naropa, Machig Labdron, Mipham, Shantarakshita, Tangtong Gyalpo, Patrul Rinpoche, Khyentse Rinpoche, Dudjom Rinpoche, Trulshik Rinpoche, Chatrul Rinpoche, Shechen Kongtrul, the two Jamgons, Karmapa,

Nagarjuna, as well as the Buddha, his disciple Kashyapa, the Dalai Lama and his previous incarnations, and many more.

I learned that when a great master dies, their body may remain in meditative equipoise and not deteriorate for many days without losing its suppleness. Even though the life force has withdrawn, the mind's nature is still present. Sometimes at the time of death, signs of accomplishment appear, like rainbows in the sky or flowers blooming out of season. There are stories of great practitioners who know when the time of death is approaching and inform their attendants to leave them undisturbed in meditation for some days—during which time, they practice for their physical body to be absorbed into light. The body shrinks until all that is left is the hair and fingernails. This Rainbow Body phenomenon is not impossible if one has trained in the practices that facilitate this level of realization in one's life.

It is more common that when the body of a highly accomplished master is cremated, relics are found in the remains as a sign of realization. These are gathered and made into medicines, like homeopathic remedies, and passed down through lifetimes. These "precious pills" carry profound healing and are said to confer the blessings of the enlightened energy of body, speech, and mind of the realized masters upon all who come in contact or ingest these. This is one way the energy of the lineage is transmitted and kept alive.

Our treasure vases were blessed with this kind of medicine.

There was not much more the vases needed after that, but nevertheless, month after month, year after year, our sangha would gather to fill the seemingly empty pots in our own humble ways. I listened to each prayer, story, wish, or song, giving everyone my undivided attention. This has been my offering, too. Doing so, I understood how deeply we all need to be heard, how much we have to share and to give.

It became clear to me that the practice of deep listening was a critically important offering. For example, Deena Metzger, who had invited me to dedicate the vase for Liberia, invited me to bring two Earth Treasure Vases to her home for her community of healers, writers, and visionaries to make offerings into. Since it was a large group, I sat outside with the vases, so people could come up one by one to make their offerings and share their prayers. I arranged two chairs beside a small table and opened myself and the vases to receive each person who came forward to speak their deepest wishes in hushed tones into my ears and place their offering inside a vase. Receiving these intimate sharings on behalf of the vases from so many individuals in a concentrated way, for several hours, I really felt like I was becoming a vessel myself.

The monks from Ajahn Chah's tradition in Thailand made extraordinarily generous offerings into the vase destined for the forest surrounding Dtao Dum Monastery. Theirs is a monastic order based on renunciation of worldly possessions, and, just like the Buddha and his disciples, these monks and nuns rely entirely on the generosity of others for all of their worldly needs. I was amazed by the offerings brought forth for the vase and surprised to discover what wealth these renunciates manifested from so little—the most generous and abundant offerings I had ever witnessed being placed into a vase. Ajahn Pasanno brought out a crystal stupa containing Buddha relics, which he discovered had recently *multiplied*, and these he offered directly into the vase. As the vase went around the large circle of monks, nuns, and laypeople, everyone gave their very most precious possessions.

Even an amulet made by the late Ajahn Chah was offered into the vase by one of the monks. I was told later that it was so highly valued that he could easily have traded it for a Mercedes-Benz in Bangkok.

One of the most thrilling moments during a vase ceremony took place in South Africa. Our host, Linda Tucker, had invited Zulu and Shangaan elders and representatives of the lion-shaman lineage she is a part of to join us at her white-lion reserve for a ceremony with the Earth Treasure Vase. As the open vase was passed around the circle, the white lions, who gathered around the periphery of the enclosure where we sat, roared each time a particularly strong prayer was offered into the vase, adding their powerful commentary to the ceremony.

The South Africa vase was also opened in the presence of the elephants in Kruger National Park and at the Makalali Game Reserve, where Hugh had worked with Audrey Delsink, a remarkable young woman who has dedicated her life to protecting the African elephants. We tracked the elephants in vehicles, and when they emerged from the bush, they slowly ambled over to gather around and show us their babies. These great beings are among the planet's most important elders, carrying wisdom across the land from generation to generation and passing their knowledge directly into the body of the Earth as they make their migrations along the songlines.

When beloved Yupik elder Grandma Rita Blumenstein from Alaska learned we were on our way to the South Pacific with an Earth Treasure Vase for the ocean, she opened her medicine bundle to access her sacred fan, which had been crafted from thirteen white-eagle tail feathers by her grandmother who predicted when she was still a girl that Rita would one day become part of the International Council of Thirteen Indigenous Grandmothers.[2] Rita revealed how it was prophesied by her people that in the future the seas would rise in the South Pacific, resulting in tremendous chaos and displacement of people all the way to Alaska—heralding a time of renewal. Then she yanked off a fluffy feather from this most sacred object for the South Pacific Ocean Earth Treasure Vase. Moved to tears, Hugh and I told her the next Earth Treasure Vase would be coming to Arctic Alaska—and she pulled off another white-eagle feather for that vase, too.

In 2007 Hugh and I took the Earth Treasure Vase to the South Pacific, and in 2008, we went to Alaska. The most meaningful offering we carried for both these vases were the white-eagle feathers from Grandma Rita Blumenstein. Grandma Rita's blessing and the prophecy she shared motivated me even more to carry out this sacred work.

• • •

In Alaska, we collaborated with Evon Peter,[3] who became tribal chief of the Neetsaii Gwich'in at age twenty-five—the youngest "elder" I have known. Evon naturally commanded respect, and I hoped he would be willing to receive a vase for Arctic Alaska. In order to determine if my request to bring a vase to his land was honorable, he questioned me thoroughly to discover if my motivation was sincere and if my credentials were connected to a true spiritual lineage. Finally satisfied, he gave his blessing and we were granted permission to come. Evon, his mother Adeline, brother Odin, and sister Princess, welcomed us to their camp alongside the Yukon River.

They are Caribou People, and their home in northernmost Arctic Alaska is called The Sacred Place Where Life Begins. The duty they have to steward their lands over time, like so many traditional cultures, is a serious matter. They do so up against the presence of the Trans-Alaska Pipeline that carries oil from those delicate northern waters across the pristine and threatened Gwich'in lands and the Arctic National Wildlife Refuge, down thousands of miles, through the whole of Alaska along the Dalton Highway to the coast where the oil is shipped away to international buyers.

I think the family was surprised that by the second day at Adeline's fish camp, we had already been visited by herds of moose and had a close encounter with a mama bear and her cub when out hiking. Both Evon and Odin carried guns, and when we came upon the bears, calmly instructed us to back up—"Now!" Later in the camp as Odin and I filmed an interview with Evon, an enormous eagle flew in and landed in a snag just above our heads. These visitations were taken by the family as signs that our prayers were aligned with Spirit. When Hugh went to fold up a tarp that had been drying in the sun, he discovered the eagle had dropped a three-foot-long feather on the ground for us—a sacred offering to our host and his family.

For our final ceremony, we gathered at dusk by the shore of the wide Yukon River and pulled our hoodies tightly around our faces to protect ourselves from the hungry mosquitos. Evon took a moment to put on his ceremonial moccasins, which were old and worn, having been passed down from chief to chief, and which he wears on such occasions. Our little group came not only from Alaska but also from Russia, Spain, France, and other parts of the US. In honor of the caribou whose life force feeds the people of those lands, Adeline offered an entire caribou hoof into the vase. Another large eagle feather was placed inside by Evon, and a friend from a neighboring tribe shared a prayer for the hands that made the vase—the first time the potter had ever been acknowledged—then gave some fur from the polar bear, the animal that is sacred to her people. I have been amazed at how much can fit into one little vase. Like the loaves and fishes, there always seems to be room for more.

That night around the fire, we melted the beeswax, sealed the vase, and tucked the little holy vessel into a handmade cedar box painted by Native Northwest Coast artist Joe David. At dawn we headed up the Dalton Highway, driving alongside the oil pipeline into the Arctic Circle, as close to Gwich'in lands as we could get. Scouting for the proper place to plant our offering, we were surprised to find surveillance cameras. It did not feel like a friendly atmosphere. We deferred to Evon to find the spot, but after much searching, we turned back. Calling on the Goddess Tara, who is known to come to help when called, I chanted mantras with great intention until we came upon Adeline's truck parked by the side of the road waiting for us. Adeline had studied the area and knew exactly where the vase should go. But like the rest of us, she had thought it only right that the Chief should pick the spot. How relieved we were to find this kindhearted, wise mother harvesting wild blueberries. Smiling, she pointed across the land to the perfect spot.

Walking on the tundra, we discovered its thick spongy ground is so soft there is no need for a mattress if you sleep outside. Fragrant and welcoming, there were no cameras here in these ancestral lands to watch our every move. We all took turns digging the deep hole. With eagle feather in hand, Evon lowered the vase into that great expanse of northern tundra, its perfect resting place. As we drove away, the midnight sun hung low on the wide horizon and a rainbow appeared, arching over us from one end of the world to the other. Touched by the light of the rainbow that lingered for miles and miles, we laughed ecstatically until finally the full moon rose enormously round and the sun set in the long red sky. Slowly and quietly, darkness descended, and we watched as other animals we had not yet seen came out to greet us on the road home. Our work was done, and now the vase would do its job to radiate the offered prayers out into the Sacred Place Where Life Begins.

• • •

Making offerings, we form a relationship with the spirit of a place and invite the presence and subtle support from unseen realms. Some cultures call upon the Ancestors. Some invite wisdom beings or lineage masters. Some call upon local spirits, devas, or angels. "Many have believed in an animated, inhabited, sacred world surrounding them, the natural world that constitutes reality," writes David Suzuki in *The Sacred Balance*. "These beliefs restore our sense of belonging, of being-with, which is threatened by our dividing, conquering brain; they provide us with rules and rituals for restoring the harmony, for reentering and celebrating the world we are part of."[4]

I have discovered that these spiritual forces are waiting to be called on. They want to be invited. And they will respond. But it is important that we not draw from them, but rather offer homage, recognition, and gratitude—that we pay our respects. *Then* we invite their presence in to assist us. We are creating a reciprocal flow, but we are first and foremost giving back. Think of how long it has been since we have acknowledged the presence of something larger and more mysterious than ourselves. Maybe they are hungry and longing for us. So we feed them. Talk to them. Acknowledge their presence. For a thriving life force to be re-established and for responsiveness to be experienced, we do not take. We give. We offer. We invite. And then we open, allowing ourselves to receive without expectation or demand. Reestablishing a relationship of reciprocity with Spirit, giving back even if we don't know exactly for what or to whom, we are humbly forming a relationship with the Great Mystery and opening to the flow of nature once again.

When people ask what to offer into an Earth Treasure Vase, I tell them to offer something that is personally meaningful, precious, or symbolic of restoring balance and bringing healing and protection—anything with life-giving properties or a healing essence. When we make our whole lives an offering, walking with steps of peace, Mother Earth is happy and responds to our intentions. Our offerings set in motion a response that takes us where we need to go. In each place I have gone, the little vessels have opened the way for the Ancestors, local spirits, guardians, and protectors to respond to our offerings, prayers, and intentions.

Once during a terrible drought in New Mexico, a group of us gathered to pray for rain. At the end of our ceremony, we made a procession down to the dry riverbed—chanting our prayers and mantras, accompanied by bells and drums, and scattering flower petals and rice. We offered sacred waters gathered from around the world into the dry river, and no sooner had this been done than we looked up to see a gentle rain falling from the sky.

Through such experiences, I have learned that we live in reciprocity with the Earth. She needs us to do our part in maintaining balance and harmony. This is our sacred trust, and to make offerings is a way to invite this balance and harmony back into our lives. As we contribute our gifts to the web of life, we are expressing a uniquely human way of participating with nature to heal the Earth. In making offerings, whether placing a stone on a cairn, giving food to the hungry, dedicating our life's work to fulfilling a deeply held calling, or sprinkling cornmeal, rose petals, or rice on the ground or in a stream, we are choosing to feed the spirit of life.

Restoring balance and harmony between the masculine and the feminine is maybe our most basic evolutionary task at this time. The Earth Treasure Vase practice symbolically enacts this sacred relationship between the masculine and the feminine through the act of placing offerings inside a vessel, then digging a hole and planting the vessel in the Earth. The vessel serves as a womb-like feminine receptacle, and our penetration, entering the opening with our offering, so very masculine. A relationship is formed between the two—the empty, receptive, pregnant space of the vessel, and the active penetrating gift of the offering. When the vase is filled until it can take no more, we dig another receptacle, a hole in the Earth, and place the holy vessel into the womb of the land like a fertile seed.

In this process, the masculine in us may go only so far as to make his offering, his gift and prayer. Then he waits for the fertilization to take hold, for the growth and development of all those prayers and offerings to take root. We never know what new life will look like. All we can do is nurture it, keep it warm and moist, and love it into this world. Then new life has a chance to become a real force to be reckoned with, and in the process, we learn how to make a relationship with the feminine beyond passivity, and with the masculine beyond the aggressive habit to dominate. In this way, together, we are participating with the Earth in bringing new life into the world.

• • •

This morning I sat under the tall spruce tree that Hugh and I planted when we first moved to our home in New Mexico more than twenty-five years ago, and I watched as the sun rose into the world. Spring was in the air, and a tiny bird landed on the very topmost branch and sang a long and beautiful song to greet the day. He turned to face me, and I knew we were sharing the moment. Suddenly, the sunlight fell onto those high branches and the feathers of my fine friend as he continued to sing out for all to hear. Just as suddenly, his mate hopped out from within the depths of the giant spruce to join him in the light. A new day had begun.

My heart swells to begin the day this way. Coming inside from this reverie, I light the candles on the altar as I do every morning and take a thick stick of earthy Tibetan incense and light it from a candle. I bow, and with each gesture, another offering is made.

Every day is an opportunity to bow down, humble one's self within the vast nature of all that is. Every step is holy; each breath, a new moment to live in gratitude. Each season, a time to remember the "family of things," as Mary Oliver says in her poem "Wild Geese."[5] Every dawn, a new day—"twenty-four brand-new hours," says Thich Nhat Hanh, to enter the present moment within the web of life.[6]

Gyatrul Rinpoche reminds us that when we put on a beautiful

new dress for the first time, to imagine wearing it as an offering. And when we walk slowly and peacefully on the Earth, Thich Nhat Hanh says, we can imagine a lotus blooming with each step and think to ourselves, I walk for you.[7]

In an act as simple as lighting a candle, we can reverently remember the bigger picture, and with each mindful breath, a larger view comes back into focus. Being aware of the sun's rise or set, the season's growing fullness or steady decline, we can ask ourselves, Is the world's light longer and warmer, or darker and colder? Where are we, where am I, in the scheme of things? What offering can I make to connect with the life force of Mother Earth more fully?

CHAPTER EIGHTEEN

BECOMING A HOLY VESSEL

My journey with the Earth Treasure Vases always felt as if I were living in a mythic landscape, carrying out an epic assignment to do an impossible task. From that first meeting with the old wise man in the cave, like Frodo and the Ring, there have been many challenging twists and turns along the way as I carried out the sacred purpose that was given to me to deliver each of the little holy vessels to its final destination. Like all mythic journeys, I have been tested many times: will I stay true to the little vessels I have been given to guard, to fulfill—even if the world dismisses, judges, abuses, or rejects me and my mission?

In every region of the world, I have crumpled in helplessness to gaze into the eyes of the many desperate souls looking for a friend. I have met fellow travelers on the path who are really only out for themselves. I have lost the way, walking on for hours and miles, in the rain, in the cold, thirsty and hungry, hot and tired. Getting sick, taking weeks to recover, being stuck in bed with my back out, barely able to walk to the toilet.

There has been the need to operate under cover of darkness with a cloak of invisibility. Bribing gatekeepers or telling tall tales to divert attention away from the shovels we carry for planting the vases. Going into deep forests, climbing high mountains, seeking the source of great rivers, all to find the hidden places where the holy vessel will be safe and well received. Getting through customs, through security, with questionable little pots and pouches full of mysterious and sometimes illegal things like earth and sand, seeds, feathers, roots, shells and rocks. Lots of rocks. Offerings from gorillas, white lions, elephants, dolphins, and horses. Waters in vials, medicinal herbs, fragrant incense, beautiful flowers wilting in plastic bags. All the medicine bundles from around the world that fill the vases with alchemical healing forces until they become the promised treasure—treasures of the highest value, full of riches no one can put a price tag on.

I have lost my way, almost giving up, time and again. Could I keep going? Will those who travel with me make it this time? Do they really understand what we are doing? Do I? Could someone please translate? Have we prepared ourselves properly? What more must I give? Offer? Let go of? Find? Whom should I trust to lead me down the path in this foreign land, through the darkness into the light?

But I keep going, never giving up. Dedicated, some say. Exhausted, I say, but I know I must continue. Filled with a deep joy for this task, even when another round of grief takes me down, gazing into the next place where healing is needed and the Earth is calling for a new treasure vase to fulfill its purpose in oceans, rivers, mountains, forests, deserts, standing stones, pyramids, volcanos, canyons, cities, countries, and caves.

There have been many mistakes, many missteps, many misunderstandings, many trials and errors, and many regrets. Each vessel has carried its own lessons. These are the shadows to be understood, the problems to be solved. The healing journey is not for the faint of heart, and practicing with the vases brings out the very things we wish we didn't have to see.

All those years ago, Charok Rinpoche said, "Just put them in the ground, they'll do the work." It sounded simple enough. But a chorus of other voices had followed his, the voices inside, chanting, "Guard those little vessels with your life. They are living beings. They can break. They are filled with the most sacred prayers and offerings—the hopes and dreams of whole cultures and communities. They carry our prayers for renewal, for a future to be possible."

And: "Are you willing to do whatever it takes? Give everything? Yes? Ok, *now* the journey begins. Are you equipped? Physically fit? Mentally sharp? Openhearted and easygoing? Spiritually trained? Can you read the maps? Have you reviewed the guidelines and instructions? Did you memorize the path? Ready, set, go!"

One foot in front of the other, one step, one breath. Present moment, only moment . . . until there is nowhere left to go but *in*.

Eventually, it became clear that the little holy vessels were in fact leading me back to my true self. All the trials and demands of carrying them out was an alchemical process of personal transformation. Each journey wore me down and tempered the parts that needed to change. I did not realize it at the time, but my vessel was being honed. And I noticed that everyone who stepped forward to help steward a vase was also being worked in this way.

Applying myself and concentrating on this activity with every fiber of my being, I offered myself up in order to carry out the purpose of the vases as if my life depended on it. Eventually I came to see myself as both the one who offers and the offering, and the separations of subject and object fell away. Over time, the Earth Treasure Vase practice evolved from one of doing to one of being. The "practice" is really about being a holy vessel ourselves.

• • •

As with all mythic journeys, helpers appear when you really need them. It was no different for me. Lama Tsultrim arrived with the Twenty-One Taras practice when I was desperate for spiritual support in Africa. And Joanna Macy appeared once again to inform the next phase of the process at just the right time to move us along with a deeper understanding. It was she who brought home how we are all "Vessels of the Holy."

I was interviewing Joanna about Nuclear Guardianship and her burying of the Earth Treasure Vase at the tritium facility at the Lawrence National Laboratory in Berkeley, California. Reflecting on her experience, she said:

> *I can see that we, ourselves, are like vessels. And that to keep offering, we must take care of what we put in our vessel. The teachings, the prayers, the glimpses of beauty, the celebrations, all make us good vessels. This revolutionizes how we see ourselves. The industrial-growth society sees us as consumers who are needy, insufficient, driven by dissatisfaction and cravings. But to see ourselves as vessels of the holy, well, that would be a revolutionary act. That would be a liberation from so much that is demeaning and tawdry and corrosive to the spirit of our contemporary economic culture.*

She continued: "To see ourselves as vessels for healing—you could say that is like a miracle if we could do that!"

She paused thoughtfully. "We are due for a miracle now," she said. "I mean, it has to happen because without it, this could be the closing chapter. But choosing to find our courage in community and solidarity, that is a miracle."[1]

I was beginning to understand that if we want to be a holy vessel and contribute to the healing of our world, it is vitally important that we cultivate the ground of our being and plant new seeds. The soil is depleted; life is out of balance. Once these seeds have been planted, they need to be watered. They do not grow into nourishing fruit overnight.

So we cultivate the ground of our being, and we wait. We know that if we disperse the energy of transformation too soon, we will not reap the benefits. We learn to trust the process, and like a vase, to contain the new energies we are cultivating. Acting too quickly, we risk perpetuating the same old stories, and even if we've had a great idea and can't wait to jump on it, we still wait until we are certain we have come to inhabit utterly new ground. Everything in our lives tells us we have to do it *now*. And *now* arrives quicker than ever as time speeds up faster and faster. But if we want to offer something truly new, if we want to really be of service, then taking another breath and allowing the energy to build within ourselves until we are aware of *embodying* a whole new operating system—*then* we are assured that our actions will be contributing to the healing of the world.

As we give over to this process of transformation and awakening, a certain ease dawns, and a new sense of creative flow naturally comes into our lives. This is when we realize we are becoming a vessel. It's not about "me" any longer. It's about being so full we contain the whole web of life and all possibilities. We are truly empty of a separate self in those moments. From here, our actions flow in response to what is arising around us, and we know with confidence we have arrived.

In spite of the conditioning that tells us we have to do, do, do, we actually don't have to do it all right now. We can stop and ask ourselves, What is skillful action? Can I wait for the right moment, not just for others, but also for myself? Can I trust that I will know when that right moment arrives? Because certainly, to be a holy vessel, a good container, we simply must care for ourselves. Many of us can barely remember how to listen to our own needs. We are so busy that we neglect and ignore our vessel at the expense of our well-being. And our world reflects this.

Many of us have become such strivers that we have sacrificed ourselves on the altar of the patriarchy over and over again. We have worked ourselves to the bone, to the point of collapse, trying hard to make a difference. Telling ourselves, "Maybe if I just keep going, maybe if I just sacrifice my own needs one more time, maybe this time it will be different."

I know I am not the only one who struggles with the feeling of not being good enough, smart enough, or successful enough. We strive to be successful and powerful, yet we're dismissed and told to be less threatening. Society tells us to be beautiful and sexy, yet we are raped and abused for our beauty and our sexuality. How many atrocities must we live through before we can stop trying to be something other than what we are, stop fitting ourselves into an unattainable image of perfection? Before we can relax into safety and do what comes naturally? Now, as the Earth screams for our attention, we must reclaim our miraculous, powerful true nature, inseparable from Her.

If we want to be the change we seek, if we want our prayers to take root, we need access to a new energy that is not conditioned by the same old ways that never lead anywhere. It takes courage to choose not to act habitually in relation to the consensus reality of the dominant culture. It is a radical act to stop. But the more we do, the more power we build into our spiritual muscles. By containing the energy we so readily dissipate and throw away unmindfully, our spiritual power grows, and a profound energy of transformation arises within us.

Too often, we think we have finally figured it out, or as we say in Buddhism, have arrived at the other shore—the shore of liberation—and we start talking about our big insight, getting all excited. Because it feels so good, we want to share that really wonderful breakthrough experience. But this, too, is something to keep to ourselves. As Gyatrul Rinpoche would say, "Don't make a big deal." Why? Because we lose the insight we gain the very moment we make a "big deal" talking about it and thinking we have arrived, grasping onto it or making ourselves special in *any* way.

When the energy of transformation is not respected or understood, we dissipate it and easily fall into habitual distractions. Then we turn around one day and wonder, What happened? Where did it all go? We thought we were really making progress, but we threw it away. We thought we had it nailed, had really understood that we'd never do it again. But it's not enough to have an insight. This is only the first step. We must harness the energy of insight and understanding and turn it into the energy of actual change.

For me, it was in the process of receiving all the offerings that are contained in those little clay pots, month after month, season after season, year after year, that I came to feel like I was filled with treasures, too.

In the course of my apprenticeship to the Earth Treasure Vases, I had to learn to hold them diligently, listen to what *they* had to say and where *they* wanted to go. They showed me they needed to be cared for like living beings, to be protected with my life. Receiving all the prayers they contain, then stewarding them with full attention every step of the way to the place where they are to be planted, I came to know that a holy vessel filled with treasures is alive with possibility, just like you and me. Whoever we are and whatever we have lived through, we are all holy vessels. We are treasures, each of us holding a piece of the medicine for a healed world.

In the meditation practice we do to activate the vases, the visualization of light feels like a key, as it serves to connect us to an awareness of a planetary matrix of energy flowing in and around the whole Earth. We visualize or sense this light flowing through the ley lines and meridians of the planet and into the Earth Treasure Vases in each of their locations, then back out from the vases into the whole area within the sphere of influence of every holy vessel.

The vases have been intuitively placed around the world with each location seen as a node in this web of light mirroring the physical web of life. During our monthly full moon meditation, we visualize light radiating from our hearts to the vases and activating them. We then visualize the vases radiating this light out to the entire region where they are buried. In this way one could say we are facilitating an enlightenment, or awakening, for the whole Earth.

This light is in us, too. We can imagine this same light moving through our own meridians, bringing healing to the knots and nodes in our physical vessel, melting and freeing the life-force energy within and enlightening our embodied experience of this precious human life.

Once in meditation, I had a vision of light so strong I could barely meet it without being obliterated. The light streamed around me—its rays almost impossible to differentiate except to notice that they were white, tinged with golden yellow. As I adjusted to the light, I noticed it formed a matrix, like Indra's Net described in the Avatamsaka Sutra. At its highest point, the light appeared to have a pattern, from which the rays flooded down. Then I became aware that holy beings were materializing in the light, and I sensed I was surrounded by a number of them in a circle like a kind of council. Some were sitting on thrones and some were standing like pyramids or mountains, very large. I understood this to be a kind of governing body, beings of light who embodied, for the benefit of my limited perception, elements of creation in a realm beyond thought, filled with an inconceivably vast primordial wisdom, awareness, and compassion.

As I sat in this vision and the awareness it generated, dakinis of the Five Buddha Families came into view, dancing in between each of these light beings. These dakinis were made of light, too, and seemed to be bridging from the realm of these vast light beings into our world. I viscerally understood how energy arises as light and sound, which coheres into colors and feelings and then takes form. I saw that everything in its unborn state is actually light—appearing like a rainbow, fully present but impossible to grasp. And I realized what is meant by the Rainbow Body or "body of light" in the Dzogchen teachings: it is this sound, light, and color, which coalesces into the five elements in our physical bodies as we take on form at conception and dissolves into light at the time of death.

In Vajrayana Buddhism, there is a teaching on the "youthful vase body" that speaks to being a holy vessel of light. Imagine the subtle channels or meridians in our bodies as pathways of awareness that travel from the inner "field" of the heart out to the organs of perception; in particular, the eyes. The inner field of the heart is described as a "crystal palace of five lights" (connected to the Five Buddha Families) where the youthful vase body resides. Imagine this youthful vase body as our inner experience of primordial wisdom dwelling within a mandala. This is our Buddha Nature. It is youthful because it is unconditioned by ordinary reality and, metaphorically speaking, not subject to old age, sickness, and death. It is like a vase because it is empty and open to receive, yet capable of being filled with the light of awakened energy, of primordial wisdom.

For us regular humans neurotically circling around and around in samsara, the youthful vase body lives inside us unrecognized. But for a practitioner who has awakened his or her awareness through the practice of meditation, the energy that naturally arises from the heart can be experienced as a vision of radiant light becoming manifest. The teachings say that this self-arisen nature, our youthful vase body, is always there, dwelling within the innate "ground" of our being.

Our reactive emotions, unconscious habitual patterns, and conditioning obscure our capacity to experience our primordial wisdom nature. But once we begin to awaken to the nature of awareness itself and peel back the layers through all the tests and trials along the path, we may start to glimpse this spontaneously present light dwelling in our heart and come to know that at the very ground of our being, we reside as a vessel of the holy—with the love and compassion we naturally embody spontaneously shining out in every direction as our offering to the Earth and all beings.

CHAPTER NINETEEN

LISTENING TO THE ELDERS

In the courtyard of the Dogon elder Guimolo Dolo's home in Mali, I climbed a ladder to look out over the roof. It was 2009, and beautiful piles of recently harvested millet lay drying in the sun. Along the river below, onions—the other main crop in Dogon Country—were growing lush and green. In the presence of this man and his land, I felt at peace.

My guide, Abdoulaye, and I explored Dogon Country, hiking up to caves where the Ancestors dwelled, through mud villages with their conical thatched roofs, past gathering places for the elders, called "togu nas," built so low that no one can stand, which is believed to reduce the chance of argument. Wandering in the marketplace and through the streets and alleys, we saw fantastic wood carvings decorating every home. It seemed ancient mysteries were alive and well in that land. We drove on tracks across the desert, red dust flying, the music of Habib Koité and the great musicians of Mali blaring. Those gorgeous sounds entered my heart and entranced me. I had entered another land behind the veil.

The jihadist groups that came to Mali the next year brought unprecedented violence and persecution that ripped the fabric of this timeless culture to shreds. I pray for peace in Mali and for the music that was outlawed into a deafening silence to sing out once again. Guimolo Dolo has passed on now, but I know Abdoulaye will always be committed to the Dogon people. As a respected art dealer and collector, his appreciation of their culture runs deep. And he supports rural doctors providing medical care in villages throughout Dogon Country.

Encountering this land behind the veil and receiving the blessings from another old wise man of the Earth opened a pathway to peace in Liberia and the other African countries that later received a vase. The Earth Treasure Vases were accomplished just as he predicted.

Following my dream to meet Guimolo Dolo led me to seek out the blessing of elders in all the lands I visited with a little holy vessel. I realized that making relations with the elders *is* the pathway to peace. It is an important key to fulfilling the purpose of the practice and bringing our prayers to life.

• • •

The Indigenous peoples of the Sierra Nevada de Santa Marta in Colombia, known as the Kogi, have been a major influence on me in carrying out the practice of the Earth Treasure Vases. *The Elder Brothers Warning: A Message from the Heart of the World* is an extraordinary book and film that brought out a powerful message from a people who had intentionally chosen to live sequestered in their remote villages and maintain their traditional way of life in what they call the Heart of the World. They regard themselves as the Elder Brothers—and we, the colonizers from the industrialized Western world, are their Younger Brothers (and Sisters). "The Younger Brother has got out of hand: he has begun to undermine the structure and stability of the whole world," writes the author and filmmaker Alan Ereira. "The Kogi demand that we behave responsibly, that we begin to take care of the world. They are demanding an ethical revolution on our part, in which greed and selfishness are tempered by awe, and by a sensitivity to the earth as a living—and now perhaps dying—totality."[1]

The Kogi, along with the Arhuaco, Wiwa, and Kankuamo, are part of four tribes in the mountains of Colombia collectively known as the Tairona people, whose solemn responsibility is to maintain balance in the Heart of the World. Offerings are like a payment to Mother Earth for all we have been given. It has been my hope that burying the Earth Treasure Vases around the planet might be received by Mother Earth as a form of reciprocity, of giving back.

In 2001 we had the opportunity to offer an Earth Treasure Vase to the Kogi through the late peace activist Shannyn Sollit and ritual performance artist Dominique Mazeaud, who were invited to share their work in Colombia. Shannyn and Dominique first brought the Earth Treasure Vase to art institutions and universities there, where the vase was filled with offerings in ceremony. Shannyn recalled, "The offerings reflected deep sadness and tender hope for a transformation of the terrible suffering of war and poverty." The vase was sealed in Bogotá with former homeless children from the organization, Ponte en Mi Lugar (Put Yourself in My Place), who had dreams of finding a better life away from poverty, prostitution, and drug dealing—the only life they had known.

From Bogotá, Asdrubal Torres, a member of the Arhuaco tribe, carefully transported the sacred vase to the Tairona leader, Ramon

Gil, for burial in the Sierra Nevada de Santa Marta. The vase spent seven years in safekeeping before it was clear to Ramon that this Tibetan offering coming from the United States was to be accepted.

When Shannyn returned in 2008, she presented Ramon with a booklet I had sent with pictures of other elders and activists that described the Earth Treasure Vase Global Healing Project. Before making his decision on the fate of the vase, Ramon did a divination. In the morning he informed Shannyn he would bury the vase.

"Ramon was clear he needed to bury the vase secretly to protect it from detection. He announced he would do so a few days later," Shannyn told me. While Ramon placed the vase, Shannyn sat above a rushing river, facing the morning sun. "I felt a tactile energy of love, healing, and protection flowing into the mountains. I saw golden-white rainbow light shining out from the Heart of the World like an erupting volcano, encircling the whole planet. This was truly among the most memorable meditation experiences in my life."

The Kogi feel strongly that the sacred sites of the world are critically important to protect. They regard these sites like elders holding the wisdom of the planet. With this in mind, we have placed treasure vases at a number of locations long revered as some of the planet's most sacred places. The Great Pyramid of Giza is one such location, and burying a vase there was a way of bringing the energy of that beacon of ancient wisdom and power into our global healing mandala. The vase placed near Avebury with its standing stones, crop circles, and powerful ley lines connect us to spiritual energies we can barely comprehend. The vase Hugh and I respectfully brought to a hidden realm on the slopes of the volcano Haleakala on the island of Maui in Hawaii is also such a place. Meditating on the full moon at

Haleakala with rainbows arcing around us, we felt our prayers travel to the molten core of the Earth. A local elder we met afterwards lovingly confirmed our purpose and told us how he, too, had dedicated his life to the protection of his people and their sacred places.

These are places where we can feel the sacred wisdom of the elders emanating from the rocks across time. Touching these holy grounds, and making offerings here, we are able to connect with a spiritual source beyond ordinary reality that is still guiding us if we are open to it. The ancient knowledge of the elders is alive.

There is a vast array of Indigenous spiritual practices around the world that hold wisdom for restoring balance and living in a wise relationship with the Earth. The Kogi got my attention early on with their warning as planetary elders to us "youngers" who have created such imbalance upon Mother Earth's natural systems. They inspired me to apprentice myself as a younger to the elders I met everywhere I went and offer them my respect for their long-held teachings on living within the web of life.

When the treasure vases were to be buried on Indigenous ancestral lands, it was only right that we bow to Indigenous leadership to guide the way. It was a process I needed to learn: to slow down, listen carefully, make relations respectfully, and not make any assumptions. The Kogi had delivered an urgent message from the Heart of the World, but I learned from the Dogon elder in Mali to respond to that urgency with considered patience. And when I did not push for quick results, a certain grace came into play that guided the process better than I ever could. Every Indigenous culture keeps alive laws of the land that maintain balance and harmony in their places. I was learning that it is necessary to seek permission from the elders to place an Earth Treasure Vase in their ancestral homelands, and when this was done properly, the blessings flowed.

The Earth Treasure Vases have been graced and consecrated by many elders around the world, and I have been transformed by each and every one: from Charok Rinpoche and Gyatrul Rinpoche to Thich Nhat Hanh and Joanna Macy, from Marian Naranjo in Santa Clara, New Mexico, to Yupik elder Grandma Rita and Gwich'in Chief Evon Peter in Alaska, from the Khoisan grandmothers in the Kalahari to my Batwa "husband" in eastern DRC, Guimolo Dolo in Dogon Country, and Mahwen and the other tribal elders in Liberia, Papua New Guinea, and Oaxaca, Mexico. All these living treasures have bestowed their extraordinary blessings. And from this, I have come to know I am not alone but am moving forward within the embrace of a holy congregation.

Forming such relationships with elders around the world, I was able to distinguish between good, even great, ideas and true spiritual guidance. The thinking mind rushes ahead. The Indigenous mind takes its time. It makes an offering. It holds space for the right moment. And it knows when the timing is right because it notices the signs and synchronicities that appear to guide things to fulfillment. This is where compassionate activity arises naturally and without effort.

The blessing of the elders is a powerful force to be respected. It is so often the elders who are the healers, and it is their knowledge and gifts that have long been ignored. Their contribution has made all the difference in the realization of our prayers with the vases. All too often, land once stewarded by the First Peoples has been forcibly taken from them. Asking permission to bring an Earth Treasure Vase to their land out of respect is already an important healing. Inviting the prayers of the elders, healers, and medicine people in the places we have gone is another way that the practice has crossed cultural and spiritual boundaries to become meaningful in every location.

Above all, Indigenous elders have taught me the importance of honoring the Ancestors. Maintaining a respectful connection to those who have gone before is a key to sustaining harmony among the people and the land. We all come from this Earth, and to the Earth we shall return. In traditional cultures, the Ancestors are spiritual guides inseparable from the land itself. To honor and acknowledge those who have come before us and invite their blessing and spiritual support, we need the elders to open the way.

As my global pilgrimage neared completion, the last of the Earth Treasure Vases would take me to the lands of the Indigenous Aboriginal Australians where I was about to experience an opening of the way by an elder like never before, whose blessing and acceptance would bring me home to a sense of belonging I never could have imagined.

CHAPTER TWENTY

WELCOME TO COUNTRY

In 2013, as I prepared to leave for Australia to bury the last of the original Earth Treasure Vases, it suddenly dawned on me that this was going to be an important trip. This vase had a big job to do; in fact, it had its own continent. I felt the Dreamtime was calling this little vessel to its rightful home.

According to Aboriginal spiritual understanding, the Dreamtime describes the relationship between people, plants, animals, and the physical features of the land. The Dreaming stories explain how these relationships came to be, what they mean, and how they need to be maintained in daily life and in ceremony. It is said that at the very beginning of time, the Ancestor Beings traveled over the land to create life and all the important geographic formations. In the Dreaming, they made the people and the rivers, streams, water holes, hills, rocks, plants, and animals. The Dreamtime recognizes the interbeing of everything. It points to a beginning that never ended—a continuum of past, present, and future within a totally integrated way of life. In his book *Voices of the First Day: Awakening in the Aboriginal Dreamtime,* Robert Lawlor writes, "This Dreaming constitutes the sacredness of the earth . . . The Dreamtime mythology sustained a culture that lived in harmony with nature and was full of vigor, vitality, and joyousness."[1]

In my own dreaming, I saw this last vase connecting with the other vases throughout the web of intention around the Earth that we had been creating through our global healing practice. I hoped that when the Australia vase went into the ground, it would activate the other vases and the global mandala would light up—coming to life as a whole network. What I did not anticipate was how much this pilgrimage would mean to me personally.

Originally, this vase had been dedicated to Australia through an antinuclear activist named Pamela Meidell. Pamela had taken the vase to the United Nations for the conference reviewing the Treaty on the Non-Proliferation of Nuclear Weapons. There, she met an Aboriginal activist from Kakadu, in Australia's Northern Territory, where there was a huge uranium mine. The activist had agreed to take the vase there but got called away suddenly, and the opportunity was missed. Pamela kept the Earth Treasure Vase and waited for a time when its destiny could be fulfilled. Time passed and eventually she graciously returned it to me.

When the time came to reconnect with Pamela, I got a synchronistic call from my colleague Christian Leahy. I could feel her smile on the other end of the phone when she gently inquired, "Would you like to meet Uncle Bob Randall, the Custodial Elder of Uluru, Cynthia?" After practically falling off my chair in surprise, I said, "Yes!" Uncle Bob Randall was an elder of the Anangu people of Central Australia, and he served as the traditional "owner," or custodian, of Uluru. One of the world's most famous sacred sites, Uluru (known as Ayers Rock to non-Indigenous peoples) is a red rock monolith in the middle of a vast desert in the center of the continent. Uncle Bob was a traditional leader, Aboriginal educator, and well-known musician whose spiritual teachings and cultural knowledge had touched me deeply. Through Kelly Wendorf, who was hosting Uncle Bob and his wife, Barbara, Christian arranged for them to visit us the next day. I lit candles on the altar and we sat in a circle sharing stories. Uncle Bob held the Earth Treasure Vase quietly for a long time and then invited us to bring it to Australia.

Through Uncle Bob and Barbara, I was introduced to another Australian, Jeremy Ball, who leads pilgrimages to sacred places around the world. Jeremy immediately engaged with the Earth Treasure Vase practice and organized the journey that brought the little holy vessel to the land of Oz. A number of friends from Open Way Sangha converged in Sydney, where we were joined by a group of Australians Jeremy had invited. We began with three days of teachings from His Holiness the Dalai Lama. To my amazement, Jeremy had arranged for our humble Earth Treasure Vase to sit on the main altar next to the Dalai Lama's throne. On the last day, as His Holiness entered the imposing stage in front of an audience of thousands, he paused and picked up the vessel, chuckling as he held it and gave it his blessing.

And what a blessing indeed! Like being given the keys to the city, that clay pot opened the door for us to be "Welcomed to Country" by respected elders everywhere we went.

Welcome to Country is a ceremony performed by Indigenous Australian elders to welcome visitors to their traditional lands. Visitors are invited to acknowledge the Indigenous custodians of the land and their long relationship with "Country" and offer respect to their culture and Ancestors. Professor Mick Dodson explains: "When we talk about traditional 'Country'. . . we mean something beyond the dictionary definition of the word. For Aboriginal Australians . . . we might mean homeland, or tribal or clan area and we might mean more than just a place on the map. For us, Country is a word for all the values, places, resources, stories and cultural obligations associated with that area and its features. It describes the entirety of our ancestral domains."[2]

With the Dalai Lama's blessing upon the Earth Treasure Vase and the Welcome to Country we received from local elders, our connection to the land and each other grew ever more potent as we moved from Sydney to Uluru in the Central Desert, north to Darwin, and on to Kakadu and Arnhem Land in the Northern Territory. As we traveled, a sense of belonging to that land took root in me.

At Uluru, Uncle Bob and Barbara Randall greeted us warmly. We were invited to camp on Uncle Bob's ancestral land and given a feast of kangaroo tail cooked on the coals of the campfire. A "songman" with a personal history as a member of the stolen generation—when Aboriginal children were forcibly taken from their families by White authorities to be "reeducated"—Uncle Bob transformed the challenges of his life through music and the ancient teachings of his Anangu people. He brought out his guitar and we listened to him sing and tell stories. His greatest teaching is about the principle of unconditional love with responsibility, called "Kanyini." This is the awareness of our connection with every living thing, formed by the Ancestors, in kinship with all life as family.

Uncle Bob describes his early life in the desert in the film *Kanyini*: "We didn't own land—the land owned us! We were living in harmony with all things, in naturalness. Our people's spirits looked good; we were beautiful people with confidence. We were walking with all big and strong things." He paused. "Then the Killing Time disturbed the naturalness, breaking the Law, taking away what was rightfully ours, and thousands of years of wisdom gone, forbidden and forgotten." Uncle Bob had lived through this himself. Heartbreakingly, he shared this history: "Broken, we were driven from Country; people were slaughtered, massacred; women and girls raped; such wrongness against the rightness of how we lived."[3]

Uncle Bob's people had lived in harmony for sixty thousand years.[4] He continued, "Us mob, lived here in the desert where everything you can see is family. The Earth is our Mother. We were born through her and she looks after us. We were disciplined, trained to look after the land and each other. 'Don't ever take more than you need' is what we learned. And being part of all that is. We're connected . . . Just being alive connects you to everything! You are never lost, never alone. The completeness, the Oneness, when every inch of land is sacred and lived in a nonrestrictive nature . . . Openness was there, we were always free. We were alive! Don't need a house when you are alive! We lived in Our-ness—no one is without. Everything was already created in a perfect state . . . We had a confidence in life . . . a niceness, a connection. We were so proud, so big, so responsible. We were so big with our sharing and our caring . . . Then everything changed and we started to shrink. Government took away our Kanyini. We are nothing without our Kanyini."

Everything changed. Today, tourists enjoy gazing at the sunset on the enormous redrock formation rising up from the desert floor from the veranda of their hotel room. People come from all over the world to see this sacred land, while Uncle Bob and his people live in poverty on the shadow side of their great landmark, on government land, in a town called Mutitjulu, where the schools have empty classrooms, the jails are full, sniffing petrol is an epidemic, and they are "floating with nothing," as Uncle Bob told us. "Thrown a line of welfare."

Every morning at sunrise, Uncle Bob took us out on the land with a view of that awesome red rock where every nook and cranny holds a sacred Dreaming story that tells of the Ancestor spirits who created the land and of events that took place there. He offered this daily prayer:

Welcome Mother Sun to Mother Earth
It is really good to see You.
May the blessings of your Light
Be the light of Love that will remain with us today and always.
From the highest point above and below me,
Throughout the Universe,
Extending beyond the horizon in all directions,
I call on All Things that Was, that Is, and that Will Be,
To come and meet with me
And create a sacred space
From which we can acknowledge the right of All Things
To live in love, light, peace, and harmony throughout their time,
As being given that right by the Tjukurrpa
To all those who desire to live according to the Kanyini Principles
Of having unconditional love for each other
And being responsible for that love
Throughout their time on the Earth plane.

In the name of all that is Sacred and Holy
So let it be.

Uncle Bob was growing old, and I watched him sitting on a ubiquitous white plastic chair gazing out over the land he calls home. Like so many of the world's Indigenous elders, he had been waiting a very long time for White "fellas" to wake up and understand their place in the family of things, and to find love and caring with responsibility—our Kanyini.

Barbara and Uncle Bob looked after us, fed us, and cared for us like family. We gathered with the Earth Treasure Vase, and Uncle Bob invited us to contribute our prayers from our Country, making sure our many lands and languages were all represented. Then he added some red earth from the ground of Uluru and spoke these words: "For the Vase and the people who love themselves, love each other, love Mother Earth and Mother Sun, and love all of Nature . . . on behalf of all of us of Indigenous ancestry, from the First Peoples of Australia to all the Great Creators of Nature, who have always loved us without condition throughout all of our natural life and beyond, I make this offering."

Not long after our time at Uluru, Uncle Bob passed away at home in Barbara's arms. His enormous love and caring had found welcome in our hearts, and Kanyini had been passed to us and into the Earth Treasure Vase.

• • •

The land down under held me and the little clay pot I carried in my backpack. Our group bonded every night around the fire as we shared our intentions for the vase and slept on the land. The feeling of belonging grew between us and that country. The art and culture of the Aboriginal people spoke to me of a vast understanding beyond time and space yet deeply grounded in the Earth. Sleeping under the stars, my consciousness was expanding within the warm embrace of my Aussie friends, who had connected to the Earth Treasure Vase even more fully than many people in other places I had been.

Leaving Uluru, we traveled to the Northern Territory, and, with the help of one of our joyously inspired drivers and pilgrimage cook, Therese Hogan, the Earth Treasure Vase ended up in the hands of Aunty Margaret Katherine Oenpelli, a Buyhmi-Jawoyn elder from Arnhem Land. Therese had formed relations with many Aboriginal elders in the region and made a special connection to Aunty Margaret. She arranged for us to meet Margaret at the Mary River Roadhouse, where we found her sitting on the grass playing cards with her "mob." After some meeting and greeting, Aunty Margaret hopped barefoot into one of our vehicles with her fancy purse, and off we went. We were bound for Kakadu, and she would be our guide. The first night in camp, Aunty Margaret dreamed about the Earth Treasure Vase and in the morning shared that she had made a connection with the vase. She understood that the vase contained Charok Rinpoche's blessings and that the vase itself had its own personality or spiritual embodiment. From then on, she called it my "Teacher."

One night, as we sat around the fire with a "cuppa" tea, she gave us all "skin names." This is the traditional way of making a proper connection between us, so we knew clearly what our relationship was to her and to each other. Giving skin names makes us kin in the Aboriginal tradition; it relates us as family. She told me without hesitation I was her "bungann" (daughter) and she, my "karang," or "mumma."

I had always wanted brothers and got three wonderful ones that night: Jeremy, our tour operator; Ben Manbulloo Emery, our expert outback guide; and soundhealer Julian Silburn. In addition, our whole group became related as sisters, aunties, uncles, in-laws, children, and grandchildren. Our global Earth Treasure Vase community became a family through Mumma that night.

Mumma Margaret did not know what an enormous healing this was for me. She gave me back a family—one that has endured to this day. After my parents died, I found the courage to tell my sisters about what had happened to me in our family. But our subsequent estrangement had left me feeling isolated and sad to lose those special bonds. I forged new family relations with Hugh and looked for sisters in other women I became close to. But becoming a daughter to Mumma Margaret and finding my long-lost brothers, along with all my other relations, filled that sore spot up and made me whole again.

In her presence, we all felt warmly welcomed to Margaret's Country. She took our hands and walked with us barefoot on the land. She loved to tell a good story around the fire or hear one, and she would laugh often and weep easily with tremendous feeling. In our Earth Treasure Vase ceremonies, Mumma would sometimes wail. As one member of our mob, Magi Whisson, put it: "It was a piercing wail from the depths of Being, a wail that held the story, and the grief, hope, and knowing of 60,000 years of continuous living culture. She wailed the Song of the Ancient Ones. She wailed Life into Being."

Aunty Margaret made it clear to me that Welcoming to Country was important for us to learn. I remember the sound of her voice calling out to the Spirits and Ancestors and how the words reached our hearts. She taught me how to do this in her Jawoyn language and wanted me to memorize the words and use them to make relations with the places I visit and the ancestral lands I know:

> *"Nagaga . . . Niwala . . . wan wokani . . . maam . . . kawanango niwala leear ingolo! Nagaga . . . Niwala . . . Nigaganai ningolo leear . . . Awan wokani maam . . . Kawonango leear ingolo!"*
>
> *"To all our elders, I bring these (white) fellas to see this place, this country. I introduce all the family to you and to this Country. To all the old people (Ancestors) here . . . I bring these (white) fellas to see your Country. I'm introducing this mob to you. I am introducing them to the land and the Spirit people in the Language."*

From Margaret, we discovered that this Welcome to Country was not just a formality to honor the original "owners" but a way to open a portal into another dimension of being in relationship to the land. Suddenly, the spirits of the trees, rocks, plants, and animals came alive and recognized us. We were no longer cut off from the land but one with it. Margaret suggested we dip our hands in the rivers, springs, and watering holes, then touch our faces and hearts (and even underarms!), then dip our hands back in the water to make a connection. Aunty Margaret showed us it is through our open hearts that we make the proper connection to Country. She taught us that the energy of nature flows around us and that when our hearts are open, this energy flows through us, too. By opening, we restore harmony between ourselves and Mother Earth.

After several days of traveling and exploring Kakadu, Aunty Margaret sat me down and said, “Honey, I support you and your Teacher”—referring to the Earth Treasure Vase—“and will do whatever you want, but this isn’t really a very good place for him.” The group had begun to sense this, too, but we did not know what to do or where to go. She explained that it floods there every year and the vase would not be safe. Then she said, “I have a very good place. You could bring him there.” I looked at Jeremy, who looked at Ben, who got out the maps. Ben reckoned if we got up early and drove all day, we would be there by nightfall.

Sure enough, we arrived on Aunty Margaret’s land late the next afternoon. After pulling into a beautiful forest of gum trees where we would camp, we brought out my Teacher. Mumma once again called out to introduce us to the Ancestors and welcome us to her Country. As the land’s custodial elder, she told us this blessing would go out on and on, forever, and that the Earth Treasure Vase was now invited to rest there for all time.

While the group made camp, Jeremy and I took off with Mumma in her “troupe carrier,” as she called their old Toyota Land Cruiser, with Daddy (David, her husband) driving, to find the perfect location for my Teacher to be placed in the deep rock wall lining that sacred valley. Daddy drove us on toward the guardian protector of the area—to “Our Lady,” an ancient and rare cycad tree. She was Mumma’s landmark, and to Her we were delivered, down the dirt track into the remotest outback.

The Aboriginal people do not bury their relatives in the ground, they place them in the rocks above. Margaret had granted permission for us to find a place for our Teacher in this escarpment and directed Jeremy and me to search. "Up there," she instructed, pointing toward the red rocks and boulders layered above the forest floor. Our eyes were wildly searching for a spot from the vehicle, and finally we jumped out and scrambled up a rocky cliff. We split up to search for a suitable resting place for our Teacher. Almost immediately I came to a perfect spot, but told myself, No, it can't be so easy; I must keep looking. But without realizing it, I kept circling back to the same place, feeling it calling out. A small tree grew up beside a rocky overhang with an opening at the bottom just big enough to slip the vase in. When Jeremy came to see, he immediately confirmed, "Yes, this is it!" We lingered, appreciating the moment, and then he left me there alone while he hurried back with Mumma and Daddy in the old 4WD to fetch the others before the sun went down.

Alone on the rocky cliffs of Mumma's land, I had time to contemplate the moment. The shadows grew long while I waited for the group. Soon I could make out the light of the full moon rising toward the distant treetops. With my back resting against a large boulder, I listened to the dingoes howling in the distance. Settling into the land of my newfound family, I caught my breath and sat, absorbed in Country. As the moon's light grew, and the sun's light faded, I became aware that I had *arrived*. The last of the Earth Treasure Vases was going to be buried *here*.

And so, recalling the Buddha, I touched the Earth, summoning Her to witness the moment with me. It was not my moment but *ours*. It was Hers. And as I touched the Earth, I felt myself to be part of a much larger tapestry woven around the world. We had succeeded in creating a matrix or mandala of treasure vases planted around the whole Earth as our offering. The vase in my hands connected them all like a key unlocking a hidden chamber. A sense of enormous relief and inexpressible gladness washed over me as I understood the assignment had been fulfilled at last.

I gazed out over the land to the opposite ridge across the valley and leaned back once more into the comfortable warm boulders that surrounded me. It had been the journey of a lifetime to arrive here, now. I breathed with the trees and felt the soft, dry dirt with my fingertips.

Touching the Earth with the vase at my heart, I witnessed this long journey through Her eyes. And in that timeless moment I watched the brilliant full moon, my constant companion, crest over the ridge as the sun set behind me. Alone in the wilderness of remotest Australia, having found my mob, summoning Earth and feeling Her beneath me, all around me, in me, I witnessed Her receiving our offering and accepting my efforts on Her behalf. And I felt Her whole vast body become one with mine, with my life and with my commitment to see this sacred task fulfilled. My body relaxed into the land, and the leaves rustled in acknowledgment.

I heard the vehicles approaching and knew my precious moment alone with Gaia would be over soon. Yet the awareness of Her permeated everything and would stay with me forever. When the group arrived, they found me rooted in Her lap with the vase held out for them to gather around. Twilight descended, and Julian played his didjeridu. Soon we joined our voices with his sacred sounds, chanting the mantra of Tara while final offerings were made into the vase. All of the earth from all of the other Earth Treasure Vase locations were sprinkled into the vase to make an alchemical medicine connecting the songlines, from vase to vase, across space and time. A little stove was lit to melt the wax, and we sealed the cork. The silks were carefully draped one by one on top, and the cords were tied. We dripped golden sealing wax onto the cords and stamped them to the silks as a final seal. David Bacon, who had constructed the boxes for the very first vases, gently placed the vase into the wooden container he had lovingly carved and which had been exquisitely hand-painted at Uluru by Uncle Bob Randall's mob for the occasion. David lowered the lid to close the vase inside . . . but with the overflow of offerings, it would not close!

Without missing a beat, David took another breath and whittled and carved the inside of the lid, burning the wood with the flame of the fire from the stove in his lap to hasten the process. We kept right on chanting, and the ongoing sounds of the didjeridu and our invocation of Tara took us deeper and deeper into a reverie of sacred time, holding us in the spell of our prayers until the lid could be sealed, too.

Suddenly, we saw fire creeping up the canyon walls toward us! It seemed the campfire below that Mumma Margaret and brother Ben sat beside had spread. It looked as if the fire were coming straight toward where we perched!

"Is everything OK down there?" I yelled.

"Yup," came Ben's reply as the orange flames flickered up at us.

"Really?" I inquired again as fear of a wildfire flooded over me.

"Yup, it's all OK," came the answer once more.

Our chanting continued, while the campfire—unleashed by Mumma to clear the underbrush, cleanse the land and empower our ceremony—burned itself out around us. [5] She and big brother Ben chatted it up 'round the fire, "drinking a cuppa tea or two and gnawin' on some biskies," as Ben put it. He had asked her then, "Mumma, what about our Teacher?" And Ben shared with me that Mumma told him "forthright" that this place would enter the Dreamtime now, and the story of the Earth Treasure Vase would be passed on from generation to generation.

With the fire burning up the undergrowth and David's crotch practically catching fire as he held the stove in his lap to char the wooden lid and whittle away, we concentrated ever more fiercely on Tara. Under the full moon light, Tara became inseparable from Gaia witnessing our prayers, and, no doubt, responding. Eventually, the lid was secured and the vase in its special container was closed properly. Jeremy laid it into the rocks, and we all sealed the opening with more rocks so it would be well hidden. Our group had become one body, with countless arms and single-pointed concentration, reminding me of Avalokiteshvara, the Bodhisattva of Compassion with a thousand arms. We sensed the offering was received, the gift accepted. The Ancestors had come.

Back at camp, relaxing by the warm (and contained) fire, we lifted our eyes to behold a canopy of stars so bright and dense they filled the deep black sky down to the horizon. It was as if we could reach out and touch them—the infinity of that star-studded sky displaying the vastness of the cosmos we live within—and we understood something of our true nature. Julian's didjeridu never ceased the whole night long. Its primordial sound carried us into the Dreamtime like the breath of the Ancestors. We could not sleep. We had, in some small way, awakened.

After I returned home from our journey, my brother Ben Manbulloo helped me to better understand the culture and ancestral ways of the people, his own Aboriginal heritage, and what had happened out there in Country. He explained that the songlines are like energetic highways—the energy system of the planet. And he told me, "This is how Dreaming stories are made. We tell the stories by the firelight to our young ones. The stories explain why things are. And I believe this one will live through words and fire for all time to come. Mumma will already be tellin' of how a group of wonderful people came out to this place, did some special ceremonies, and camped and enjoyed her Country, and I promise you that when the young ones go to Jawoyn Country, they will hear the story of your Teacher."

I was in an altered state for a long time after Australia. The separation between the dreaming and waking state blurred. A portal had opened, and the light around me looked different. All I wanted to do was sit around the fire and "sing up them songlines."

Aunty Margaret's passing in 2018 left a big gap in my heart, but her warm embrace lit up my life and brought the global journey with the Earth Treasure Vases to fruition. Her unconditional love for me and her acceptance of the vases was among the greatest gifts of my life. Sitting around the fire, she saw into the nature of my Teacher, and she opened the way for the vases to enter the Dreaming. The songlines came alive and connected the Earth Treasure Vases around the whole Earth. The global mandala was awakened, whole and complete, back to the beginning of time and forward into future generations. In her eyes and in her cackling laughter, this was made clear. Her heart expressed itself so purely.

Margaret Katherine embodied a vast view of unconditioned awareness (the Dreamtime) completely connected to Country, and this brought everything together for me. Aunty Margaret was a living treasure, a holy vessel of healing, open to Spirit, pouring her love into the world. I am forever grateful to be her daughter, to have held her hand, walked with her for a while, and sat around the fire, listening to her stories.

SECTION FOUR

COLLECTIVE AWAKENING

CHAPTER TWENTY-ONE

INDRA'S NET

Almost every morning, I walk with my dog, Jala, out on a long mesa that overlooks the entire Rio Grande Valley. This morning, a lone coyote howls and yelps incessantly. Jala and I stop to listen and try to locate his presence, antennae out. The coyote's wailing finally comes to an end, and the mesa is silent again. As we continue on our walk, we are alert, sniffing some fresh scat and stopping to determine where the coyote has gone.

We make our way up to where the Ancestors dwell—land that was once a Native pueblo long ago and where I have counted five hollows that must have been their ceremonial kivas. There are pottery shards on the ground everywhere—painted lines on bits of clay, the broken remains of the life once lived here. I feel the spirit of the Ancestors and call out for their blessings like Aunty Margaret taught me, expressing my gratitude and praying for our future as I take in the presence of Los Alamos National Laboratory across the valley.

The chilling calls of the coyote reverberate. What is this trickster trying to tell me? I walk up onto the highest mound on the old pueblo land, picking up a painted shard along the way. I sit, then carefully place the potsherd back on the land where it belongs. Jala digs a cool dirt bed next to me to curl up in as I look out across the vast expanse. My gaze falls on Area G, as it so often does, and my heart quickens. I touch the Earth and call on Gaia to help me face the knowledge that our country is gearing up for more bombs, not fewer. I am painfully aware that the Environmental Protection Agency is threatened, as new roads encroach on this sacred mesa from all directions. It feels like only a matter of time until the coyote call is silenced forever.

In the next breath though, I notice new grasses coming up from the parched Earth, thanks to recent rains. And I am transported back to Santa Clara Pueblo, also visible across the valley at the base of the Jemez Mountains, where the recent ceremonial dances for their annual Feast Day are still echoing through me. The drumbeat, the songs, the dancers whose feet keep the rhythm of the drum, men's bare chests coated with paint, rattles shaking in their hands, wrists tied with evergreen branches, and the women's headdresses—standing tall above the crowd—decorated with feathers, painted hummingbirds, butterflies, and rainbows. The line of dancers stretching from one end of the plaza to the other in a gorgeous cycle of honoring and renewal.

• • •

As we took on the assignment of global healing more and more deeply, our collective prayers for healing and protection began to take root in the body of Mother Earth. And when the Earth Treasure Vase was planted in Margaret's ancestral land, our global healing mandala came to life as a whole. This living mandala with all its nodes radiating light in every direction reminded me of the Buddhist teaching of Indra's Net.

This teaching, illustrating the interconnectedness of all things, is found in the Avatamsaka Sutra, or Flower Ornament Scripture, where abstract truths, like the idea that the whole universe may be reflected in a particle of dust, symbolically convey the vast range of Buddhist teachings. Thich Nhat Hanh describes Indra's Net like this:

"Indra's net is a vast, cosmic lattice that contains precious jewels wherever the threads cross. There are millions of jewels strung together to make the net, and each jewel has many facets. When you look at any facet of any one jewel, you can see all the other jewels reflected in it. In the world of the Avatamsaka, in Indra's net, the one is present in the all, and the all is present in the one. This wonderful image was used in Buddhism to illustrate the principle of interdependence and interpenetration."[1]

Like those jewels, it is through each other's reflection that we experience our wholeness. When we each feel that we are being witnessed, the net sparkles with awareness and healing feels possible. But if it feels like the world is not present or our community is not holding us in our suffering, then we feel hopeless and isolated. We are a microcosm of Indra's Net in both our beauty and our pain.

The Earth Treasure Vases offer us a way to collectively bear witness to the truth of suffering and our commitment to heal it. We may be conditioned by patriarchal views to believe this is not enough, but this bearing witness is the critical first step: seeing clearly together. Feeling together. Remembering the infinite reflections within Indra's Net, we see we are not alone. Operating within an awakened collective, anything is possible. Each of us is a jewel radiating light in every direction, like each treasure vase, filled with infinite potential on every node of the mandala.

I don't imagine we can ever wrap our arms around the whole of it. But bringing our sensitivity and our kind attention to each other and the lands we love is what heals. If no one comes when we are calling out in desperation, life feels pointless. Being heard and being held is perhaps the greatest gift we can give to each other now. To recover from our isolation. To find the courage to go on.

The thing is, when a little clay pot is involved, our ability to listen is magnified. And our heart's longing is given permission to come pouring out. We don't need to yell. Every time a fragile little vase is passed around a circle to receive our tender offerings, we receive the strength we need to look at things we so often protect ourselves from seeing. Bearing witness to our vulnerability and listening deeply, with the support of a group, becomes the key to unlocking the treasures buried deep within. No longer turning away from the hard things, we can act with awareness, and new possibilities come to light.

The vases receive our visions and dreams. They come alive—and so do we—with the healing we are calling for. Our intentions create the causes and conditions within us for transformation to be possible. And the outdated systems that have gotten us into this mess and disconnect us from our true nature can be seen for what they are.

In the world of interbeing, our true nature is not separate from the life force of Gaia. She is infinitely creative, and so are we. We need to no longer be limited by our lack of imagination. For instance, we can imagine that the Los Alamos National Laboratory could be repurposed for the restoration of life instead of causing untold death and destruction. Or, remembering the women of Liberia who ended a civil war, we can stand together to end the war against nature.

Inspired by Indra's Net, through our visualizations, prayers, and meditations, we can see ourselves as active participants in the process of collective awakening and unlock the key to our survival. When we practice together, sending our love to all beings, we discover our interconnection—each of us aware of being a facet of the whole. This lays the foundation for a new operating system. Indeed, many of us are already in the process of cocreating that new operating system for an awakened planetary culture. Just as our own old, outdated habits, addictions, and patterns of conditioning need to be released in order for us to grow and evolve individually, many of our ways of living life on Earth need to die, too—the habits that are no longer contributing to the whole and are blocking the evolution of life. We can see these now for what they are—self-centered and self-serving habits that use resources and energy for a purpose that benefits only a few and not the whole of creation.

Living and practicing the way of awareness teaches us to work different muscles than the ones we are conditioned to believe are going to get us where we need to go. It's easy to fall back into our collective agreement that the world is a terrible mess and there's nothing we can do about it. The dominant culture tells us this every day. But our awareness, especially when cultivated collectively, gives us another view. The mycelial network shows us how we can work to restore balance to the web of life. To be planetary healers we must choose to focus our attention, with all our hearts, on the path of restoration—and to imagine that the healing is accomplished and the vitality of the Earth is completely restored.

Practicing awareness through meditation, we are nourishing and strengthening that which *helps.* From out of the wellspring of love and caring come solutions—the gestures of healing and compassion to alleviate the suffering around us. If we identify with how awful things are, we *lose* energy, get sucked into the mire, and can't move, becoming more and more reactive and depressed. So we practice to cultivate a joyful mind and a good heart and the world becomes a better place instantly. With every breath, we can cut through the old ways that hook us into the dying system that gives power to the few.

Looking into the vast web of interbeing and recognizing each other reflecting back the beauty and goodness that is our true nature, like the sparkling jewels of Indra's Net, we see we are not separate and can trust we are arriving at a collective awakening.

The time has come to operate together, with our shared intention for restoration and peace. The lone coyote is howling for his tribe. He cannot survive alone.

CHAPTER TWENTY-TWO

SACRED ACTIVISM

I was not the only one to be healed and transformed by the prayers contained in the little clay pot in Australia. Each one of us in the outback that full-moon night was forever altered by our experience. As we sat together in silence around the fire at the center of our circle, under the sea of stars, our thoughts and feelings settled into a vast and timeless weaving of story and place. The power of prayer entered our hearts and we knew something good had happened.

I wanted to rest in what I had experienced in Australia. To once and for all drop the sense of urgency I felt and heed the words of Guimolo Dolo in Mali. I knew the deed was done and needed to take it in. Something had happened, was happening. I recalled how Gyatrul Rinpoche used to say, "Slowly, slowly, step by step." Change happens, but not as fast as we might wish. Thich Nhat Hanh always counseled us to stop and breathe in order to arrive fully present in every moment. These great masters did not push us. They knew better. They were pointing to the need to be with ourselves in order for the wisdom gained from life-changing experiences to naturally arise in its own good time. I did not know what was coming from all this, but I heard the words of my friend, the Nigerian author Bayo Akomolafe, who perhaps said it best: "My people say, 'The times are urgent. Let us slow down.'"[1]

So I took a breath. And another. And I offered my prayers "up them songlines" once more, trusting in something so much larger than myself.

"Our prayers have an impact," writes Buddhist teacher Thanissara, who speaks to the need for a dharma in response to the Earth's suffering. "Each of us is called to contribute whatever we can . . . Together, we should dedicate our prayers and undertake ceremonies and rituals of acknowledgement and restoration, generating a circle of sacred intention and engaged response around the globe."[2]

Simply put, prayer is nothing more or less than an intention. And when we share our prayers or intentions, the universe responds. Getting clear on our intentions is the first step. To do this, we need to stop thinking; settle our busy, worried minds; and find that calm place within to relax. Once we have settled the monkey mind, we may feel our whole body relax, and then we can more easily get in touch with our heart's calling, for this is where our prayers or intentions dwell. Not in our head, but in our deepest heart of hearts.

This intentional energy of the heart sends a message out into the world, rippling out like waves, where it meets the shared prayers and intentions of others, and where it activates a universal responsiveness that can be trusted. A call will come in, an unexpected guest will arrive, a piece of information will be shared with us that holds a key to our understanding, an introduction will be made—and a solution will suddenly be available. Synchronicity opens the door for our prayers to be realized.

But it's up to us to pay attention to the signs and omens and not to miss the response or casually dismiss it as unimportant. Maybe the response comes in a form that is different from what you wanted, so you look away because it is not what you expected. Or you don't feel deserving, so you ignore it. Staying open and out of judgment is the key that unlocks a stream of support for our deepest prayers to come true.

Lakota Grandmother Rita Long Visitor Holy Dance stated, "The prayers are very sacred. It is something that you gotta put your mind to, not just because you're saying it. You gotta mean it!"[3] In Tibetan Buddhism they say you need to pray so hard the hair on the back of your neck stands up or tears stream down your cheeks. Taking action is the next step. The Dalai Lama is adamant: "I always believe peace must come through action. Not just prayers. Not to wish. We have to work!"[4] The work will feel good when you are fulfilling your prayers. Even if it's a lot of work, there will be a flow to your actions when you are certain that what you are doing is aligned with a larger flow connected to the universe. This happened so many times with the Earth Treasure Vases. Once I'd get clear and form an intention about where the next vase was to go, I would be amazed to watch the connections that would pop up in my life pointing in that direction, facilitating its journey.

Sometimes I *thought* I was clear and knew exactly where the next Earth Treasure Vase was to go, but in fact it was just my idea and not actually connected to something larger than myself. At those times, it felt like I hit a brick wall: it was clearly time to stop and open to further guidance.

But when it was right, I felt it, like Grandma Rita says. It's like following the clues in a treasure hunt. You catch the whiff and off you go. It's not really "you" in control, but something so much larger that is calling the shots. Neema Namadamu calls this larger force of the universe The Coordinator. Her husband, Danny, refers to God. My Native American friends refer to Great Spirit. These days I say that it is Gaia responding to our prayers. It doesn't matter to me how you identify this universal force, just as long as you recognize that when you get out of the way, a spiritual force—or the web of interbeing, perhaps—can operate. And when it does, you are in greater alignment with what you are actually supposed to be doing with your life. When you take action from there, you are contributing to a better world.

• • •

My first taste of this kind of sacred activism was in the early 1980s when I took part in a telepathy experiment conceived by the late Mary Payne of the Esalen Soviet-American Exchange Program and Joan Steffy, PhD. It was four decades into the Cold War between the United States and the Soviet Union, and we were a part of a growing movement in citizen diplomacy, working to thaw the tensions between those two superpowers and build friendships with our peers there. A group of Californians in the Human Potential movement gathered to link telepathically with a group in Tbilisi, Georgia, led by a psychic healer and artist named Viktor Krivorotov, who was involved in Russia's movement to explore "hidden human reserves."

After developing a scientific protocol to telepathically send and receive images and undertaking the experiment for many months, we realized we had fallen in love with our Georgian friends. One of the American participants, Avon Mattison, who went on to found the international nonprofit Pathways to Peace, coined the term "telempathy." We felt it was the empathic connection that was allowing us to have such successful results and certain that making a heartfelt loving relationship with our Soviet friends was exactly what was called for. At the end of our first extended telempathy experiment, we had become so strongly connected with the Georgian community that a number of us traveled there to meet our friends in person. It was a glorious journey filled with loving intentions for peace and healing across the political boundaries that had previously separated us.

I went on to initiate a regular full moon meditation so that we could continue to "meet" with our Soviet friends every month and send our prayers out for planetary peace. Soon we invited others from around the world to join us in meditation at that time as well. This ongoing synchronized meditation, begun in the early 1980s, would eventually form the basis for the Earth Treasure Vase practice every full moon.

Looking back now, I can see that the telempathy experiment created a strong foundation for our work with the Earth Treasure Vases and for what we now call sacred activism. Prayer had left the monasteries and was finding new avenues of expression in our current times.

"When the inner joy Mother Teresa spoke of, the joy of compassionate service, is married to a practical and pragmatic drive to transform all existing economic, social, and political institutions, a radical and potentially all-transforming holy force is born. This radical holy force I call Sacred Activism," Andrew Harvey writes in his book *The Hope: A Guide to Sacred Activism*, which helped popularize the term. Andrew defines a sacred activist as "someone who is starting to experience the inner joy and outer effectiveness of this force, who knows that the profound crisis the world is in is challenging everyone to act from our deepest compassion and wisdom, and who is committed to being, in the face of growing chaos, suffering, and violence, what Robert Kennedy [the brother of JFK] called 'a tiny ripple of hope' and a 'center of energy and daring.'"[5]

David Nicol, cofounder with Leslie Meehan of the Gaiafield Project, developed an academic thesis on what he calls "subtle activism" and published a book describing the basis for it. It was thrilling to see a wider public recognizing the validity of the kind of activism I had been quietly engaged in for so many years. David describes subtle activism as the idea that "focused collective meditation and intention can powerfully and measurably contribute to social change and collective healing. It grows from the idea that there are many effective ways—some newly emerging, many as old as humanity—to positively influence social change other than overt political action." In his book, *Subtle Activism: The Inner Dimension of Social and Planetary Transformation,* David writes, "Subtle Activism is really a modern name for an age-old practice, adapted to the structures of contemporary society."[6]

So many of the old ways of working for social change are not helping any more. The fundamental and pervasive changes we must make to survive, much less thrive, require radical new ways of thinking and living. The Earth Treasure Vase practice combines both the sacred and the subtle forms of activism. Synchronizing our meditations around the world every full moon for a greater impact magnifies the effect we can have individually. And with the Earth Treasure Vases planted in the ground, the global mandala of people and places we have established has become a powerful anchor for the prayers and intentions of subtle, sacred activists worldwide.

When I first met Thich Nhat Hanh, I was struck by his teachings on Engaged Buddhism. This was the hook that got my attention and let me know I had found my teacher. It is vitally important to sit on a cushion in the comfort of our home and take time out in retreat to deepen our understanding. But if our practice does not also help others in a real way, then it is not effective. In his book *Peace Is Every Step,* Thich Nhat Hanh writes, "When I was in Vietnam, so many of our villages were being bombed. Along with my monastic brothers and sisters, I had to decide what to do. Should we continue to practice in our monasteries, or should we leave the meditation halls in order to help the people who were suffering under the bombs? After careful reflection, we decided to do both—to go out and help people and to do so in mindfulness. We called it Engaged Buddhism. Mindfulness must be engaged. Once there is seeing, there must be acting . . . We must be aware of the real problems of the world. Then, with mindfulness, we will know what to do and what not to do to be of help."[7]

Engaged Buddhism asks us to live in such a way that every step, every breath, is a meditation, a prayer for the world. We engage each activity, no matter how small, as if it were benefiting others, living every aspect of our lives in service and with mindfulness. This is not to say we sacrifice ourselves and override our own needs. Because self and other are two sides of the same coin, what truly benefits me also benefits you. The trick is to know what is truly beneficial, what will really serve us in any given moment.

Thanks to Thich Nhat Hanh, Andrew Harvey, and David Nicol (and more recently many others), the notion of sacred activism has been seeded in our collective consciousness. Yet many still dismiss the work of sacred activism as not really doing anything.

We might ask ourselves, Where does change actually come from? How does it happen? Where does it begin? What actually brings about healing? Looking deeply, we can see that all impulses toward change and the actions that arise to bring change about begin with awareness. And awareness is cultivated by listening to that quiet, still voice within. Awareness, even before thoughts have the chance to get our attention, gives rise to an impulse, and when that impulse is fueled by the energy of compassion, the insights that come and the actions that are born from those insights can heal the world.

We have learned that every thought has an effect. Action comes from somewhere. Whatever arises in the mind can be seen as energy, and this force can be directed consciously when we have developed our concentration. A subtle realm of energy is operating within and around us all the time. The worldview of the dominant culture's rational mind does not accept the presence of a mysterious, unexplained, invisible reality. It's time to break free of this limitation and find another path—a path that takes us where we really want to go. A path, as Charles Eisenstein would say, "to a more beautiful world our hearts tell us is possible."[8]

In the Buddhist tradition, every time we sit down to practice meditation, we cultivate the Bodhisattva Vow, committing ourselves to be of benefit to all sentient beings. At the end of every meditation, a Dedication of the Merit is recited as a reminder that the goodness we have generated is not just for ourselves but to be shared with all beings. Buddhists have been practicing sacred, subtle activism for thousands of years. The Earth Treasure Vase practice combines both the subtle and the sacred, and engages us to go out into the world to make direct relations with places and communities that need healing and protection.

Training in a dedicated meditation practice, our intentions form the basis, or aspiration, for our actions. Feeling what we care about deeply, we discover our heartfelt motivation is naturally aligned to our true calling. This is where "right action" comes from. Slowly, slowly, as we transform our own suffering and attachment to a sense of self, we not only see the good that is possible, but also know what to do to relieve the suffering of others more and more effortlessly. We learn to feed the spirit of the potential good instead of dwelling in what is not working. We are less inclined to fall into the darkness of despair or hopelessness.

But practicing meditation is like working out. You have to build muscle to get strong. The actions that come from a practice made strong by energy and muscle, along with a relaxed capacity to see clearly, is very powerful. More powerful than we can imagine with minds conditioned by self-centered habits and desires, the actions that come from an awakened heart-mind are effective. They take us where we need to go—into full participation with the web of life. Through surrendering all that is familiar, we arrive at a place where anything is possible.

This is the shift in consciousness we've been hearing about. As Einstein is believed to have said, we cannot solve our problems with the same thinking we used when we created them.[9]

This leap into the Great Mystery does require faith—but not belief. Belief asks us to surrender our power and volition to an external authority we must believe in. Faith is simply trust in a universe that is much larger than we are. It is faith in the possibility of all sorts of things we could never have imagined, and faith in our own true nature and our relationship of interbeing with all that is. Letting go of a conceptual or predictable orientation, getting out of our own way, and trusting something so much larger is at work—this is what Gaia is inviting us into. This is the kind of activism that the Earth is calling us to now.

• • •

As a result of finding my Aussie mob and becoming family, the global community gathering to cultivate the practice of the Earth Treasure Vases became fully connected. Our prayer circle was growing, and every month on the full moon, we would learn about the outcomes happening from burying the Earth Treasure Vases around the world.

Not long after Wendy Johnson buried a vase deep in the duff of that old-growth redwood forest, the State of California purchased ten thousand acres of the land where the vase had been buried, including a portion of the Headwaters Forest Reserve, protecting it from further logging.

The treasure vase we "buried" in the ocean, filled with deep-hearted prayers and saltwater tears, catalyzed a new chapter in the work of the folks at the Biosphere Foundation. They turned their attention to coral reef restoration and stewardship programs with local communities, and are now making a difference by replanting, regrowing and "gardening" the coral reefs. Against all odds, the reefs respond. The foundation's ship, *Mir*, is carrying out hands-on educational work in the Coral Triangle, and a beautiful land-based community center has been built in Bali with environmental programs dedicated to the stewardship of land and sea.

The vase buried in Liberia inspired Christian, Harper, and Annie to build not one but four Peace Huts in conflict-prone regions of the country as safe places for reconciliation, conflict resolution, trauma healing, and community empowerment—all guided by the practice of mindfulness. And they have dug wells in each location. Their national radio program, *Conversations Under the Peace Hut*, has brought the teachings of mindfulness to the public and helped transform violence into peace and aggression into kindness and compassion.

But the depth of the transformations may be best measured by an observation from Christian. In a recent conversation with Harper, he remarked: "The sound of the bell is so important to me. It is the sound of awakening. It brings you back to your true self, to your mindful breathing. The first time I heard it was like an electric shock. This is what I need, I thought. We all need something in our lives to replace the ugly parts. Now, whenever emotion comes up, I listen to the sound of the bell *within me*—even when I hear the *ba-boom* of the gun in the streets. I've replaced the sound of the bullet with the sound of the bell."

After hearing about the importance of Congo's forests to the whole planet, Neema and her organization, Hero Women Rising, joined forces with the Women's Earth and Climate Action Network (WECAN) to start a reforestation project. WECAN trained Congolese women to gain skills and build understanding about local and international environmental protection laws. They learned the value of women's leadership, and developed hands-on knowledge about caring for local ecosystems, including growing and planting trees on damaged lands. As Neema says, "We know that the difference we make not only affects our world but the rest of our planet."

As for my mob in Australia, on that first trip in 2013 I had secretly brought with me four more Earth Treasure Vases from a second generation of vases I had received as a gift from Jim Casilio, who had been with me on that seminal trip to Charok so long ago. Back then, he had also requested and received 108 smaller Earth Treasure Vases that Lama Tsultrim had made at the same time as the ones I worked with. Jim knew that many more people had asked for vases than I had to offer and kindly sent us forty more of these smaller Earth Treasure Vases. These came to be known as the "second-generation Earth Treasure Vases" and are now going out through other stewards around the world.

These four vases traveled with me throughout our time in Australia—from Sydney with the Dalai Lama to Uncle Bob's home at Uluru and to Aunty Margaret's ancestral homeland. On the last night of our pilgrimage, I passed them to our newly formed Aussie Earth Treasure Vase mob. A year later, I returned for Aunty Margaret to bless and dedicate those first four second-generation vases. Aunty Margaret requested that we take one of these to a fifty-thousand-year-old rock shelter covered with paintings called Gabarnmung, which was only accessible by helicopter.[10] As its Traditional Owner, she chose this ancient hidden land to receive the first of the second generation of Earth Treasure Vases and invited us to travel there with her the next year.

In 2015, I flew to Australia for the third time. I could not imagine a more spectacular place to begin the next cycle of this practice. The ancient Gabarnmung site had recently emerged from the folds of time and is surely destined to become a World Heritage Site and be counted among Earth's great sacred places. Only a handful of archeologists have ever even seen it—and it was Margaret who served as the living elder bringing it to life for them. There, we were able to weave the thread of deep time into the web of loving care for the planet. It was as if the Great Spirit of Gaia and all the Buddhas and Bodhisattvas, Ancestors, elders, and lineage masters who have ever watched over this project and practice, guiding and assisting in its realization, said, "Here. Add this place into the ingredients that make up the whole of the mandala. Allow the energy from this location, from before human history was recorded, to enhance and support the prayers that will carry life throughout space and time into the next age." Of all the pilgrimage places we have ever been with this practice, we know with Gabarnmung that our work will carry on.

With the second generation of Earth Treasure Vases, a new cycle of our sacred activism began. As more and more people recognized the worthiness of a little clay pot filled with prayers and offerings and engaged with this practice, an Earth Treasure Vase stewardship council was formed to oversee the distribution of the vases that remain and make sure they are spread around the planet in a full embrace. We now have a community process to pass vases on to those who request them.

While that first little holy vessel of the second generation was being placed at Gabarnmung, two other vases were being buried at the same time: one above the Ottawa River in the unceded territory of the Algonquin, an Anishinaabe people who have occupied the entire Ottawa watershed for thousands of years, and one in the original garden at Findhorn, in Scotland. Not long after that, two more vases went out in Australia, one to Purnululu in the Kimberley region, and one on Didthul Mountain in Walbunja Country, in the Yuin Nation. Another vase was taken to the Hanford site, a nuclear "reservation" in the state of Washington, and placed downstream from that repository of radioactive waste along the shore of the Columbia River; and yet another went to Mount Ryozen above Fukushima, Japan. As part of an initiative called Wise USA, we buried a vase in Kansas, in the beautiful tall-grass prairie in the heartland of America, and another vase was taken to the edge of the sea in northernmost Arctic Alaska near the village of Utqiagvik, in a region that is sinking into the melting permafrost.

At the center of the mandala, here in New Mexico, I am still concerned that the activities at the Los Alamos National Laboratory may never be resolved. But Marian Naranjo says she has seen much transformation since we first directed our prayers there. For her, being able to bring back a sacred connection to the lands around the lab, to pray and make offerings in places like the Valles Caldera where her Ancestors once dwelled, is to sustain balance and put in motion the energies that may yet transform that place for the benefit of future generations.

After a decade of getting to know each other, Marian, who is an acclaimed potter, agreed to teach us how to make earthen vessels in the tradition of her people. In 2021, a new group of committed stewards gathered in the land of the Tewa people at the center of the Earth Treasure Vase Mandala in northern New Mexico to bring together the Native American and Tibetan Buddhist traditions in the making of what is now a third generation of holy vessels. With our own hands, we worked the local red clay flecked with mica into beautiful little pots to carry our prayers for healing into new locations across the land.

• • •

In his book *Climate: A New Story*, Charles Eisenstein writes, "If we could identify one thing as *the* cause, the solution would be so much more accessible. But what is comfortable is not always true. What if the cause is a thousand interrelated things that implicate all of us and how we live? What if it is something so all-encompassing and so intertwined with life as we know it, that when we glimpse its enormity we know not what to do? That moment of humble, powerless unknowing, where the sadness of an ongoing loss washes through us and we cannot escape into facile solutioneering, is a powerful and necessary moment. It has the power to reach into us deeply enough to wipe away frozen ways of seeing and ingrained patterns of response. It gives us fresh eyes, and it loosens the tentacles of fear that hold us in normality."[11]

For me, it has been the experience of "powerless unknowing" that has helped me the most to stay on this path of prayer into action. In surrendering to the ungraspable, somehow solutions that had not been imagined before become available, solutions that are unconditioned by the old thinking, solutions that are, in fact, the rightful actions that naturally flow from an open heart. A heart that thinks like a planet and feels like a mother acts like Gaia Herself. The only thing to do is participate in the restoration of life on Earth. The job is so huge we cannot grasp the assignment, narrow it into focus, or slice it up into manageable pieces. We must be willing to open so wide that, even if for only a moment, we take it all in. And like gazing at the stars in the sky or the grains of sand on the shore, we become aware of both our insignificance and our importance. Our rational minds shut down and we are humbled by the majesty of the Great Mystery, the jeweled net of Indra that goes on and on.

In following the thread of this assignment, I have seen what can arise through the power of prayer. I have developed an unshakable faith in our human capacity to transform suffering into beauty and heal the deepest of wounds. I have witnessed Christian Bethelson transform from a desperate man of war to a humble man of peace. I have watched communities join together across tribal, religious, and national boundaries in their shared prayers for the lands they love. I have observed forests regrow after a devastating fire in the vicinity of an Earth Treasure Vase. I have been amazed by a gigantic eagle feather dropping into our camp, heralding endless rainbows after the vase was buried in Arctic Alaska.

• • •

I light the candles on my altar as I do every morning and take a thick stick of earthy Tibetan incense and light it from a candle. I turn the globe of the Earth, gaze at the figures of the sacred feminine collected on my journeys, and bow to a statue of Buddha in the posture of Summoning the Earth. The smoke of the incense rises through the feathers, stones, and crystals that have also made their way into the current configuration of objects I venerate. A precious work of calligraphy by Thich Nhat Hanh sits among the rocks. Inside a perfect circle he drew, it reads, "I am in love with Mother Earth." A painting depicting the songlines of Aboriginal women's circles from Australia lays opposite this calligraphy, supporting a picture of my adopted mother, Margaret Katherine, and my beloved mentor, Joanna Macy. To these and all my precious teachers and friends, and numerous beings too many to name, I bow.

At the center of the altar is the last of the original Earth Treasure Vases. It was named the Mama Vessel for the way she is patiently holding space for the second- and third-generation vases to find their destinations and be buried by those who will steward them. When all is said and done, a hundred Earth Treasure Vases will serve as anchors for our mandala of prayers in the body of the Earth. The Mama Vessel waits, and reminds me to be a holy vessel myself.

CHAPTER TWENTY-THREE

MOTHER GAIA

In 2009, Lama Tsultrim had rekindled the practice of Tara in me, and I received the spiritual support I needed to take the treasure vases to Liberia, Congo, South Africa, Avebury, and Hawaii, and to Australia—three times. With each step along the path, my sense of connection to Tara deepened. I called for her support, and she came when called, becoming my spiritual friend, ally, and protector.

And yet, I was increasingly yearning to form a direct relationship to the Earth as a sacred being, a living goddess. I was coming to feel Tara was gently guiding me to realize that she was, in fact, inseparable from Gaia. At first, this was just a feeling, then a growing sense of perception crept up on me, and finally Gaia appeared to me.

One morning in 2016, with the candles lit and the Mama Vessel holding court on the altar, she came to me. I had been in retreat for several months attempting to reconcile what the path had opened up around the world and what was still left to do. I was sitting on my red cushion meditating, when suddenly from my heart, with overwhelming emotion flooding through me, I felt her presence arising.

As the feeling of her presence came alive in my body, I sensed the need to listen deeply, as if to a far-off sound coming closer. My senses were finely tuned—body, speech, and mind alert to what was happening—as the sound grew more audible until I was able to hear what I realized was her mantra sounding loud and strong and very clear:

OM GAIA MANDALA SIDDHI PHALA BHRUM AH

As the mantra penetrated my psyche, it began to flow around and around in my heart. I concentrated on the sound, reciting the words over and over, and as I did, I experienced Gaia's form appearing. She emerged dimly at first, almost imperceptibly, as I learned to see with new eyes and hear with new ears. But slowly she grew brighter and clearer. Similar to the description of Tara I was familiar with, I saw the goddess Gaia with a bright full moon shimmering beneath her, one leg folded in meditation and the other extended—stepping out into the world. Gaia's body was golden brown like the very skin of Mother Earth, and she was clothed in the green and blue of trees and plants, of oceans and rivers and the blue skies of this beautiful living planet. When she looked at me, the expression on her face seemed to change like the weather, sometimes smiling, but then turning serious or even scary.

Gaia appeared with four arms, the top left expressing the mudra of offering protection, and the top right in the mudra of supreme giving and healing, like Tara. But in her other pair of hands, she held an Earth Treasure Vase at her heart from which she poured blessings of primordial wisdom nectar into all beings and into the songlines and meridians of the Earth. Within her enormous planetary heart was the Sanskrit seed syllable for Earth, *Bhrum*, beaming golden light in every direction. And from the sound of that *Bhrum* arose the whole Earth. She was a living breathing planet in the form of the most beautiful goddess I had ever seen. The sound of her mantra flowed out into the world and as it did, brilliant light filled with love shone in every direction and activated all the Earth Treasure Vases in every location around the entire global mandala of healing intentions and prayers that had been planted in her holy ground.

OM GAIA MANDALA SIDDHI PHALA BHRUM AH
Oh Mother Earth, mandala of life, may the fruit of your spiritual powers be realized!

For many moons, I continued with the practice of Tara while reciting Gaia's mantra during my sitting and walking meditations. I did not think I was permitted by the lineage masters to change the sadhana from one of Tara to one of Gaia. But eventually I had to accept that Tara was guiding me to bring forward a new practice of Gaia. I needed her now more than ever and sensed she might be needed by others, too. So, with a feeling of confidence that I had Tara's permission, one day I went ahead and substituted the name Gaia for Tara and the words of the sadhana began to change to express Gaia's nature more directly. A new practice was taking root in my life.

There is an old oak tree at the little river's bend on our land, and when I knew this was the practice to which I would give all my attention, I went down to the river and placed a small figure of Tara—now Gaia—under the branches of the oak tree. I wanted her to take her seat on the ground within the circle of stones and crystals I had gathered for my outdoor shrine. I found a silver bowl that had been my grandmother's and filled it full of fresh, flowing river water. Offering this to Gaia while reciting her mantra, I touched my head to her sacred ground and then hung prayer flags from Grandmother Oak's twisted branches. The leaves rustled above my head and I rang the bell to mark the beginning of a new cycle of dedicated practice I knew would take the rest of my life to unfold. Then I took my seat back inside and poured the practice of the Sublime Mother Gaia into the world.

• • •

It is clear to me now that Mother Earth had been waiting for me to recognize our interdependence. Tara evolved into Gaia to show the way of interbeing, embodied in a vastly powerful image of the sacred feminine with endless creative capacities to take care of life.

The Vajrayana teachings say that when we visualize a deity we are not imagining an external entity we must believe in like a God. Instead, these imagined beings point to aspects of our own innate nature: the capacity for wisdom, compassion, and enlightened activity that dwells within.

We do not think Buddha is a god or Tara is a goddess existing *outside of us* to believe in. Their nature is *in us*. All of the enlightened qualities are already in us. We just have to peel back the layers to connect with them and receive this connection that we have invoked. Practicing this way, we come to realize that we embody these same qualities.

Since our mind's essential nature is unconditioned primordial wisdom awareness, as we awaken to this awareness within ourselves and claim our true nature, we bring it into our lives, to Earth, because we *are* Earth. Merging the light of pure awareness and the ground of our being within the glorious matrix of life, we arrive, ever more present, to offer ourselves in service to all beings. We do not need to seek an enlightened, transcendent source of refuge outside of ourselves. Bringing our direct insight and spiritual experience to Earth is the next evolutionary step of humanity—to wake up as One with Gaia and with all life. The opportunity now is not about transcending. It is about embodying.

The mantra was spinning in my heart, but to fully embody Her and integrate the practice of Mother Gaia into my life, I needed to walk Her into my blood and bones, breathe Her air, and make an offering to Her back where it all began. I needed to return to Nepal.

CHAPTER TWENTY-FOUR

HEAD OVER HEELS

Finally, in 2018, it was time to honor and integrate the journey that began at that cave in Charok and go back to Nepal.

Lama Tsultrim had taken me there in the first place and agreed to guide my journey back. His father, a highly respected lama named Kyabje Kyaprok Tulku Rinpoche, had recently passed away. His death was accompanied by many signs of spiritual accomplishment. Lama Tsultrim had been present for his father's passing and presided over the ceremonies of the forty-nine days following his death. In Sherpa culture, the lineage is handed down not only through reincarnation but also from teacher to student and from father to son. With his father's passing, Lama Tsultrim inherited the seat at Tolu Gompa. Having demonstrated great interest in the dharma from the time he was a small child, he had studied closely with both his father and Charok Rinpoche and entered his first long retreat at the young age of twelve. Now in his sixties, he knew it was his responsibility to carry on the lineage after his father was gone.

The lineage Lama Tsultrim inherited goes back seven generations. The land of his Ancestors around Tolu Gompa, where he was born and grew up, has always been a place of practice. Lama Tsultrim's father had invited Charok Rinpoche to take up residence at Tolu Gompa and to help redesign the monastery. Charok Rinpoche lived there, found the best artists and craftsmen to paint the beautiful temple, and held the seat at Tolu Gompa with Lama Tsultrim's father until the last years of his life, when he went back to the cave at Charok to live in retreat, cared for by his reclusive daughter, Ani Pema Chodron. I met him there in 1990, one year before he passed away.

Tolu Gompa became one of Nepal's most treasured monasteries. Eventually, however, Lama Tsultrim's family moved away to live in Kathmandu, and his father only returned to Tolu Gompa to uphold the annual ceremonies. Lama Tsultrim moved to the United States to establish a dharma center in New Orleans. But Tolu Gompa was always in his heart, and whatever money he raised he would take back to his monastery to make repairs and keep it alive. As fate would have it, in 2005, his dharma center in New Orleans was destroyed by Hurricane Katrina. And then in 2015, Tolu Gompa was almost completely leveled by the massive earthquake that ripped through Nepal. It took him seven years, but the center in New Orleans had been rebuilt. It was now time to restore Tolu Gompa.

So I gathered a small group of friends and Earth Treasure Vase collaborators, and two extraordinary filmmakers, and off we went to Nepal. Beginning the pilgrimage at Tolu Gompa, we would see the place for ourselves and assess what it would need to be rebuilt. It seemed like this was the least I could do for all Lama Tsultrim had given to me.

For five weeks, we trekked through the Solukhumbu region, covering 120 miles, to first visit Tolu Gompa and then walk far up into the mountains to return to the cave at Charok. We traded off carrying two of the second-generation Earth Treasure Vases in our backpacks—one for Tolu Gompa and one for Charok—as offerings of gratitude and renewal, weaving these key locations into the Earth Treasure Vase Mandala.

Back in the culture and tradition I loved, my devotion to the dharma was reawakened. I wept in the sacred places that still held much meaning for me and bowed down to honor the teachings I have learned so much from. It was good to be back in my spiritual home.

Arriving at Tolu Gompa, I was overcome with a sense of belonging to be in this stunningly beautiful place. Filled with heightened energy in spite of the altitude, I ran up to the top of the highest hilltop overlooking the monastery where the vast view of the entire Himalayan range stretches as far as the eyes can see. Every nook and cranny surrounding the temple seemed to hide a cave or rocky outcropping carved with mantras or imprinted by the body of a great master who practiced there. I wandered among the rhododendron trees blooming pink and red and white, and I meditated, gazing out on the highest mountains in the world.

But the old temple was crumbling. The earthquake that devastated Nepal had taken its toll, and all that still stood was the main temple—the gompa. We had come to offer our support for the rebuilding of this hidden gem. Everyone had brought offerings from home to place inside the Earth Treasure Vase that was to be buried there.

The day after our arrival, many lamas from the region gathered at the temple for a daylong puja, or ceremony, to Tara. Their chanting, accompanied by the sound of trumpets, drums, and the large cymbals that punctuate their prayers, entered my heart. The fragrance of burning juniper branches, freshly collected from the forest, wafted through the air in a smoke-offering called *tsang* to restore balance and harmony far and wide. All day long Tara was invoked and the old gompa came alive. Finally, I brought the Earth Treasure Vase to the altar glowing with butter lamps and lovingly decorated with red rhododendron flowers. The global mandala of Earth Treasure Vase locations was invoked, and the vase was passed to the group to receive the offerings they had brought especially for this occasion and to share their prayers for this place.

We had been there for many hours, and as the ceremony concluded, we sat quietly in the fading light with only the butter lamps illuminating the hall. All of a sudden, Lama Tsultrim reached into the folds of his robes and pulled out a pointed red hat, and before I knew what was happening, he placed it on my head and pronounced me a lama.

His attendant monk, Lama Thondrup, wrapped me in a ceremonial shawl, and with that, I was "enthroned." The group gasped, then clapped. Lama Tsultrim laughed heartily. I was stunned speechless. I felt honored and humbled, but I couldn't help asking, "What does this *mean*?" He responded that he was recognizing me for all my years of devoted practice with the Earth Treasure Vases and chuckled again.

It was an unprecedented move since I had not traveled the traditional route to deserve this honor, even if the Earth Treasure Vase practice had come to me from his lineage master. But Lama Tsultrim was clear: I had dutifully carried out the instructions I received from Charok Rinpoche, and he felt my dedication to bringing healing and protection to the Earth deserved recognition. This, along with my many years of devoted dharma practice, he said, was more than equivalent to the traditional three-year retreat one undergoes to become a lama. And he told me that to receive this honor at Tolu

Gompa, Charok Rinpoche's seat, was a special blessing. He said he thought Charok Rinpoche would have wanted this for me, too.

I was taken aback. Disoriented. In spite of how far away from the lineage teachings Mother Earth had taken me, in that moment I felt bathed in the radiant blessing of the spiritual tradition that had been my home path for so long. And for a moment, sitting beside Lama Tsultrim in that dusty old temple with a red hat on my head, I felt deeply complete. I relaxed and received the blessing that was being bestowed.

My friends were elated and wanted to celebrate. I felt honored and grateful but chose to be quiet and reflective. Becoming a lama, like receiving the transmission of dharmacharya from Thich Nhat Hanh, came to me unexpectedly. I found myself feeling unworthy, like I had not done enough to deserve such a title, and a tiny bit cornered. Did becoming a lama mean I had to become a dutiful practitioner within the lineage I was being asked to uphold? Or was it truly a celebration of my creative efforts to bring the dharma into service for the Earth? How was I to hold this title with integrity now?

I was worried there was an expectation that I would not be able to meet. I tried to shake these feelings, so it helped when, after everyone left, Lama Tsultrim asked me to give him back the hat on my head so he could return it to the statue above the altar! Maybe this was all a big joke, I thought to myself as I watched him climb up the rickety altar and replace the red hat on the clay head of one of the lineage gurus looking down on us. But he made it clear I would get my own hat when we got back to Kathmandu.

• • •

Leaving Tolu Gompa a few days later, I was still mulling over these events. To have been recognized as a lama for all my years of carrying out the practice I had been given was a profound acknowledgment. But I felt confused because I didn't know where it fit into my life now. The Buddhist teachings informed every aspect of my life, yet the wider I traveled and the deeper I went in service to the Earth, the more I felt it is not the lineage lamas or even the Buddha who is my teacher, but Gaia.

Walking away from the spiritual home that had claimed me as a lama was bittersweet. I would miss the view from those hills, but was relieved to have some distance from the discomfort I felt in accepting this new title. We left a generous donation for the rebuilding of the temple and the little vase full of promise—sealed and ready to be buried—sitting on the altar inside the gompa. Its job for now was to continue to hold all of our prayers and intentions for this place until Lama Tsultrim was ready to go to work on reconstruction.[1]

For many days, we walked a long, hard path from Tolu Gompa toward the cave at Charok, which is tucked into the Everest region, above Namche Bazaar. A kind of unraveling took hold of our group as we each grappled with our own personal issues. Pilgrimages often activate the shadows in our psyches—our fears and unresolved issues—and despite our elevated view, this one was no different. Lama Tsultrim seemed to withdraw into his own inner world, and so did I. As we trekked up the mountain path, I became painfully aware of how a spiritual system that promises perfect enlightenment must certainly come to terms with the darkness. I could feel the presence of deeply held secrets that had been kept hidden for centuries, covered up in brocade. And I had the growing sense that the Earth Treasure Vase we gave to Tolu Gompa was working to catalyze the healing needed there now.

As we continued up the very path where I had once formulated the question for Charok Rinpoche about how to bring healing and protection to the Earth, I felt overcome by how much healing is still called for in this world. After so many years of making these journeys, I had come to see how, when we form an intention to truly heal, our hidden wounds rise to the surface. Acupuncturists, like master practitioner J.R. Worsley, call this the "law of cure." For the healing of our world, the places where pain and suffering have been ignored or denied in order to keep the old systems intact must be exposed. How else will we transform and evolve?

Our little group carried the other Earth Treasure Vase up the mountain to Charok Rinpoche's daughter, Ani Pema Chodron, and to the mythic cave hermitage tucked above thirteen thousand feet. With the vase's burial there, this place, too, would become a potent acupuncture point on the living body of Mother Earth. Hidden yogis had practiced for generations in the caves and huts all over the mountainside of Charok. The view of the clear sky, along with the privacy and quiet, was a great support to their practice in retreat.

At age nineteen, Ani Pema Chodron had chosen to devote her life to her father and his teachings and had sequestered herself in the cave ever since. She was almost eighty now and had not left Charok for thirty years. She lives in solitude with her nephew, whom she has trained to be the resident lama. Lama Tsultrim told us that if she were a man, people would flock to sit at her feet. As it is, an occasional visitor comes seeking her advice or blessings; otherwise, she is left alone in the rugged high mountains that surround her. I was filled with curiosity to see her again and wondered if she would remember me. I found it significant that we were going to see the old wise *woman* in the cave this time. Her father was long gone, and the times were calling for women's wisdom to emerge and guide us. But I remembered Ani as being extremely shy and wondered if she would be forthcoming with teachings or keep herself at a distance. I also wondered how she would receive the Earth Treasure Vase.

I was full of anticipation as we walked slowly up the path through a forest of juniper and rhododendron. The low clouds lifted as I finally came out into the open in front of Ani's gate and stepped inside to glimpse the hermitage for the first time in thirty years. Crossing the threshold, I turned the large prayer wheel that sat next to the old stupa. Ani was inside practicing, so the group took the opportunity to set up our tents. I found my old camping spot on the edge of the world, looking straight out at the towering peaks across the valley far below. A raven appeared at my tent door and peered in, cocking its head curiously. The lichen still draped from the trees and the old path was still a soft carpet underfoot.

Ani Pema Chodron kindly gave us time to arrive and then emerged with a welcoming smile and invited us inside for tea. We sat along the wall of her kitchen on a wooden platform covered with colorful Tibetan rugs behind low tables. The cave had been remodeled since I was there. The walls of the back end of the "room" that adjoined the cave, once blackened with soot, were covered with a red, white, and blue striped tarp, and wooden cupboards had been installed. Burning precious wood was no longer permitted by the government, so Ani now squatted next to the burners of a propane stove and heated water, stirring powdered milk into the tea and adding plenty of sugar. She poured the tea into porcelain cups and placed them in front of us with much encouragement to drink.

I took my cues from Lama Tsultrim, who sat quietly, asking about her health and getting reacquainted. I practiced patience, the custom in Sherpa culture being to respectfully wait before jumping in with too many enthusiastic questions. I offered her a white khata scarf of respect and a full-length, burgundy down coat, a gift from my friend Linda Wylie who knew Ani in years past. She accepted these with much embarrassment. Then I brought out a booklet of photographs from all the Earth Treasure Vase pilgrimages I had made for her to see how far and wide the practice had gone since I received it from her father. She held the book with care, turning the pages slowly to look at every page, asking questions for Lama Tsultrim to translate, and expressing her happiness as she took it all in.

Finally, we let her know we had brought an Earth Treasure Vase with us and hoped she would accept it and allow us to bury it there at Charok with her. She asked me to bring it to her. I ran down to my tent and then back up, huffing and puffing from the altitude, and found her and the group in the gompa—a little room next to the kitchen that was her temple with walls covered in paintings of the peaceful and wrathful deities of the bardo. We stood in front of the altar as she unwrapped the beautiful container studded with turquoise and lined with copper, handcrafted by sangha member Juan Handelin back home. Then, opening it together, we brought out the treasure vase nestled inside. Ani humbly accepted the vase and set it on the shrine for safekeeping. She explained that she would need to consult with her nephew, who was the lama now, about when and where the vase was to be accomplished. We learned he was away overseeing ceremonies in a nearby village but would return soon.

While the vase took up residence on her altar, she invited us to climb the stairs to see another little room. On my previous visit, this had been the outdoor veranda where I met with Charok Rinpoche and asked him my question. Now this was an enclosed bedroom and her personal practice space. One by one we filed in to see the thin pallet she slept on with only a heavy, burgundy, cape-like coat lined with sheepskin fur to keep her warm. The main feature of this room was the jeweled silver stupa that contained the relics of her father. Standing about three feet tall, it was housed behind a glass case with other statues and sacred objects where it could be venerated safely. We quietly made our way past Ani's bed-seat on the floor, then bowed in front of the altar and touched our foreheads to the stupa with respect.

The next morning, we learned that her nephew, Lama Tenzin, had returned. He and Ani had done a divination and determined that the best time to bury the Earth Treasure Vase was that very day at 10:00 a.m.—we had one hour to prepare! At the appointed time, we found Ani and Lama Tenzin waiting for us in the kitchen. The young boy I met thirty years ago had matured into a tall, handsome young man, who—through Ani's training—held responsibility for all the ceremonies. I was sad to see that even though she was the highly accomplished elder, she deferred to him in every way, making it clear that her status as a woman made her secondary to a male lama.

Lama Tenzin greeted us with smiles. Then, showing the greatest respect for Ani Pema, he took charge of the ceremony. Ani crouched on her little stoop next to the stove, just as she had thirty years before, while Lama Tenzin carried out the puja for the vase according to tradition. When it was time to open the vase and make our final offerings, I gave it to Ani to hold while I made each of the many offerings of earth I had collected from treasure vase locations around the world, naming each location for Lama Tsultrim to translate. When I finished with these and the other precious offerings I had brought, each member of the group came forward to make their own offerings and prayers. The final offering was from my friend Ginny McGinn, who solemnly placed a small red coral figure of a goddess on the very top of the other offerings as she called upon the power of the sacred feminine to realize all of our prayers for the Earth. I watched Ani's face break into a wide grin when she understood what Ginny—and we all—were praying for. She nodded excitedly.

With that, we closed the vase with the cork and sealed it forever. Ani laid the five colored silks one by one over the top and tied the cords securely around the neck of the vase. I gave her a stick of golden sealing wax to drip onto the cords while I held the vase and she stamped the wax. Then we placed the vase, wrapped in khatas, inside Juan's beautiful wooden container. Ani picked up the flag of the Earth that I had carried with me as an altar cloth all around the world, now quite threadbare—and wrapped the container in it. Then, with a nod of her head, she let us know it was time to go outside.

Everyone carried something for the burial: shovel, pickax, bells, rice and dried flowers, fresh juniper and a little burner, and a tray of cookies and fruit that Ani had prepared. As we made our way in a long procession out of the cave, suddenly Ani and Tenzin stopped to point out, just above us on the path ahead, two splendid wild mountain goats (Himalayan tahr) standing like sentinels in the very spot we were going to bury the vase! They stood perfectly still watching us approach, their long, silky brown fur shining in the midday sun. As we got closer, they turned and slowly walked on, gently indicating we could follow. For a Capricorn like me, this was a pretty good sign.

We gathered in a small clearing at the base of the rock wall that stretched down to the cave's entrance far below. Lama Tenzin and Lama Tsultrim stood together chanting invocations and prayers to the local deities and verses of the traditional Earth Treasure Vase burial ritual. Ani stood to the side and behind the two lamas, listening attentively. When the time came, Lama Tsultrim asked his daughter, Sonam, the youngest person in our group who still had both her parents, to break ground. Sonam, a strikingly beautiful young woman, and her brother Jigme were visiting Charok for the first time. Jigme was an enjoyable traveling companion and charming host with a wide smile who helped us have fun, and Sonam brought with her a quiet appreciation of our shared experience and an inherent kindness toward everyone. She stepped toward the rock face that towered above us on the grassy knoll where we stood. We expected Sonam to have to break through hard ground, but the dirt was soft and welcoming. Everyone took turns digging the hole, then Sonam lowered the vase into the Earth. On top of the vase, we tossed dried rose petals and lavender I had brought from my garden, and with the smoke of the burning juniper wafting around us, we covered the little vase up for good, with bells ringing. The deed was done, the circle complete. Charok had entered the mandala now.

That afternoon, I found myself up on an enormous boulder, looking down on the hermitage, reflecting on what a rare and precious place it is—and Ani, a rare and precious being in this world.

The Earth Treasure Vase, embedded in this holy land, would absorb what was here and contribute it into the global mandala. Like Tolu Gompa, Charok, too, felt like my spiritual home—the place where I had received the most important teaching of my life from an old wise man on the other side of the veil, who bestowed unfathomable riches upon me that had borne such great fruit. Lama Tsultrim joined me on that big rock along with Jigme and Sonam. Being there together with their papa and seeing this cave where his root teacher and his spiritual sister, Ani Pema, lived in retreat was a special moment in their lives as a family. Lama Tsultrim was emotional as he told me that Ani had instructed him to return to live at Tolu Gompa, to claim his seat and take responsibility for passing on what her father had transmitted to him.

The shadows grew long, and I went to sit on the stoop of Ani's doorway, hoping she would emerge and we could have a little private time together. I was reviewing my photos when she came out and sat down with me, interested to see images of Tolu Gompa. We sprawled out like girls, side by side on our tummies, to look together at the little screen. Suddenly, the last image appeared—of me in the lama hat, sitting next to Lama Tsultrim inside of Tolu Gompa after the enthronement. I did not know if Lama had told her yet and worried maybe she would disapprove. But she exclaimed, "Oh, you look good!" and we laughed and laughed. Then she invited me and Lama Tsultrim, who had joined us, inside and served us warm potatoes that we peeled with our fingers and dipped in a hot chile cheese sauce—my favorite—as Lama Tsultrim explained how he had made me a lama. Then he requested Ani to transmit the lung (oral transmission) for the lineage to me.

At first she deferred, saying that the young Lama Tenzin would do it. But I told her I felt a connection to her and to please bless me herself with this honor, so she went ahead. Lama and I knelt on the floor in front of her, side by side with heads bowed and palms joined, as she read the lung for the Konchok Chidu lineage teachings. I had the profound sensation that she was pouring the transmission into me, from one vessel to another, just as it is said in the old texts. But now I was experiencing it firsthand, and I wept.

Afterwards, drinking tea, Lama gave Ani an updated version of the list of lineage masters that included the names of her father and his father, which could only be added after their passing. He had thoughtfully prepared this knowing he was coming to see her. He then requested her to transmit the lung for the lineage masters to me as well. Again, we bowed and knelt down side by side in front of her as she read the names of all the lamas I was spiritually connected to now. Emotion welled up in me again as she placed the pecha (written text) on my head at the end.

As she brought the ceremony to a close, I asked her if she would bless my mala (prayer beads used for reciting mantras). She nodded and invited me to come near. I sat at her feet, and as she held my mala in her lap, she showed me how to put my hand right behind hers, following her fingers in moving the beads while we both recited the mantra *Om Mani Padme Hung*. She told me to imagine myself as Chenrezig, the Bodhisattva of Compassion, as we did the mantra together circling the 108 beads all the way around. It was a deeply intimate moment, to be so close, with me almost in her lap now, breathing her breath as we recited the mantra together, moving the beads in unison. I realized this was the real enthronement: my spiritual empowerment as a lama was passed to me by Ani Pema Chodron, like nectar being poured from her vessel into mine, with Lama Tsultrim by my side.

• • •

Finally, I knew it was time to bring the practice of Mother Gaia forth. What better circumstance would I have to share this with my fellow pilgrims than in the very place where my path of service to the Earth was born? For some years, I had worked privately with the Gaia Sadhana, all the while feeling that she was needed in the world, but worried I would be criticized by the lineage masters for adapting the famous terma of Chokgyur Lingpa into a practice of Gaia. Several lamas, including Lama Tsultrim, told me to keep it to myself and let it ripen. But for how long, I wondered? I let Lama Tsultrim know I would like to teach the Sadhana of the Sublime Mother Gaia to the group while we were there, and he consented.

In the morning, wrapped in a soft, fuzzy yak-wool blanket, I climbed up to the top of the huge boulder overlooking Ani's cave below, surrounded by snow-covered peaks and fluttering prayer flags. The group made a loving circle and I brought my vision of Gaia out into the wider world.

It was my first teaching as a lama. I gave the transmission and shared my commentary, and then we practiced together. When we were done, the group sat hushed and wordless. The Sadhana of the Sublime Mother Gaia had been born. I was aware of the treasure vase nestled in the ground against the cliff nearby and the blessing of that place entering the global mandala.

The cave at Charok is found among the highest mountains in the world, where yeti are real (Lama Tenzin told us he had heard them many times), where clouds part to reveal the presence of mountain goddesses, where rhododendron trees bloom tall and the rare danfe bird entertains, where snow leopards appear every winter (Lama Tenzin showed us pictures of them he had taken on his phone), where fragrant incense is made from the medicinal plants growing on the hills, and where, in spring, the wild irises poke up their stubby purple flowers to greet the world anew. I prayed this place would remain protected and unspoiled. It is a Pure Land.

• • •

Our time was flying by and we were to leave the next morning. I wanted to ask Ani to pray for us. To tell her how our world is coming apart, how there is unprecedented climate change, war, and social injustice. I wanted to tell her that women are still struggling for equality but are rising now to bring more balance to our world with their leadership. And I wanted her to know that many of us are seeing the possibility of a collective awakening, because we know it is going to take all of us to bring about the changes that are needed. I yearned for advice from the old woman in the cave, to hear some words of wisdom to take back to our lives far away from this protected refuge that, according to prophecy, will be a safe haven in times to come.

I imagine that if we had stayed with Ani for weeks or months, she might have given us a teaching or some advice to take home. But in our short stay, this did not emerge. Instead, she served us tea and more tea as she stood on the edges, always a little behind the lamas, ready to jump into service at any time. And although she is a profoundly accomplished practitioner, she does not see herself as a teacher. Just a lowly woman in service to her lineage lamas doing her best to dutifully practice day and night, undisturbed her whole life long. Her humility was a sign of realization, of course. But there was no life-changing teaching to us from her. She did not talk about the teachings; she simply lived them.

Upon our departure, Ani Pema offered each of us her blessing, placing a white khata around our necks. We left her and the Earth Treasure Vase there, the latter buried high above her hermitage, and walked toward Thame Monastery, Charok Rinpoche's birthplace. I hoped Ani would remember our prayers were with her, too.

• • •

I always yearn to stay forever in the remote places I have been. Maybe someday I will. But, after enjoying the lama dances of the Mani Rimdu festival as a celebration of our time in Nepal, it was time to leave this magic land behind the veil and return to the world of dust. Departing Thame, the trail wound through freshly planted fields budding green. We trekked through forests of gnarled old red, pink, and yellow rhododendron trees and passed under elaborately painted gates with prayer wheels to be spun. Above us, the towering mountain goddesses poked up through the clouds.

On the last night of our trek, I dreamed of two circles around two wellsprings, one larger and one smaller, with prayer flags of the five colors around all the edges. The small one was very private and personal, and the larger one was public. They were for me to draw from in different ways, but the smaller one was just for me. It was very sacred. I kept returning to these springs all night long.

The next day, the rains came. Most of the group left early to walk the final leg of the journey with Lama Tsultrim and make sure we had seats on the plane back to Kathmandu. But on this misty morning, I walked alone, slowly, contemplating what had happened to bring my global healing journey full circle. I was still wrestling with my conflicted feelings about being made a lineage lama when Gaia was calling to me now.

And then, my ankle turned on a slippery rock. Suddenly I lost my balance and went over the edge of the mountainside. It was a sheer, steep drop-off, and the moment I fell I left my body. As I was tumbling head over heels down the slippery slope, I momentarily returned to consciousness, realized what was happening, and told myself, Cynthia, you are falling head over heels down the mountain, and there is nothing to stop you. I was acutely aware that it was several thousand feet straight down to the raging river and boulder-strewn canyon far below, and I left my body again.

An eternity seemed to pass when suddenly I came to an abrupt stop. I opened my eyes and found myself spread-eagled, backpack on my head, water bottles and trekking poles strewn here and there, but alive. I had no idea how I could have come to such a sudden stop. There was nothing but slippery wet grass on the steep mountainside in every direction. I checked my body and found no major injuries. A little banged up but not paralyzed and no broken bones. *Alive.*

I tried to stand up but was shaking. The terrain was so terribly steep and slippery I could not find firm ground to stand on. A wave of panic passed through me. I could not get a foothold and was deathly afraid that if I tried to move, I would slip and fall again, and then it really would be the end. I looked up to see the edge of the trail a hundred feet straight up. I had no idea how I was to get from here to there. The only thing to do was to start calling for help as I wondered if I would ever be heard and looked up into empty space.

A few minutes later, a head poked over the edge and looked down at me. "Help! Please help me!" I yelled. A man appeared and disappeared. Then he threw me a rope with a hefty rock tied on its end. Amazed, I grabbed it! I hung to it like a fish on a line, trying to get a foothold or pull myself up. But there was no traction, and I could not see how to maneuver myself to get up to the trail. The Sherpa porter who heard my call handed off the rope to his friend and somehow managed to climb down that steep slope to, miraculously, position himself under me and push me up the hill. In a shocked daze, I oriented toward one small, craggy tree root sticking out of the mud above me. From there I crawled up to the trail, where, on level ground, I could stand.

My leg was injured, but I had to walk another two hours to meet the group and hopefully make the last plane out of Lukla. I had no idea how much time had passed and if the three members of the group who were behind me had passed me by now or were still behind. I hugged my savior and thanked him profusely and took off in a total state of shock fueled by adrenaline. Twenty minutes later, my three companions came running up from behind, having heard what had happened from the man with the rope.

Lenya Reese, who is my doctor at home, was in this group of three, and in that moment I could not have been more grateful that she had decided to join this trek. She nursed my wounds and patched me up. Our trusty guide, Bijay, took my backpack and held me by the hand, placing himself between me and the edge of the trail for the rest of the way, apologizing over and over for letting me walk alone, for not being there with me. I have no idea how I made it but for the combination of their loving care and my adrenaline.

When we finally stumbled into Lukla to find the rest of our group, another round of shock swept over me. Lenya cleaned my wound again, cut off a deep layer of skin, and bandaged me up all over. My leg was starting to swell, and the pain I had not let myself feel before was setting in. Lama Tsultrim kept repeating the words "You are lucky to be alive," telling me that people fall off those mountain trails more often than you might think and that many don't come back.

He was convinced Tara had come to my aide. Surely, he said, it had to be divine intervention that saved me.

But I had not seen Tara in that moment. I relived my fall over and over, as it did seem that *something* had intervened, and kept asking myself, What stopped me? How is it that I am still alive? These thoughts echoed through me day and night, along with the disturbing realization that, literally, I had *fallen off the path.* What did it mean? Symbolically, the "Path" is all-important in the dharma teachings. Once you have found the Way, you stay on the Path. But I had fallen off it. I felt like an addict falling off the wagon or some sort of fallen-away angel, and I was filled with shame.

Back in Kathmandu, I hobbled downstairs for dinner and discovered a special seat waiting for me in the dining room, where the group had gathered, a pointed red hat resting on the chair. Lama Tsultrim stood by with a sly grin on his face, as a smiling Lama Thondrup grabbed a red tablecloth off the next table, draped it over my shoulder like a shawl, and placed the hat on my head. In this way, my enthronement continued. But I was hurting and did not feel like laughing.

The next day, as I was trying my best to circumambulate the Great Stupa of Boudhanath for the last time, Lama Thondrup appeared to escort me back to the hotel with my own proper lama's shawl under his arm. I was taken to my room, where the final ceremony of my enthronement took place. Lama Thondrup arranged me in a large chair and draped a brocade dress over my shoulders and lap. He covered the table in front of me with more brocade and set the ritual implements of a lama—a bell and dorje, and a small two-sided drum called a damaru—in front of my seat. Then he put a headdress of black hair with a tall topknot on my head, and, over that, the crown of the dakini was tied into place. Brocade tails fell on either side of my face.

I was sweating and feeling foolish when Lama Tsultrim's wife, Ang Dawa, arrived with Ginny to celebrate the moment. Ang Dawa's gaze fell on me and a warm feeling passed between us. She came forward and presented me with a long white khata and an envelope filled with rupees, saying that she did not do this for show but because "I sincerely feel this is so right and you deserve it." When she stood back, I could see that, to her, even though my headgear was tilted and the brocades hanging down on either side of my face were lopsided, none of it seemed to matter. My appearance as a dakini moved her deeply. But Lama Tsultrim was not around. His absence from this final enthronement ritual seemed to underline the fact that I was on my own forging a new path. Maybe it was not so bad that he wasn't there as a higher authority to tell me what to do.

• • •

On our last night, after our farewell dinner, Ang Dawa shared some of her personal history. She told the group her mother had died when she was just over a year old, and she had been raised first by her grandmother and then by her mother's sister—her "twin mother." She revealed that her twin mother had been severely abused by a high lama because she could not give him a child to continue the lineage. Her twin mother had been given to this lama in an arranged marriage, without her consent, and to maintain their prestige, the family covered up the abuse. But Ang Dawa witnessed it firsthand, and at age fourteen she called a meeting with the local authorities to ensure the safety and security of her twin mother, according to the Indigenous ways and legal customs of her people. Thanks to Ang Dawa's intervention, the abuse was stopped.

Ang Dawa also revealed that when she was on her way to college at eighteen, she was promised in marriage to Lama Tsultrim by her uncles. She wanted only to continue her education in order to stand up against the class, gender, and ethnic discrimination she had suffered, so she ran away before the marriage ceremony. But she was followed, kidnapped, and forced into the marriage. Luckily, she said, her husband is a kind person, and they have three wonderful children together. But this was the beginning of Ang Dawa's advocacy for the rights of women and all human rights in Nepal. She went on to be elected to Parliament and the Constituent Assembly representing the Sherpa people, and has dedicated her life to serving women and girls and reforming the laws that allow for these abuses to continue in Nepal.

Ang Dawa's stories revealed the kinds of things I had suspected were hidden in the shadows. Deeply shaken by my near-death experience, I struggled to reconcile the issues of abuse within the guru system and on what terms I was to accept being made a lama. In spite of it all, I felt a sense of belonging to that land and was deeply moved to have received Lama Tsultrim's recognition as a lama at Tolu Gompa and Ani's blessing and transmission in the cave at Charok. But what haunted me was the sense that something had saved me on that mountainside when I fell off the path.

Finally, Lama Tsultrim came to say goodbye. We sat down and I poured him some tea. I sensed he, too, was troubled. I knew he was concerned about fulfilling Ani's instructions to return to Tolu Gompa to serve as resident lama and lineage holder. And I was worried I could not fulfill the role of a lama. I noticed that in some ways we were both caught by the system we loved. I worked up my courage to ask him directly about the inequality and continuing abuse of women within the Vajrayana. He responded like other lamas before him when asked these questions, saying, "It is only through the blessings of the lineage masters that the path of liberation is available to us. And if we judge or criticize our teachers, we cut ourselves off from the possibility of enlightenment." He added, "The great masters are free, Cynthia. Their view is like the sky, unconditioned and vast. Do not be attached to what happens on a relative level because on the absolute level, there is no problem. There is no difference between the capacity of men and women. Do not allow yourself to get caught by your negative criticism, and remember that there have always been great female practitioners in the dharma."

I heard his words as if in a dream. I felt my love for him and my gratitude to have been steeped in the teachings, but my heart sank as I dropped into a deep well of silence. Though I had wished for a different response, I had expected him to express this traditional view. There was no possibility of any further conversation. He was asking me to believe in something I could no longer trust. I knew I was going to have to find my own way to new ground. I saw how I had been caught—not by my criticism—but by deferring to an external authority I wanted to believe was omniscient. Devotion is one way to open the door to spiritual awakening, but when a spiritual belief system demands blind faith, it is dangerous. In these times, for collective awakening to flower, healing is called for within the power structure of the Vajrayana system itself. I had literally fallen off the path struggling to come to terms with these issues.

• • •

Back home, it took weeks to recover from the painful fall. Over and over I found myself back on the side of the mountain, glued to the ground, frozen. It was a miracle I survived. Still shaking in my bones, I would ask, *What stopped me?*

Then one day, in a flash that rippled through my whole body, the answer dawned: it was the *Earth* who caught me! It wasn't some beautiful, imagined deity or lineage master, but Gaia who grabbed me to Her. I could still feel myself pressed to Her side, held ever so tightly. There on that precipitous mountainside covered in shiny grass, She had my back. "I've got you," She seemed to say. "You are not going down that mountain. Not yet."

The moment this became clear, I felt reborn. My search for an enlightened teacher or mystical deity was *really* over. It had always only been Her. The ground beneath my feet. The deeply rooted tree at my back. The rhododendrons and the roses.

I *had* fallen off that old path. And *She* caught me. I had landed within the safe embrace of the Earth, my true source of refuge and the greatest expression of the teachings and catalyst for awakening I could ever hope to find.

On the last day of our pilgrimage, a final lesson was needed. I still had not gotten the message, and "Lama Cynthia" needed a wake-up call. It took a near-fatal fall from grace for me to realize my own true path in this life.

I am simply head over heels in love with life on Earth.

CHAPTER TWENTY-FIVE

BUDDHA GOTAMI

Returning from Nepal, I could feel Ani Pema Chodron's singular presence in her cave, free from the relative world most of us inhabit, contributing her peace to the world, and praying for all beings. Knowing she is there is a great support to me. And the still-palpable magic behind the veil in those high mountains is a blessing for the world to protect and keep alive.

And yet, I understood that places like Tolu Gompa need to be opened up to the light of a new day. This is a place where the wisdom of an ancient and authentic lineage could be brought *forward* to model a thriving community living in harmony with the Earth and shining the light of bodhicitta into the world for the benefit of future beings.

I also knew I had to keep finding my own way through the old system to new ground. I reminded myself that the Great Mystery often hides in darkness, and the seeds that germinate to bring forth new life do so in Earth's dark soil.

I could feel the Ancestors accompanying me, saying, "As long as abuse exists, full liberation is not possible. The gap between this world of samsara and the rarefied air of the deities and gurus must be bridged. Our awakening today needs to unite the worlds of relative and absolute truth in the understanding that there is not one without the other. We cannot close our eyes before suffering. Not anymore."

The path I am following now is aligned with a new turning of the dharma wheel. Today, our practice must include the trees and the rivers and address the greed of the few along with the starving of the many. To truly serve all beings, our spiritual lineages must embrace and empower women, the Indigenous, and people of color worldwide. Those who have carried the burden of injustice in connection to Mother Earth for so long can no longer be ignored. If we are to have any hope of a collective awakening, all of the hierarchical systems that hold power over others need to be recognized as the very systems that are destroying the planet.

With Gaia at my back, I felt supported to consider the old stories in new ways. Given that these times are vastly different from the time of the historical Buddha Shakyamuni, Siddhartha Gotama, I found myself reimagining the story of the historical Buddha. How might the Buddha appear today?

I was taken by surprise when it struck me that I could imagine the historical Buddha as a woman. Not that the Buddha *was* or *should be* a woman, but that as a woman myself, I could *imagine* him and the way his teachings were transmitted in a new way—a way I could identify with, that breaks through the hierarchy and brings us down to Earth. I was not fantasizing about what *could* be but simply imagining that *a woman could embody the same qualities and accomplishments as the historical Buddha.* This made the Buddha's realization seem personally attainable. It was liberating to imagine his person in a feminine form.

With this new imagining, I felt radically empowered to claim my own experiences on the path of awakening as valid. It had never occurred to me that I had a choice in how I identified with the Buddha. I was well trained to never question authority. Like so many women around the world, even those who are independent or rebellious, I have been conditioned to be subservient.[1]

This shift in perspective woke me up. Giving her a name—Buddha Gotami[2]—brought a renewed sense of joy and excitement to my relationship to the dharma. Just this was enough to shift the whole landscape. And so here is a new version of this famous story.

• • •

There was once a woman named Lady Gotami of the Shakya clan. She was a beautiful young woman, privileged with every comfort, but she knew, somewhere deep inside, this was not all there was to life. She went through the motions of fulfilling her duty as a daughter, then as a wife and, soon after marriage, a mother. She tried hard to be good and tell herself she was happy. But her dissatisfaction grew, and she wondered what lay beyond the walls of her insulated life.

It was unheard of in those days for a woman to go out unescorted, but one day she slipped out beyond the protection of her home and family to explore the wider world. She was shocked by the many things she saw in her brief outing, but what affected her most strongly was coming face-to-face with suffering. She had never known such terrible things existed. For the first time, she saw poverty and disease. She encountered old age and even looked death in the eyes. And when she returned to the safety and comfort of home, she was not the same. She felt uncomfortable with having so much when others had so little. In light of such profound suffering and inevitable death, she could not understand the purpose of life. She realized she must seek an understanding about the human condition, and she knew she would not find the answers to her questions at home.

Gotami pondered her predicament long and hard—it took courage to consider leaving her family behind. Each time on her brief ventures out, she saw what a limited view her sheltered life was giving her. She worried she would get caught, but she knew she had to break free. Finally, one night she took off her earrings and removed her necklaces, bangles, anklets, and hair ornaments. She stepped out of her beautifully embroidered silken dress and picked up a used cotton sari cast off by one of the servants. Then, taking a last look in her mirror, she combed her hair, tied it back in a simple braid, and covered her head with a shawl. She wrote:

> *Dearest Rahula, my beloved son, I am so sorry to leave you and your father while you are still so young. But I must go now and answer a call deep in my heart to seek the truth of this precious human life. I do this not just for myself but also for you, so that I might become a better mother to you, my love. You will be deeply adored and well taken care of by your grandmother and grandfather, and by your kind and generous father. Please take care of each other and know that I love you with all my heart. I promise, one day I will come back for you.*

She left the note along with her wedding ring on her pillow and turned away. Gotami went quietly through the familiar darkened halls to the stable where her trusted horse waited. She rode as far as she could before releasing her horse, confident he could still find his way back home without her. She continued on foot.

Gotami wandered from place to place for a number of years. She carried a small bag across her shoulder for provisions and mostly slept on the ground. Everywhere she went she asked, "Who is the wisest person in the region I can study with?" After years of study and practice, she became quite learned and even experienced some valuable insights from her many teachers, but still, she knew there was more. Finally, on the brink of starvation from extreme renunciation and deeply exhausted, she collapsed under a tree by a river and stopped. When she opened her eyes, she did not know how long she had been there. A young shepherd girl had brought Gotami some fresh yogurt, and she held out a cup of water and wiped her brow. Gotami's head had been laid on a pillow the girl had made for her from tall, soft grass.

Gotami looked up and noticed the leaves of the tree shading her were shaped like hearts, and a gentle breeze was cooling her fever. It took her many days to revive and for her skin and bones to fill out once again. Every day she bathed in the river and her new friend brought her a simple meal. Nourished by the food and the flowing river, her strength returned, and one day she knew it was time to sit up at the base of that beautiful tree and settle her mind. She took a few deep breaths—and looked deeply into her heart.

Slowly, Gotami saw what she had not been able to see before. She breathed into the moment and felt a kind of clarity arising within her. As she continued to breathe, connecting her body and mind and relaxing deeply, she began to see the interdependent nature of all that is. Gotami perceived the arising and falling away of phenomena and understood how our attachment to a sense of self creates the causes for our suffering and the endless round of birth and death. Her own sense of self fell away as an infinite spaciousness dawned—and "Gotami" was no more. She recognized her habit of grasping at what was familiar as everything dissolved into light, and then she let go—and a Buddha was born.

Buddha Gotami rested in this state of awareness free from all concepts, a state as vast as the universe. Time fell away . . . and when the morning star caught her eye, she realized the Great Perfection of all that is. In that moment, she experienced her own nature of heart and mind mirrored perfectly by the Earth, the stars, and the interdependent web of life. She reached out and touched the ground she sat upon, summoning the Earth to witness her enlightenment.

Then an overwhelming compassion welled up in her, and she saw a path leading from suffering to liberation through awareness. Gotami had seen into the interconnected web of life—it was vast beyond conception, empty of a separately existing self. She had understood her part of the whole and how to live in a harmonious relationship with the Earth and all beings. And she saw a path of living in awareness free from suffering. She saw that this path of liberation had the qualities of gentleness, of nonharming, of loving kindness, and of caring and compassion, and that it was filled with a radiant light of joy that led to equanimity and peace.

Touching the Earth steadied her and grounded her awareness in the power of the moment. She had Awakened. She had seen the Way—a Way free from extremes and intimately connected to all that is. She knew she was Home—and she touched the ground to call upon this Earth, the Maha Bodhisattva, the greatest of Awakened

Beings and Mother of All, to recognize and support her breakthrough to freedom as only She could do.

Gotami sat with this awareness for days as it flooded through her being. She walked, gently touching the Earth with each step, breathing in and out, inviting this new understanding to penetrate her being. With each passing day, more and more was revealed to her about the path ahead and how to live and cultivate what she had seen.

Finally, she became aware of her son and knew she had arrived at a liberating vision that she could pass on to him, for she had never forgotten her promise. She had also left behind many wonderful friends that she had made during her years of searching, and she wanted nothing more than to find them and tell them about the noble path of liberation and awakening she had discovered.

As she touched the Earth again and again, she knew unshakably that her discovery was not only hers but was available to everyone—that Buddhahood is within us all and can be lived with every breath and each step.

She hugged her young friend and said goodbye, setting out once again, strong and fearless, having faced the truth and liberated herself from the bondage of self-clinging. When Gotami found her friends, she invited them into a circle to sit with her so she might share what she had seen. They immediately recognized she was not the same person they had known before—she was transformed. As they listened to what she shared, they recognized the path of awakening for themselves—and so began the life of the Awakened One, Buddha. Her teachings became known as the Dharma, and the community around her, or Sangha, was born. That little circle of friends accompanied Buddha Gotami to reunite with her family, and everywhere she went she invited people to come around in a circle and hear the teachings she shared, and soon enough, her spiritual friends offered the teachings as well. She invited everyone to practice so that they, too, could liberate themselves in this very life. Eventually a large community grew up around her, and for forty-five years she openly shared her understanding until she passed away at eighty, having served countless beings to find the path of awakening.

• • •

Through her many years of practicing meditation, Gotami had developed the capacity to witness her own experience, and when her awakening came, she knew she was an intimate part of the whole Earth: the trees, the stones and grasses, the clouds and stars, the animals and birds, and her young friend who brought her food. In that moment, when she was struggling to release the last shred of her attachment to a sense of self, Gotami reached out and touched the ground beneath her. She called upon Mother Earth, summoning the vastness of the entire web of life to support her. In so doing, her gesture of touching the Earth to witness her realization brought an unshakable and uncontestable confirmation. Gotami's awareness of interbeing became conscious in her own embodied experience.

And when that timeless moment passed, as all things do, and she returned to everyday awareness once again, she was sitting on the Earth, with a river flowing nearby, leaves rustling in the trees overhead and the morning star twinkling in the sky. She had come home to the ground of her being, her own true nature in a precious human life on Earth.

Soon after her awakening, Gotami sought out her friends, her family, and most importantly, her son. She was committed to integrating them all into her life and practice community. She had become a Buddha, but she was also still Gotami, a woman and a mother. She had no desire to renounce her family or her family name, but rather to bring her newfound awareness to bear on her worldly life while also practicing to sustain a vast view of the perfection of wisdom. As the path evolved in response to her teachings, she did not separate these aspects of her life; she simply embraced all with loving kindness and compassion.

Drawing deeply from this story today, whether we identify with Shakyamuni Buddha or Lady Gotami, we, too, can claim our birthright as a Buddha-to-be. And like the Buddha, we can summon the Earth into our lives as an ally. When we take our seat upon the lap of Mother Earth, we become aware of our participation in the process of creation. The Buddha understood this—all Buddhas do. This great story—the only story of spiritual awakening in which the central figure invokes the Earth as a witness to their enlightenment—shows us that the ground of our being, where enlightenment happens, is the Earth Herself.

In ancient India, the Earth Goddess Prithvi supported and witnessed Gotama/Gotami's awakening. Incredibly, Prithvi was seen holding a treasure vessel into which she received offerings to restore balance and harmony, bring abundance and fruitfulness, and set all things right on Earth. Prithvi not only offered her riches, but also her lap, that we may find our seat at home in the womb of creation.

• • •

I, too, summoned the Earth in the outback of Australia. My motivation in touching the Earth was not (sorry to say) to witness my enlightenment. Rather, I wanted to invite Her to witness that final Earth Treasure Vase offering and receive it. I wanted to make our relationship conscious and let Her know of my undying effort to serve the healing and protection of the Earth. When I did, I found myself in a state of fathomless peace, hushed and humbled by the immensity of the view I was granted, looking into the heart-mind of Mother Earth as She responded to my summons and received our offering.

And when I realized She had arrived, I saw She had always been there. And then I saw it was actually I who had been summoned all those years ago; for surely, She recognized me as a vessel in service to Her and called on me to carry out our relationship of interbeing and reciprocity. My summoning of Her was a response to Her summoning me! And for a whisper of time, "I" was no more. There remained only the gesture of response and the responsiveness, in an act that extends forever then falls away as the summons arises once again. The offering, the one who offers, and the recipient, inseparable within the mandala of life unfolding.

CHAPTER TWENTY-SIX

THE ORACLE'S MESSAGE

It has taken me a lifetime, but I have learned to stand up. My journey has gone from taking refuge in the Earth to calling on Tara for help, to imagining Buddha Gotami, to forming a living relationship with Gaia. I am anchoring myself in a new location now, a new node on the mandala. Here, at this new node, the path is changing direction as the sources of spiritual guidance and refuge shift from an external masculine authority to an internal feminine knowing.

I am no longer conflicted about becoming a lama. I hold it as an honorary title. Lama Ngawang Tsultrim recognized me for my dedication to the Earth and for carrying out the practice of the Earth Treasure Vases, given to me by his teacher, Charok Rinpoche. But I am not trained as a lama in the Konchok Chidu lineage teachings, and I know I will not be able to uphold the tradition as expected. I honor a nonhierarchical spiritual path now, informed by many cultural traditions from around the world.

As I attempted to come to terms with my long journey, I realized that as a Western woman, to be whole, I needed to understand the roots of the culture that has conditioned me. There are two primary sources—the Judeo-Christian Old Testament and the ancient Greek myths. Both these traditions capture deep truths that we have unconsciously carried for millennia and form the basis of Western civilization. For me, the place to start looking was within the Greek myth of Gaia.

• • •

It is said that the original homeland of Gaia was in Delphi. Long before the reign of the gods of Olympus—who established their power through manipulation, rape, and war—a sisterhood of priestesses could be found living there in service to the Earth.

The myth tells us that in the beginning there was only the primordial darkness of the void. This vast space was the womb of all creation. And out of this chaos, energy and matter separated and the Earth took form—Gaia was born. Her yearning for another gave birth to Ouranos, the sky. They embraced and loved each other, and life on Earth began.

But Gaia did not only give birth to the beautiful web of life. The ugly and terrible also issued from her union with Ouranos. She loved all Her children equally, but when Ouranos discovered these awful children, he found them unacceptable. He was angered and repulsed. He rejected Gaia and split himself off from Her—unable to tolerate the dark, wild, and untamed beings she had borne. He wanted things to be different, to control the outcome, to have his way.

But Gaia was the Mother of All Creation: an Oracle, prophet, and truth-teller. The Great Mother's home on the slopes of Mount Parnassus quaked with Her contractions, activating intoxicating fumes that rose from the cracks and fissures of Her sacred ground, the "navel of the Earth." Here, Gaia's voice was heard by the priestesses who were devoted to Her. Above Her gaping chasms, they sat upon a tripod to absorb the mists rising from Her womb into their own wombic opening. Breathing Her vapors catalyzed their own clear seeing and truth-telling. This source of knowing was a wellspring of direct, embodied understanding that did not arise from the thinking mind.

Gaia was served well by Her priestesses. They took care of Her and the land they loved, and She provided them with everything they needed. Soon She gave birth to a large serpent, a cross between a snake and a dragon—sometimes male, sometimes female, and sometimes both, depending on which version of the story you are told. The names given to this serpent, whose purpose was to guard and protect their Mother, the Oracle, were Python and Delphyne.

To the ancients, Gaia's sanctuary in Delphi was the center of the world, and it was marked by a great stone, or Omphalos, to represent Her navel and Her connection to the primordial darkness within Her fertile womb. Like the lap of Prithvi where Buddha sat, Gaia's "navel" was where wisdom seekers came to commune with the Goddess for nearly two thousand years. Gaia's temple priestesses were called the Melissae, and the women serving as the Oracle became known as Pythia, after Mother Earth's serpent-child, guardian, and protector.

Many spiritual and shamanic traditions across the planet speak of the serpent. The energy of the snake represents the kundalini shakti that lives at the base of the spine, and which, through yogic practices, can awaken our own clear vision, healing powers, and inner wisdom. Additionally, the snake's capacity to shed its skin symbolizes transformation, and two coiled serpents reflect matter and spirit joined as one. In Mesoamerica we find the plumed serpent Quetzalcoatl and in Native American Pueblo culture there is Avanyu, a water serpent and guardian-protector who sustains life and brings needed change and transformation. In Aboriginal culture, the Rainbow Serpent bridges Heaven and Earth, opening a portal between dimensions.

All these serpents herald power and goodness, but from the patriarchal perspective, Gaia giving birth to a serpent was an abomination. The story they told was that Her temple at Delphi had been flooded and covered in slime, and the terrifying serpent threatened the land. So, Apollo, the god of light, decided it was his job to put things right. He may have intended to do good, but blinded by the power of his godliness, Apollo entered into battle with the Python and killed it, tossing its remains under the Omphalos stone at the navel of the world.

Having conquered the serpent, Apollo then seized Gaia's power and claimed the Oracle as his own. The god of light succeeded in destroying the living connection to the land and forcefully commanding the Oracle to speak for him. After that it was Apollo who became known as the great prophet and healer, not Gaia. Her sovereignty faded as order triumphed over chaos, light over darkness.

Apollo also fought with Eros, the god of love. To retaliate, Eros shot an arrow into Apollo's heart to make him obsessed with a beautiful young maiden named Daphne. But Eros also shot an arrow into Daphne's heart compelling her to reject Apollo. She wanted to be free, and the more Apollo lusted after her, the farther she ran from him. He chased her, trying to grab her, to have her for himself, and just as she was almost taken, she called on Gaia for help. Gaia's body opened to save Daphne, who was instantly turned into a laurel tree rooted deep in Earth's soil, crowned by beautiful branches reaching up to the sky. Her leaves became a potent medicine for the Pythia.

Artist and writer Catherine Brooks states, "What happens when the Primordial Mother is defeated by the solar hero? At Delphi, the space of contemplation and communion with the Great Goddess was covered by a monumental temple complex. Over time, the ritual offerings made by pilgrims changed from traditional honey cakes to excessive riches which packed numerous treasuries built below the temple. Large statuary donations of heroes and gods overflowed the streets and Delphi became a theater of faith, opulence, and power."[1]

Not unlike stories in the Old Testament, this myth, as told by the ancient Greeks, became a part of the canon of Western civilization—a story that grants permission to colonize Earth and celebrates violation, rape, and war. It is a story that normalizes harm and abuse of the feminine. Wild uncontrollable nature did not fit into the ideal of "civilization" that gods and men sought to create. By cutting off the dark feminine, attacking love, and raping the innocent, patriarchal culture has destroyed the Earth and dominated the Western world ever since.

But in Gaia's realm, time is not linear. Her power as an Oracle to speak the truth and reveal the past or future is not rational. And many of us are hearing Her message and feeling Her oracular energy in our own bodies. The coiled serpent, long dormant, is suddenly rising from our wombs to herald a new awakening. We know Gaia in our blood and bones. The memory of living in harmony resides in our DNA.

• • •

Like many women and men of European descent, I have distant ancestral memories of having been a healer and caring for my homeland. Just as there is intergenerational trauma and internalized oppression, there are also the memories of being vessels of healing and wisdom. We know that the separation of matter and spirit is not the way to wholeness. Father Sky and Mother Earth need each other for life to flourish in balance.

It was as if the Oracle was already speaking to me when it became clear that I needed to take an Earth Treasure Vase to Delphi and offer it to Gaia. The snake had to be resurrected and made whole, the Oracle brought to life again. After dedicating this treasure vase, many members of our Gaia Mandala community from around the world responded, and for months we gathered virtually to reflect on the healing that the vase for Delphi was awakening in us. We discovered how strongly this ancient story was alive in each of us as we faced the ways we are still living with the harm and abuse of the feminine encoded in this myth today. We read and wrote and made art. Our dreams began to speak to us as we became conscious of the mythic threads we were weaving into the vase—and into our own lives. Those who could not travel to Greece sent offerings, and when it was time for our pilgrimage group to depart, our "dreaming hive" held us firmly in its loving embrace.

• • •

Arriving in Athena's land, our group of fourteen women and one man was welcomed by Poliana Dimitropoulou on the Hill of the Muses overlooking the Acropolis. Dressed in dark green with slender, expressive hands and long auburn hair pulled off her sculpted face, Poliana introduced us to the traditional ways of approaching the sacred sites respectfully. She taught us hymns in ancient Greek and led us in ceremonial dance movements as a way to enact our intentions and offer them to the land. She showed us how to make offerings of olive oil and bread, milk and honey, seeds and wine, which she also fed to the Earth Treasure Vase as her blessing. We were moved when she let us know that the Ancient Greeks worked with vases as sacred objects within their ritual life as well.

Our next stop was the island of Naxos, where Ariadne was abandoned by Theseus after giving him the red thread to lead him out of the labyrinth on Crete. But there, she met Dionysus. Their union was fruitful, the island was fertile, and, unlike most of the other gods and goddesses of Olympus, they stayed together.

We invoked their presence, eating and drinking the fruits of that land and celebrating the divine sweetness they shared. We also visited the Temple of Demeter, on a wild hill overlooking the fields of wheat, grapes, and gnarled old olive orchards. We had already encountered Demeter and Persephone at Eleusis near Athens, and were ready to journey into the underworld as part of a renewal ceremony that would prepare us for Delphi. We wanted to meet the Oracle fresh and free of the worn-out old stories we carried that no longer served us—the stories we had inherited, the ones we had identified with over the course of our lives that held us back.

Early the next morning we made our way to the edge of the sea for a ceremony. The high winds had settled down overnight and the day dawned bright and clear. Dressed all in white, we made a quiet procession to the beach, walking down into a small bay held by two welcoming arms of land. Under the warm sun, beside the clearest turquoise water lapping at the shore, we formed a circle on the sand as if we were seated on Gaia's ample lap. Tenderly, we placed offerings in the center of our circle and poured libations onto the land. The honey, the olive oil, the wine. Some bread and seeds.

To bear witness to the pain we each held, we sat in pairs and listened to one another's stories. When this part of the ceremony was complete, we ritually cleansed each other by placing fragrant chamomile and rose, lavender and sage, damp from soaking in bowls of warm sea water, upon each other's wounds. Nikole Rosaria, our pilgrimage coleader, kept her drum beating while she lovingly sang to us until we all felt a budding sense of liberation. As for me, some deeply held issues were finally set free. I made my way into the sparkling water and was invigorated by a delicious tingling all over when I dove in and swam out to luxuriate in the blue-green, crystal-clear Aegean. I could've floated there for hours, supported by the sea's buoyant embrace. Back on shore, we savored the taste of juicy melon, ripe olives, bread, and fresh island cheese.

The next day, our vessels newly honed, we left the island, ready to meet Gaia and receive Her wisdom. We approached Delphi with heightened awareness. I sensed we all quietly yearned to receive a message from the Oracle. But like Tara, Gaia is within, not outside us as a separately existing entity or being. Her message would come from our own direct experience, and it was my hope that, walking the sacred lands of Delphi, we might claim our own oracular nature.

• • •

After resting for the night on Mount Parnassus, we made our way to Delphi. On the drive, I was suddenly alerted through a repetitive sensation on my cheek that something wanted to be known.

An energetic caress sent shivers through my body, and it happened again and again, as if a feather were tickling me. I knew I must pay attention.

In Delphi, our first stop was at the Castalian Spring. Once a large bathing pool amidst a lush grove, today the spring water runs from a spigot near the roadside. This is the water that the Pythia purified themselves with before entering the Oracle. Petitioners, often traveling from afar to seek the Oracle's wisdom, would also stop there to cleanse and prepare themselves. Our little band of pilgrims received the waters from the spring, entering even more fully into the moment we had anticipated for so long. My cheek still tingled.

Above the spring is the main Temple of Apollo where the site of the Oracle can be found perched on the steep hills. The whole temple complex stretches over a vast area of the mountainside; below the spring, on a grassy terrace surrounded by pines, olive trees, and rocky outcroppings, is the smaller temple to Athena Pronaia.

We walked slowly down the hill from the spring to the Temple of Athena Pronaia. I carried the Earth Treasure Vase in a bag across my chest—alert for whatever was trying to get my attention. In the shade of a spreading pine as the sun grew hot, our guide spoke about this lesser-known temple. After her introduction, we each wandered off to find our spot and enjoy our own experience in silence. With the vase in its bag on my lap, I sat looking directly at the ruins of the Tholos—a round temple structure with three tall pillars still intact.

Strong feelings swept over me as I gave my attention to this place. I knew nothing about the site prior to my arrival—but as I faced this small, round temple, untapped feelings surfaced and tears began to fall. I moved closer to sit next to the base of the circular temple.

A sign read: "The function of this building is still unknown; it was possibly associated with the cult of Mother Earth, the first divinity worshiped in the sanctuary."

I gazed at the stones, the three remaining columns that towered above me, and the remains of those that had fallen. Round temples were uncommon in ancient Greece. I felt so at home—the temple was only a little larger than my own round temple at home in Santa Fe. This place felt very familiar.

Looking through the fallen stones into the space in between, time fell away and I realized I was . . . *there. Then.* I saw myself walking up the steps rising around the circular platform, up to what would have been the main temple area. Tending the altar, sweeping the temple floor, gathering the offerings, preparing the ceremonies, conducting them: I had been doing this in the company of other women for a long time. We knew what to do to maintain balance and harmony and to commune with the Goddess Gaia. This was our job.

We conducted ourselves with much beauty and grace, flowing in and out of the seasons. A peaceful air was present as we enacted the rites and rituals we knew must be done and listened for Her instructions. Our knowledge arose from the Earth Herself, from the land we cultivated, and from our hearts, open and full of trust. I wept to touch these memories—for that is in fact what it felt like: I was remembering how it was.

But the tears were also grief-stricken. The longer I sat gazing across time, the more I became aware that what we knew then about how to live was eroding. I saw that changes had been put in motion to take power and control over the land, over Her, over us, and over the rites and rituals of our priestesshood. Our oracular nature was being used politically and we had to conform. I saw myself going through the motions to keep the balance alive, but I knew it was only a matter of time before this way of life would be lost. I understood viscerally the importance of what we did, and it broke my heart to realize these life-affirming ways were no longer respected. Our access to Gaia's wisdom was fading as the priests of Apollo told us what to do. I kept on enacting the old ways as if my life depended on it, as if all of our lives depended on it. Our ceremonies and offerings kept us in right relationship with the living Earth. By participating in Gaia's creative life force, we were perpetuating the wheel of life. The great flowering of culture in ancient Greece was testimony to this.

I was desperate to do what I could, while knowing there was no way to change the inevitable course of events that the gods were beginning to dictate through the men in power. Their ways were too much, too violent, too strong. There was nothing I could do except continue to go through the motions and try to keep our prayers alive for the sake of future generations in the hope that all would not be lost forever.

This swirling vision stretched across lifetimes as all sense of time vanished in a continuum of birth and death playing out over millennia. I could no longer see the temple in front of me, the intricately carved stone flowers and animals at the top of the towering pillars. The thick grass at my feet and the wildflowers poking out from the rocks all fell away. I was transported through a swirling tunnel, rushing through time as the memories accelerated. I saw men coming with their swords and, later, their guns. At first, gently and seductively. Later, they did not care. They took what they wanted and we suffered the consequences. I saw how I have been compelled, even possessed, to try my best to find a way to reconnect with this ancient source of peace. I realized I have been feeling my way in this lifetime, trying hard to remember what to do, lost in the folds of time, searching for a way to reestablish harmony with Mother Earth and repair the damage done since we lost our connection to Her—and to ourselves.

In rapid succession, I saw there were so many of my lifetimes when only tiny steps were made; in some, none at all, when other lessons needed to be learned. And then, in this lifetime, I found myself in a Himalayan cave with an old wise man, being given some holy vessels to bring as offerings to restore our relationship with Earth, an answer to my deepest prayer. Still, not remembering exactly what to do, I continued to feel my way, possessed by a desperate need to fulfill a vow I made way back then.

It was hard to breathe as this vortex of visions unfolded, and I did not feel the hot sun burning the skin on my arms. Past and present dissolved into a continuous thread, and I saw how I have always been trying to find a way back to what I knew in my heart, the coiled serpent of my DNA finally awakening in this life to fulfill my prayers. All the journeys and pilgrimages. The suffering and abuse. All the desperate cries for help, all the betrayals, the losses and the great loves, circling round and round with the ever-present commitment to keep going, to find my sisters and tenderhearted brothers, to form a global prayer, to make the offerings that will once again awaken Her in us and protect life.

My body was shaking as I gradually returned my focus to the temple ruins before me, the stone I sat on, the blue sky. I unwrapped the vase and opened it there. Holding it out I plucked some of the stubby chamomile growing at my feet and placed it into the vase along with some of that very earth. Suddenly a guard at the site marched over, shouting, "What is that you are holding? What are you doing?" Before the vase could be seized, I quickly put it back in its bag and wiped my tears. "It's nothing," I said, and moved away—the time clearly not yet ripe to allow such ceremonies to be conducted out in the open.

That afternoon, our group toured the rest of Delphi, but I felt little more arising except the confirmation of what had been done when the patriarchy took power and Apollo's rule was elevated above all else. The myth of his light brought great wealth to that land . . . and eventual ruin. The serpent was long gone, Gaia's voice swallowed in silence.

• • •

Our group stayed that night above Delphi on Mount Parnassus. The next morning, I walked up the path to the Corycian Cave with my trusted collaborator, Nikole, while the rest of the group stayed behind.[2] A practitioner of an oracular tradition that traces its roots back to the priestesses known as Melissae, Nikole has kept bees for many years. Through her Sicilian bloodlines, she is also a musician steeped in the Italian tarantellas, a drumming lineage that honors the Dionysian rhythms and rites along with many other Mediterranean wisdom streams. Nikole informed our group that the Corycian Cave was held sacred by the Melissae, and in ceremonies there, they listened to the ways of the bees, divining how to live in harmony with nature.

As we hiked up the path to the cave, we were listening too, and in Nikole's presence, I perceived the bees humming all around us, feeding on the nectar-rich pollen hanging off the branches of the bushes and abundant wildflowers. Gaia was dressed in a beautiful gown that day! Outside the opening of the cave, we buried our noses in the sweet grass and fragrant herbs that covered the ground like a soft blanket. We offered bread and honey and slowly entered Her holy womb. No guards here, only an opening as deep and wide as could birth and rebirth countless generations of ecstatic nymphs and singing bards, who have kept the memories alive to this day.

We explored Her caverns and caves, past huge phallic stalagmites rising up from the floor. The cave stretched back and in, deeper and deeper. We placed our foreheads under crevasses like perfect yonis opening into Her ever more deeply. Amid dripping moisture and slick damp Earth, far into the cave we found a still clear pool of water and crystalline walls sparkling in the light of our headlamps. Crawling on hands and knees, ducking under rock until we could go no farther, we settled ourselves and brought out the vase.

And then the realization dawned—we two were fulfilling the vow we had made back *then*, to bring this sacred offering to Her. Shivering, we felt the ripples going out across time. A state of awe enveloped us both and we knew with certainty we had arrived to fulfill this vow together. Gazing into Nikole's eyes, I dropped more and more fully into this new awareness, and in that moment it felt as if my cells were being rearranged around a new point of reference. Slowly, we made our way back outside to explore more of the area.

Later, returning to the group, we shared our delight in finding the perfect home on Mount Parnassus for the holy vessel to be planted. That night, with candles lit, we prepared the vase for its burial and everyone made their final offerings. While the group sang the Gaia mantra and Nikole played her drum, I took a needle and some red thread and we each sewed the severed parts of the serpent back together—represented by the slinky fabric I had brought that was once a skirt I wore in my younger years. We sealed the cork with beeswax and draped a piece of this "snakeskin" over the cork and tied it beautifully with the five colored cords. We then dripped golden sealing wax onto the cords and stamped them with a dragon. It was clear the vase wanted to be buried directly in the land, and now She was dressed for the occasion.

Fellow pilgrim Kat had brought with her a beautiful omphalos she had crafted with a fantastic blue-green snake wrapped around it. The next day, on the full moon, this was buried at the base of the hill, as protection for the vase, which found its own private place high up on the mountain. Before the burial, the group entered the cave, spiraling one by one into the center of the enormous central chamber. It felt as if a portal opened and access was granted. We invoked the mantra as we had so many times—*Om Gaia Mandala Siddhi Phala Bhrum Ah*—then sat or wandered in the body of the Earth Herself, quietly waiting like expectant mothers while a smaller group of us took the vase and placed it forever in Gaia's embrace.

Returning to the others, we were welcomed by the soft angelic sound of their chanting echoing in the cave. We shared warm hugs all around and then, as we absorbed the experience of our mission accomplished, we spontaneously erupted into songs of praise and ecstatic dancing.

Our outpouring complete, we shouldered our day packs and

made our way from the cool darkness of the damp cave towards the opening that let in the light. Once outside in the warm sun, we sat down on the blanket of soft green grass and brought out a picnic. Biting into our sandwiches, we suddenly heard the sound of buzzing bees and, looking up, right above the cave's entrance, we saw them. Nikole shouted, "It's a swarm! It's a swarm!" and excitedly told us that this meant a new Queen had just been born, and in the bright light of the warm sun, she was being ecstatically carried within the safety of the swarm to her new hive. We were witnessing the Queen's one and only day outside in the sunshine and fragrant land. Nikole reminded us that in ancient times, the Melissae would observe the behavior of a swarm as a form of divination, and where the swarm flew held meaning and answers. We knew Gaia was speaking to us then, as the large cluster of bees, buzzing loudly, transported their newly crowned Delphic Queen directly over our heads to her new home in the east.

• • •

A new dharma door opened for me that day. After planting the vase as our offering, it was as if the bee nymphs lifted the veil and showed us a way forward through the eastern gateway towards a new dawn, bringing us into alignment with the spirit of Gaia. The rituals of re-membering that our little circle of pilgrims conducted everywhere we went reconnected us with the roots of Western culture beyond our conditioning, to recover our wholeness and reclaim our sovereignty. Together.

Walking through this new door, I shed an old skin. I know now that there was once a community of priestesses who lived in service to

Gaia. I was one of them. I have touched the Earth in Her cave, sat in Her lap, entered Her womb. Her story has come to life for me, much like the Buddha's story did when I went to India so many years ago to walk in his footsteps and sit under the Bodhi Tree. Gaia is no longer a myth. She is alive with each breath and every step.

Mysteriously, in ways I will never understand with my rational mind, a Tibetan lama in another cave heard my heart and gave me a way to make the offerings that finally led me back to Her. Now the snake bites its tail, and we are held within the wholeness of its Ouroboros.

EPILOGUE

I walk up the hill to make my final prayers as this book comes to completion. Standing at the base of the Sangre de Cristo Mountains, grieving in the depth of my soul, I accept now that we might not make it.

The pilgrimage in Greece revealed more of the root causes that contribute to the feeling we are living through a bad dream. Most of the time I feel convinced we will awaken to see our way out of this mess. But the wind is pushing hard today, and I have to hunker down and brace myself against it. All these years, I have refused to believe it could really be the end. But today, I feel the grief. Life on Earth is in a precarious balance that could tip at any moment. All caution is blown to the wind. And the wind is blowing strong.

I feel myself collapsing under the weight of this grave sorrow. Then I hear Gyatrul Rinpoche, my dear old root teacher, admonishing me and calling me by the funny name he gave me long ago: "Stand up, Sausage!" So, I get up and stand tall and strong, the wind pounding me in the face. But I do not turn away. Even if the end of life on Earth is near, I will meet the gale with all I've got.

Coming out of my reverie, I realize that if I go toward what is ahead, the wind is at my back! And by harnessing this gale-force wind, I know we will get the job done.

• • •

My fall off the mountain in Nepal had been the wake-up call I needed to finally accept Gaia's summons. I stopped resisting and began to teach the Sadhana of Mother Gaia. Her mantra poured into the world as more and more sisters and brothers took their seats in the circle beside me to learn this new practice. Going to Delphi to offer Gaia the Earth Treasure Vase brought unshakable clarity. Guru Yoga has given way to Gaia Yoga. My current inquiry is: How do we wake up collectively? What will it take to arrive at the other shore—the shore of liberation—*together*?

The goal of individual enlightenment is no longer the main focus. Instead, I am excited about the great adventure of a collective awakening. I thrill at the prospect that, together, we may realize our commitment to the liberation of *all* beings and usher in a time when the relative and absolute realities are integrated in compassionate awareness. Out of the field of our shared intentions for life on Earth, what will be revealed as we embody the healing solutions that arise from the experience of *we*?

I will never forget hearing Thich Nhat Hanh quietly say in the early 1990s that "the next Buddha will take the form of a Sangha." Then, during the Paris Climate Talks in 2015, his words struck home again:

"We live in a time of collective awakening. . . . One of the signs that we are beginning to wake up is our ability to come together as a species to face the global challenge of climate change. . . . It is only by continuing and deepening this process of awakening that we will be able to save the planet and make a future possible for our children and their children. Awakening is the foundation of every change."[1]

All over the world, there are those who recognize we are part of something so much larger and are waking up to a relationship of interbeing with Earth. It is our collective vision and creative caring that is catalyzing the next turning of the wheel, opening that new dharma door.

The implications of a collective awakening are shattering to our sense of individuality. Our identification with a separate sense of self will no longer be the organizing principle for life on Earth. Our evolution as a species and as a planetary culture depends not only on our realization of this, but our embodiment of it. Living our lives in a profoundly transformed way and connecting our communities in service to Mother Earth is where hope can be found.

We know this: we breathe the same air, drink the same water, and grow the same rice and beans in the same soil as our Ancestors. The animals, trees, flowers, and insects all share this land, air, and water with us, too. Future generations depend on us. The great invitation of our human incarnation is to live in such a way that we naturally care for one another based upon our relationship of interdependence.

This is the Buddha's insight of interdependent origination that catalyzed his enlightenment. Buddha awakened, and we can too. Will we hover on the brink of collective suicide and succumb? Or, perched on the brink of a collective awakening, will we choose to live a radically new life in alignment with Gaia?

• • •

I don't know if a little clay pot filled with prayers and offerings actually does protect and heal the Earth. There is so much I cannot explain. But it's not a matter of belief. Maybe it is as simple as "This is because that is," as Thich Nhat Hanh would say.

This was the assignment I was given. And I was compelled to continue through thick and thin because of what our Earth is going through. Over and over, I have been brought to my knees to bow down in honor of the glorious cycles of Nature that have guided me on the path. I'm in awe as the little yellow wildflowers valiantly poke up from the dry red dirt here in New Mexico every spring. And just the other day I was stunned to witness a brilliant rainbow around the sun as it set in the western sky. Running to the highest hill in that sublime moment, I beheld a divine pink hue spreading over the land as the space above turned red, then purple and a heavenly deep blue with a hint of green radiating out on the clouds high above—the whole world bathed in rapturous light.

Not to be outdone, the bright full moon rises up over the mountains to shine a path through the darkness. Month after month, year after year, I return from my wanderings outside to sit in the round room where, each full moon, we focus on a little clay pot in the center of our circle. Beloved moon, you have been the most loyal of companions, our beacon and great awakener. You connect us in a shared moment all around the Earth and steadfastly support our meditations around the world. In your light, we are united as we steadily continue breathing in and out, flowing with the river and the tides. Your monthly renewal reminds us of the cycle of life and death: the season's turning, the trees growing, the spring coming with her new buds. Then, all is gone again into the darkness of winter, but not before the fullness of summer and the bountiful harvest, the delight in what is possible from one little seed. One little clay pot planted in the ground of our being.

When the full moon illuminates this world of dust, is this not an utter magnificence? Witnessing the wonder of the moon rising over the mountain peaks or setting across the vast ocean, the waves' constant rhythm through the tidal pull—sometimes lapping calmly; other times crashing with a deafening roar—we are reminded of the Great Perfection we live within. The cosmic dance of sun and moon, Earth and stars, is a rhapsody of stunning beauty beyond words. This life, the endless round . . . is a miracle.

We need to do much to restore balance, wherever we are. It will take lifetimes, generations to accomplish. But what else is there to do? This is the work of our times, and we must dedicate ourselves to it region by region. Slowly, slowly, step by step, we shall arrive, feeding the spirit of life on Earth, not the spirit of destruction. As the old story crumbles around us, we each have the opportunity to turn and face the light of a new day. With eyes open, standing up tall, we will do whatever we can to protect beauty and heal suffering.

• • •

I write this as the longest night of the year envelopes the northern world in darkness. The life force of Mother Earth is hibernating now. It is cold, yet the almost full moon sparkles in the early dusk, shining brightly on the body of the Mother. The plowed garden lies fallow in the cold of winter. Snow covers the ground. Coyote tracks follow the course of the little river in the trees. The sun goes down early. But in a few days, this long dark night will begin to turn, and the light will come. A longer, warmer time will again be ours. The dog runs with her stick under the stars that emerge twinkling.

Once, years ago, I dreamed I was standing with my beloved Hugh, looking out over a vast and beautiful landscape. A rainbow appeared nearby—just a foot away from where we stood. We realized we could get on it. As we stepped onto the rainbow, it turned into a solid path of luscious green grass lined with wildflowers, arching up into the sky.

Somewhere I heard that if we open to infinite possibilities, infinite possibilities will appear.

May it be so.

ACKNOWLEDGMENTS

This book is a remembering of places and times, a telling of stories I have lived through thick and thin, a meditation on the glorious web of life, and a prayer for healing, enacted over and over with each passing moon. At times I have felt as if I have been living a myth, called as I was onto an unmarked path through diverse cultures and communities, dark forests and high mountain caves, bearing witness to the beauty and sorrow of life on Earth. Every step of this mythic journey has been an initiation into trusting what I cannot see, something so much larger than myself.

To walk this path and attempt to fulfill this global healing prayer, I have been assisted by a multitude—seen and unseen, in the flesh and gone beyond. I acknowledge all of those who have come before, who walk with me now and who will come after. I bow down to the enormous community that has accompanied me on this path of global healing.

To everyone who has ever held an Earth Treasure Vase or passed one, warm hand to warm hand around the circle, thank you for your contribution to the healing of our world. To everyone who has ever stewarded an Earth Treasure Vase or is doing so now, my deepest gratitude. To all of you who have traveled on pilgrimage with a little holy vessel, I give thanks. And to everyone who has ever sat in our circle on the full moon (in person or virtually) and participated in our global healing meditation, made an offering, or voiced your prayer into one of the clay pots, I add my breath to yours that our prayers may be realized. My amazement only grows for all of you who are part of the fabric of my life and this global mandala of healing intentions for Gaia. This book may look like my story. But it is *our* story.

To David Wilk of Easton Studio and Prospecta Press, thank you so much for publishing this book. Working with you has been a dream come true. Jeremy Townsend, your support in managing the project has been a gift. Barbara Aronica, your artistic expertise in designing the book and collaborating on the cover has fulfilled my vision beautifully. And copy editor, Phoebe Mogharei, many thanks!

To photographer Ed MacKerrow with In Light of Nature Photography, I can hardly believe my luck in finding your gorgeous image of the full moon rising over the mountains right behind our home. To Gonzalo Rescalvo with Abzzolum Digital Art, your creativity gave full expression to my vision for the cover. Steve Alexander, thank you so much for your crop circle photos, and Karen Alexander, thank you for the way you taught us to see those "temporary temples." And to my dear Rachel Bliven, I'm so glad you entered my life all those years ago. It was such fun to be photographed by you!

To everyone else whose photos and video documentation have been featured here or have been part of this journey, I thank you for bearing witness to the extraordinary events we have lived through. In particular, my love, love, love and joy, joy, joy goes to Katie Teague and Andre Lambertson.

For help in refining the story, pushing me where I needed to go, and "braiding" all the threads, I give thanks to my master editor, book doula and beloved wise impeccable writer friend, Christian Leahy, for whom I have the greatest respect. Thank you for taking on this project so completely and giving so much for so long. Your integrity is unmatched and I could not have done this without you.

To Arnie Kotler, our long friendship and your wisdom in the world of book publishing has been such a help, and your guidance, a great relief. Sandie Sedgbeer, your generous support is also deeply appreciated. And to editors along the way, Bonnie Badenoch, Jennifer Browdy, and Diana Rico, thank you.

To Sarah Drew, from our very first walk in Tennessee Valley when you said I ought to write a book, you kept the candles lit unwaveringly every step of the way. Thank you, my beloved sister dakini and angel ally.

To Wendy Johnson who engaged strongly with the Earth Treasure Vases early on, thank you for your enthusiastic partnership, spreading the word, encouraging me to write, and playing a key role in three locations.

To dear friends who read the book at various stages and whose feedback has been so helpful: Christian Bethelson, Elizabeth Christine, Corinna Chung, Stephen Comee, Sarah Drew, Carroll Dunham, Charles Eisenstein, Trudy Goodman, Dahr Jamail, Wendy Johnson, Harper Karmon, Arnie Kotler, Kendall Kalkstein Laird, Joanna Macy, Ginny McGinn, Leslie Meehan, Deena Metzger, Neema Namadamu, Marian Naranjo, Danny Walters, Linda Ward and Hugh Wheir.

Other treasured friends who have each contributed something important to the writing: David Abram, Ian Baker, Kate Cook, Andrew Harvey, Brad Laughlin, Julian Silburn, Mirabai Starr, Katie Teague, Duong Thao Trinh and Jeff Vander Clute. Stephen Comee, thank you very much for your assistance on the glossary. Richard Grossinger, I am grateful for your feedback. David Nicol, our time collaborating on full moons and teaching together was a special era in the evolution of the Gaia Mandala. Thank you for your vision and engagement.

I gaze now at the world treasure map so beautifully crafted for this book by Tracy Seidman before her sudden and untimely death. After mapping many private lands and homesteads for individuals and local communities, she turned her attention to imaginatively mapping the whole Earth and the Center of the Mandala for this book. This was her final project, and I thank her for giving everything. Tracy's map was completed by Marty Peale, who refined the geography and added the Earth Treasure Vase locations and creative flourishes that brought the map to life for these pages. Thank you, Marty, for picking up where Tracy could no longer go and bringing your mapmaking skills and artistic sensibility to completing our treasure map so lovingly.

The lineage masters, teachers, elders and ancestors I have been blessed to know are the living treasures whose guidance and support along the path have opened so many dharma doors. First and foremost, to His Eminence Kushok Mangdon, Charok Rinpoche, who gave me a purpose I could never have imagined. To Lama Ngawang Tsultrim Zangpo Rinpoche, your spiritual friendship has been the gift of a lifetime. Thank you for your open-hearted response to my quest and your unconditional assistance, trust and recognition. Please accept my gratitude for blessing me with the very surprising title of honorary lama and for your ongoing support for my unusual path of the dharma as it is unfolding now. And to Ani Pema Chodron, whose life in the cave continues to be an inspiration.

To the late Gyatrul Rinpoche, my beloved teacher, I offer my deepest gratitude for all the teachings and empowerments you bestowed upon me. Through the circumstances of your passing into Parinirvana, my faith has been restored.

To my first Dzogchen teacher, Namkhai Norbu Rinpoche, I offer my gratitude and respect. And to his student, Jim Casilio, whose companionship on the path opened worlds for me. Without you, this never would have happened. Thank you for letting me come along.

To Lama Tsultrim Allione, I give thanks to you for your teaching and support over all these years. Your feedback on several memorable occasions and our discussion of certain points, along with your kind words offered in this book's foreword, mean the world to me.

To Robert A.F. Thurman, thank you so much for your enthusiastic response to reading this book as expressed in your extraordinary foreword. I am honored to have received your guidance and deeply moved by your friendship and support.

In the Zen lineage of the Order of Interbeing, I give thanks to my root teacher, the Venerable Thich Nhat Hanh, to whom I bow in gratitude. The gift of knowing you and receiving your transmission is beyond words. To Sister Chân Không, I am so grateful for your enduring friendship and generous support for our Liberian friends. To Brother Phap Lai, thank you for meeting me on the path and your dedication in supporting Christian, Harper, and Annie through thick and thin. And to the monks and nuns of Plum Village, you inspire me beyond measure.

To my adopted Mother from Arnhem Land, Aunty Margaret Katherine Oenpelli: I hear your laugh when I walk the land and call upon you here where I live. Thank you for naming me your daughter and welcoming "my Teacher" to your land. Your embrace was a healing balm that opened a view into the vastness of time and space.

And to the mighty Australian ETV mob, including most especially my brothers Jeremy Ball, Ben Manbullo Emery, and dear Julian Silburn, whose sound healing has enhanced this practice and our global healing mandala immeasurably. To my special "lovelies," Magi Whisson and Eva Iken, your vision and friendship in embracing the ETVs so fully has filled my heart with joy. May we find ourselves out bush around the fire singing up the songlines once more.

To Joanna Macy, for forty years, your teachings and friendship have shined a light on the path I have walked. I have learned so much from you.

To Marian Naranjo, wise woman and respected Tewa elder of Santa Clara Pueblo, thank you for teaching me how to live on this land with respect for the mannerisms of your people. I am humbled to learn so much from you.

Thank you to Vickie Downey, Tewa elder of Tesuque Pueblo, for blessing the Earth Treasure Vase at the center of the mandala and inviting the Ancestors of this land to accept our offering when this all began. Your presence, along with the Gyumed monks from Dharamsala who performed the ceremony that day, opened the way.

Deena Metzger, thank you for your vision of healing for this world. Your invitation to consider Liberia changed my life forever. Thank you Cyndie Travis for your work with *everyday gandhis* that led me to Lofa County.

To Christian Wolo Bethelson, in you I have witnessed a miraculous process of transformation. Thank you for trusting me, and for your courage to go the distance. And to my dear friend, Harper Momolu Karmon, your selflessness is a teaching we can all learn from.

To my Congolese sister, Neema Namadamu, thank you for welcoming me so unconditionally to your homeland. Together with your husband, Danny Walters, you are examples of the holy spirit at work.

To Clare Dubois, founder of TreeSisters, and Chameli Gad, founder of the Awakening Women Institute, you each have extended your sisterhood to me and poured your love into the Earth Treasure Vases along with so many members of your communities. I thank you for receiving me by the river's edge.

Cynthia West, your poetry speaks to the heart of life on Earth and your art illustrates the ceremony that life is. You are a true source of inspiration to me and our Gaia Mandala Sangha. Thank you so much for accompanying me in all the ways you do in life, practice, and in writing this book.

To Roshi Joan Halifax, I honor the many paths we have shared and how far we have come. Thank you for your teaching and friendship. To Ken McLeod, I give thanks for your spiritual friendship and clarifying teachings. Linda Wylie, I honor you as one of the rare few who have actually been there. The fragrance of burning *tsang* gathered on that mountainside is a blessing we share. And to my dear friend, Joanna Harcourt-Smith, I miss you every day.

To my sisters, Karen Kalkstein, Emily Jurs Sparks, and Christy Papadakis, we have been through a lot in this lifetime. I am grateful for your enduring love. I honor our parents, Florence and Gene, who gave us the gift of this precious human life. I sense them with me still and feel their support, along with that of our Grandmother Helen, who became a writer ahead of her time, and her father, the publisher Gardner Cowles.

To my beloved niece Kendall Kalkstein Laird, thank you for your fierce honesty and compassionate understanding. And to my step-daughter Mariah Harley Wheir and her brother Will Wheir and his family, I love you all so much.

To Alliance for the Earth's generous funders, deep bows of appreciation to each of you, along with all the members of the Gaia Mandala Global Healing Community whose regular donations keep us going. None of this could have happened without your support.

To the Earth Treasure Vase Stewardship Council, your engagement in the practice of the Earth Treasure Vases has been a profound support every new moon. Your collective vision has illuminated how and where Gaia is calling us and has feed me so deeply.

To the former staff of Alliance for the Earth, including Judy Herzl, Christian Leahy and Anna Molitor, the work you did was heroic. And to the Board of Directors of Alliance for the Earth, I thank you for your devotion in seeing it through. Ginny McGinn and Jeff Vander Clute, your heartfelt service, past and present, has kept Alliance for the Earth alive.

Here at the hub of the Gaia Mandala, a very special deep bow of gratitude to Elizabeth Christine for the depth of your engagement over these many years and your beautiful leadership in the Gaia Mandala. The prayers keep turning with the help of three beloved colleagues: Nikole Adele Rosaria Manieri, Rick Jansen and Rasul Luisa Bravo. Your assistance, leadership, creativity and engagement are a gift from Gaia. Nikole, what you brought to the pilgrimage in Delphi was an important part of opening that new dharma door. I heard the oracle in the beat of your drum and the memories of a Gaian priestesshood were reawakened. Thank you.

Finally, I offer my infinite gratitude to Mark Lumbard for your generous life-giving support in the writing of this book. Through you, so much has been possible for me and for Alliance for the Earth. May it return to you a thousand-fold.

To the Ancestors upon whose land I walk, I thank you for the blessing that allows me to be here. I am forever grateful for this land that supports me, the mountain from whom the waters flow, the garden that feeds me, the flowers that enchant me, the coyotes, bears, birds, and Jala, my best friend and companion, and now, Santo, the newest addition to our fur family.

My infinite gratitude goes most of all to my husband Dr. Hugh Wheir, who has been by my side every step of the way, from the time the vases arrived in their trunks from Nepal; on every full moon in our home, offering your prayers, joining me and so many others in meditation; holding me through each pilgrimage; taking care of me when I returned; patiently waiting for this book to be written and offering your incisive feedback and words of wisdom when needed. Thank you for all you have done to keep me going, for our healthy healing home, for the food you have grown and meals you have prepared, and for your enduring love which has sustained me. Your partnership means the world to me, my beloved muse.

ENDNOTES AND CITATIONS

Prologue

1. Joanna Macy, *World as Lover, World as Self: Courage for Global Justice and Ecological Renewal* (Berkeley: Parallax Press, 2007), 151.

2. Thich Nhat Hanh, quoted in Macy, *World as Lover, World as Self*, 95.

Section One: Answering the Call

Chapter One: The Path

1. For thirty years I lived with the understanding that Charok Rinpoche was 106 years old when I met him. But then, nearing the completion of writing this book, I learned from Lama Ngawang Tsultrim Rinpoche that he was ninety-six when he passed away. A mythic tale is hard to come by, and this news was hard to accept. But I hope you will agree, regardless of his actual age, all that unfolded from meeting him was extraordinarily meaningful.

2. "Meditation boxes" or *gomtri* in the Tibetan language are the typical tantric wooden meditation seats where the male or female practitioner remains throughout day and night. Generally, it is applied in three-year retreats. However, some apply this method all life long. Erik Pema Kunsang, *Blazing Splendor, The Memoirs of the Dzogchen Yogi Tulku Urgyen Rinpoche* (Boulder, Rangjung Yeshe Publications, 2005), 160–161.

3. Since radioactive waste comprises multiple substances with varying lifespans in different durations of time, it is difficult to estimate how long it will take for radioactive waste in general to decay completely. However, as of January, 2009, *Scientific American* claimed that plutonium, one of the primary elements used in nuclear weapons, would have fatal effects on humans for at least 250,000 years. David Biello, "Spent Nuclear Fuel: A Trash Heap Deadly for 250,000 Years or a Renewable Energy Source?," *Scientific American*, January 28, 2009, https://www.scientificamerican.com/article/nuclear-waste-lethal-trash-or-renewable-energy-source/.

4. Edwin Bernbaum, *The Way to Shambhala: A Search for the Mythical Kingdom Beyond the Himalayas* (Los Angeles: Jeremy P. Tarcher, 1989), 64.

5. Ian Baker, *The Heart of the World: A Journey to the Last Secret Place* (New York: The Penguin Press, 2004), 10.

6. Baker, *Heart of the World,* 26.

7. This chapter appeared in a modified form in *Tricycle*. Cynthia Jurs, "Earth Treasure Vases," *Tricycle: The Buddhist Review*, Summer 1997, https://tricycle.org/magazine/earth-treasure-vases/.

Chapter Two: Stepping Stones

1. For more information on Oddiyana, see:
https://en.wikipedia.org/wiki/Oddiyana
https://www.rigpawiki.org/index.php?title=Oddiyana

2. Thich Nhat Hanh was eventually allowed to visit Vietnam again and made several important trips there with members of his extended community. Then, in 2014, Thay had a stroke that paralyzed half his body and

prevented him from speaking. Finally, in 2018, Thay indicated he wished to return to his homeland and was given permission to return at age ninety-three. He lived out his days at his home temple, Tu Hieu Pagoda in Hue, until his death on January 22, 2022, at age ninety-five.

3. Thich Nhat Hanh, *Interbeing: Fourteen Guidelines for Engaged Buddhism* (Berkeley: Parallax Press,1987), 6.

Thich Nhat Hanh goes on to say, "If we combine the prefix 'inter' with the verb 'to be,' we have a new verb, 'inter-be.' To inter-be and the action of interbeing reflects reality more accurately. We inter-are with one another and with all life." *The Art of Living* (New York: HarperOne, 2017), excerpted in "Interbeing," *Awakin*, https://www.awakin.org/v2/read/view.php?tid=2619.

He continues, "To be means to inter-be. A flower has to inter-be—with the sunshine, the cloud, with everything else. She doesn't have a separate existence. So being means interbeing. Existing means coexisting." "To Be Means to Inter-Be," Plum Village, July 12, 2021, https://plumvillage.app/to-be-means-to-inter-be/.

4. Open Way Sangha was the name of our sangha in the early years when I began to teach in the tradition of Thich Nhat Hanh and carry out the work with the Earth Treasure Vases. Elsewhere in the book we refer to Alliance for the Earth, which is the nonprofit organization that serves as the fiscal entity for our global healing work. Nowadays, our community is called the Gaia Mandala Global Healing Community, or simply Gaia Mandala.

5. Thich Nhat Hanh, *Call Me by My True Names: The Collected Poems of Thich Nhat Hanh* (Berkeley: Parallax Press, 1993), 73.

Chapter Three: The Terma

1. For more information on the terma tradition, see: http://www.rigpawiki.org/index.php?title=Terma.

2. For more information on peace vases, see: http://peacevaseproject.org/.

Chapter Four: The Bomb in My Backyard

1. In a personal conversation with Marian Naranjo on August 31, 2022, she shared that there were 125 pueblos before the Spanish came to what is now known as New Mexico.

2. Although I have had trouble documenting this, I was told by Marian (on August 31, 2022) that the "towering volcano" was the size of Mount Everest and that its explosion sent rocks hundreds of miles. She says she remembers seeing images from the first space shuttle, which showed lava from the Valles Caldera in Chicago! For more information on that explosion:

Fraser Goff, "The Valles Caldera: New Mexico's Supervolcano," *New Mexico Earth Matters*, Winter 2010, http://npshistory.com/publications/vall/nmbgmr-winter-2010.pdf.

3. Greg Mello, founder and executive director of the Los Alamos Study Group (http://www.lasg.org), shared in a personal communication with me on October 15, 2021, that this is a secret program so there is no single place where complete information can be found, but these links might be helpful:

- Los Alamos Study Group, "NNSA Pit Production Strategy: No Clear Goals, Plans, or Likelihood of Success; Production at LANL Has High Risks and Costs, Few or No Program Benefits" (online PowerPoint presentation, updated

Oct 3, 2020), http://lasg.org/presentations/PlutoniumPit-Workshop_1Oct2020.pdf.

- Los Alamos Study Group, "Presentation to the Radioactive and Hazardous Materials Committee of the New Mexico Legislature" (online PowerPoint presentation, Sept 9, 2020), http://lasg.org/presentations/LASG-RHMC-slides_9Sep2020.pdf.
- Los Alamos Study Group, "LANL Pit Production: Fifth Failure in Progress" (online PowerPoint presentation, Sep 30, 2021), http://lasg.org/presentations/LASG-SantaFe-public-mtg_30Sep2021.pdf.

In addition, as of April 28, 2021, the Department of Energy's National Nuclear Security Administration approved the Los Alamos Plutonium Pit Production Project at Los Alamos National Laboratory to produce thirty pits per year. "NNSA Approves Critical Decision 1 for Los Alamos Plutonium Pit Production Project," US DOE's National Nuclear Security Administration, April 28, 2021, https://www.energy.gov/nnsa/articles/nnsa-approves-critical-decision-1-los-alamos-plutonium-pit-production-project.

As of May 26, 2021, the *Albuquerque Journal* reported that LANL has started to expand their plutonium-producing sites into Santa Fe, NM. *Albuquerque Journal* staff, "Big development on the nuclear horizon," *Albuquerque Journal*, May 26, 2021, https://www.abqjournal.com/2394598/big-development-on-the-nuclear-horizon-ex-huge-growth-at-lanl-in-plutonium-pit-production-raises-ethical-issues.html.

Finally, the most recent info comes from Tewa Women United, which sought public comments to oppose the expansion of plutonium-pit production to thirty pits a year by 2026:

Tewa Women United, "Action Alert: Submit Public Comment on LANL's New Sitewide Environmental Impact Statement (SWEIS)," accessed May 17, 2023, https://tewawomenunited.org/2022/10/action-alert-submit-public-comment-on-lanls-new-sitewide-environmental-impact-statement-sweis.

4. Laura Paskus, "Groundwater War: New Mexico's Toxic Threat," New Mexico PBS, updated April 26, 2021, accessed July 7, 2023, https://www.newmexicopbs.org/productions/groundwater-war/2021/02/24/forever-chemicals-found-in-los-alamos-waters/.

5. Rebecca Moss, "Cancer-causing chemicals appear to spread in regional aquifer near LANL," *Santa Fe New Mexican*, September 15, 2017, https://www.santafenewmexican.com/news/local_news/cancer-causing-chemicals-appear-to-spread-in-regional-aquifer-near/article_7f368ea7-120c-57fe-ade7-aa6561db190a.html.

6. An independent report completed by the students of Worcester Polytechnic Institute in 2020 concludes, "Chromium concentrations at laboratory borders are increasing and continue to pose a risk to the adjacent Pueblo." Charles A. Carlo et al., *Plutonium-239 and Chromium-6 Contamination at Los Alamos National Laboratory: Analyzing Contaminant Migration and Assessing Remediation* (Worcester, MA: Worcester Polytechnic Institute, 2020), i.

On February 24, 2021, the New Mexico Environment Department sued DOE for its continuing procrastination on cleaning up nuclear waste at LANL, which poses hazardous impacts on people's health in neighboring communities. *Albuquerque Journal* staff, "State Sues DOE over LANL

Cleanup," *Albuquerque Journal*, February 25, 2021, https://www.abqjournal.com/2363558/state-sues-doe-over-lanl-cleanup.html.

In 2023, the DOE responded with a strategic vision for the cleanup of legacy contamination, including the plume of hexavalent chromium. "Los Alamos National Laboratory Strategic Vision: 2023–2033," Office of Environmental Management, Department of Energy. accessed July 12, 2023, https://www.energy.gov/em/los-alamos-national-laboratory-strategic-vision-2023-2033.

However, plume cleanup was halted in late March, 2023, by New Mexico state regulators due to ongoing concerns that the current treatment process is not fixing or containing the problem. Scott Wyland, "LANL Plume Cleanup Halted Due to Water Concerns," March 31, 2023, updated April 1, 2023, https://www.santafenewmexican.com/news/local_news/lanl-plume-cleanup-to-be-halted-due-to-concerns-about-water/artile_7381e37c-cd98-11ed-ab67-4fe506af6dc5.html.

7. Gregory Hooks, and Chad L. Smith, "The Treadmill of Destruction: National Sacrifice Areas and Native Americans," *American Sociological Review* 69, no. 4 (2004): 558–75, http://www.jstor.org/stable/3593065.

For an excellent overview examination of the legacy of the nuclear industry in New Mexico from those most impacted, please read:

Myrriah Gomez, "Nuclear Nuevo New Mexico: *Colonialism and the Effects of the Nuclear Industrial Complex on Nuevomexicanos*." (Tucson: University of Arizona Press, 2022)

8. Joanna Macy, *World as Lover, World as Self: Courage for Global Justice and Ecological Renewal* (Berkeley: Parallax Press, 2007), 120–122.

9. "Lifeways," for Marian, is a better, more inclusive term than "ceremonies." She emphasizes, "Everything is a ceremony to our people!" In a

conversation on August 31, 2022, I asked her how she would define "lifeways" and she responded: "The ways, the mannerisms, and the beliefs of the Tewa people, including the annual events of our seasonal calendar that are upheld for our survival."

10. To save the lab, firefighters engaged a back-burning solution to divert the direction of the wildfire, which sacrificed six thousand acres of lands on Santa Clara Pueblo. Kyle Dickman, "Feeling the Burn," *Outside*, July 1, 2011, https://www.outsideonline.com/outdoor-adventure/environment/feeling-burn/.

11. Marian observes: "LANL is located at the edge of a rift valley. Santa Clara Canyon is the biggest fault line in the area and it burned. We were so worried because if it 'slipped' it would be a catastrophe. It's only three miles from LANL." She reminds me there is only one way up and one way down to drive in and out of Los Alamos in an emergency—and no one realizes this. Marian indicates that it is not a matter of "if," but "when" the sleeping volcano beneath LANL will awaken. "We just don't know when . . ."

In our conversation on August 31, 2022, she went on to say how we need to stop the production of nuclear weapons, clean up the waste in the area, and educate people on what "sacred" means. This would provide jobs and be a great demonstration of something positive—and good for tourism, too!

12. Due to tritium's unstable form, people are exposed to a small amount of it every day. Our bodies can eliminate it through urination in ten days, demonstrating that natural tritium is nontoxic. However, artificial tritium, created through nuclear-weapons production, appears in great amounts and causes cancer when its disposal is not handled properly. In this way, its radiation is fatal. More information on health risks caused by tritium

exposure can be found at: https://www.scientificamerican.com/article/is-radioactive-hydrogen-in-drinking-water-a-cancer-threat/.

13. Macy, *World as Lover, World as Self*, 185.

14. Joanna Macy and Chris Johnstone, *Active Hope: How to Face the Mess We're in without Going Crazy* (Novato: New World Library, 2012), 148.

15. Macy, *World as Lover, World as Self*, 195.

16. See: Tewa Women United, https://tewawomenunited.org/.

Chapter Six: Pilgrimage

1. Thich Nhat Hanh, *Present Moment Wonderful Moment: Mindfulness Verses for Daily Living* (Berkeley: Parallax Press, 1990), 57.

Section Two: Hearing the Cries of the World

Chapter Seven: Planetary Acupuncture

1. Jelaluddin Rumi, *The Essential Rumi,* trans. Coleman Barks (New York: HarperOne, 2004), 36.

Chapter Eight: A Thousand Arms

1. Vessantara, *Meeting the Buddhas: A Guide to Buddhas, Bodhisattvas, and Tantric Deities* (Glasgow: Windhorse Publications, 1993), 140.

2. Vessantara, *Meeting the Buddhas*, 144.

3. For Wendy Johnson's full story, see: Wendy Johnson, "A Prayer for the

Forest," *Tricycle: The Buddhist Review*, Fall 1998, https://tricycle.org/magazine/prayer-forest/.

4. Keridwen Cornelius, "Biosphere 2: The Once Infamous Live-In Terrarium Is Transforming Climate Research," *Scientific American*, October 4, 2021, https://www.scientificamerican.com/article/biosphere-2-the-once-infamous-live-in-terrarium-is-transforming-climate-research/.

5. Thich Nhat Hanh said this in Plum Village one summer in the early 1990s, and it rippled through us like a prophecy. Later that year he spoke to this at Spirit Rock in California, which was quoted in *Inquiring Mind*. Thich Nhat Hanh, *"The Next Buddha May Be a Sangha," Inquiring Mind* 10, no.2 (Spring 1994), https://www.inquiringmind.com/article/1002_41_thich-nhat_hanh/.

Thay also writes in his book *Teachings on Love*, "I am more and more convinced that the next Buddha may not be just one person, but he may be a community, a community of love. We need to support each other to build a community where love is something tangible. This may be the most important thing we can do for the survival of the Earth. We have everything except love. We have to renew our way of loving. We have to really learn to love. The well-being of the world depends on us, on the way we live our daily lives, on the way we take care of the world, and on the way we love." Thich Nhat Hanh, *Teachings on Love* (Berkeley: Parallax Press, 1995), 141.

Chapter Nine: Twenty-One Taras

1. Miranda Shaw, *Buddhist Goddesses of India* (Princeton: Princeton University Press, 2006), 353.

2. The text is the "Profound Essence Mind Treasure Tara Mandala Sadhana: Essence of the Two Accumulations," revealed by tertön Rigdzin Choguyr Lingpa. The practice was transmitted to me by Lama Ngawang Tsultrim Zangpo Rinpoche and appears on page 27 in the unpublished practice materials for the use of practitioners at Dhognak Tharling Dharma Center.

3. Lama Tsultrim Allione, *Green Tara: Explanation and Commentary* (Machig Publications, Tara Mandala, July 2020), 8–9.

Chapter Ten: The Sound of the Bell in Africa

1. See the excellent documentary film *Pray the Devil Back to Hell* for the full story of how the women stopped the war in Liberia: https://www.forkfilms.com/pray-the-devil-back-to-hell/.

2. Ellen Johnson Sirleaf and Leymah Gbowee also shared the Nobel Peace Prize in 2011 with Tawakkol Karman from Yemen.

3. Truth and Reconciliation Committee of Liberia, *Final Report*, vol. 3, title 12, "Towards National Reconciliation and Dialogues: The Palava Hut or Peace Forums," https://www.trcofliberia.org/resources/reports/final/volume-three-12_layout-1.pdf.

4. It was the women of WIPNET (Women In Peacebuilding Network) whose idea it was to change the name.

5. It was Prince Johnson who killed President Samuel Doe. Johnson is now a senator for Nimba County, Liberia.

6. In Thich Nhat Hanh's tradition, the bell is considered a bodhisattva because its sound invites us to wake up. Likewise, the practice of mindfulness is a practice of nonviolence, so we never "hit" or "strike"

the bell; instead, in Thich Nhat Hanh's teaching, we "invite the bell to sound."

Chapter Eleven: Do Not Close Your Eyes Before Suffering

1. Jelaluddin Rumi, *The Essential Rumi,* trans. Coleman Barks (New York: HarperOne, 2004), 36.

2. At Plum Village, in the early days, they sold handmade little pieces of wood with various gathas printed on them to hang on the wall as a reminder. I bought this gatha written on a little wooden plaque and to this day it sits above our kitchen sink near our compost bucket. Often, there is a rose in a little vase right next to it.

Over the years the language of some of Thich Nhat Hanh's gathas, like the Mindfulness Trainings, which were originally called "precepts," have changed slightly. But this is the way I learned it.

At the first retreat with Thich Nhat Hanh that I organized at the Ojai Foundation, he gave a whole teaching on the compost and the rose. The next morning, we made a special flower arrangement (as we did each day) for his talk: we placed a pile of compost in various stages of decomposition and stuck a beautiful pink rose in the center of it.

3. Thich Nhat Hanh, *Interbeing: Commentary on the Tiep Hien Precepts,* (Berkeley: Parallax Press, 1987), 34.

Chapter Twelve: Reckoning

1. Thanissara, *Time to Stand Up: An Engaged Buddhist Manifesto for Our Earth—The Buddha's Life and Message through Feminine Eyes* (Berkeley: North Atlantic Books, 2015), 60.

2. Thanissara, *Time to Stand Up*, 91.

3. The occurrence of babies being cut out of pregnant women and cooked is something that I heard about more than once while educating myself about the situation in the DRC. The rule of law does not operate in the DRC. It is very difficult to prove things and there is much that is covered up, especially terrible atrocities like this. That does not mean it does not happen. My Congolese collaborator, Neema Namadamu, who reviewed this chapter, did not highlight this issue to say it was inaccurate.

The brave 2007 documentary film by Lisa Jackson, *The Greatest Silence: Rape in the Congo*, won a Sundance Film Festival Special Jury Award and features firsthand commentary from rebels and survivors. Lisa Jackson, *The Greatest Silence: Rape in the Congo*, aired April 8, 2008, on HBO, https://www.youtube.com/watch?v=MNq0WmW2nV0.

For an overview: Max Fisher, "A Congo Mother Survives Cannibalism to Save Her Children: Why Her Photo Matters," *The Atlantic*, April 26, 2012, https://www.theatlantic.com/international/archive/2012/04/a-congo-mother-survives-cannibalism-to-save-her-children-why-her-photo-matters/256405/.

4. "DR Congo: 48 rapes every hour, US study finds," *BBC*, May 12, 2011, https://www.bbc.com/news/world-africa-13367277. In May 2011, US scientists found that forty-eight females, on average, are raped hourly in the Democratic Republic of Congo, which totals up to over 420,000 over twelve months. These 2011 findings (using data from 2006 to 2007) remain the baseline, although it is difficult to track the incident of rape due to many factors. A 2021 report from RAINN notes: "True prevalence rates of rape are difficult to measure. UN Women reports that 51 percent of ever-partnered women have experienced physical and/or sexual intimate partner vio-

lence in their lifetime, with 37 percent experiencing such violence within the past 12 months. One of the most comprehensive studies in DRC concluded that approximately 1.69 to 1.80 million women reported having been raped in their lifetimes (with 407, 397–433,785 women reporting having been raped in the preceding 12 months), and approximately 3.07 to 3.37 million women reported experiencing intimate partner sexual violence." Rape, Abuse, & Incest National Network, *Sexual Violence in Six African Nations: A Call for Investment*, 2021, 21, https://www.rainn.org/sites/default/files/Africa-Report-2022.pdf.

5. RAINN, *Sexual Violence in Six African Nations*, 20–21.

6. "Gendercide" is a term coined by Congolese activist Neema Namadamu.

Chapter Thirteen: The Heart of . . . Darkness?

1. I am aware that calling the Democratic Republic of the Congo "the Heart of Darkness" could be considered offensive to the people of that nation. I hope that through this writing my readers will see beyond this well-known label and realize that as Neema Namadamu has said, Congo is an Eden deserving of our protection and love.

2. UN Peacekeepers have not left the DRC since their mission started in 1999. They still have over eighteen thousand troops in the country, but some believe that their capacity to "keep peace" is negligible at best. Claude Muhindo Sengenya, "Why we're protesting against UN peacekeepers in DR Congo: 'Who will come to save the Congo? Only us young people,'" *The New Humanitarian*, August 18, 2022, accessed July 24, 2023. https://www.thenewhumanitarian.org/2022/08/18/why-we-re-protesting-against-un-peacekeepers-dr-congo. .

3. "Democratic Republic of the Congo: Economy," Global Edge, Michigan State University, accessed April 18, 2023. https://globaledge.msu.edu/countries/democratic-republic-of-the-congo/economy. For more information: https://enact-africa.s3.amazonaws.com/site/uploads/2022-05-03-research-paper-29-rev.pdf.

4. Oluwole Ojewale, "What Coltan Mining in the DRC Costs People and the Environment," *The Conversation*, May 29, 2022, https://theconversation.com/what-coltan-mining-in-the-drc-costs-people-and-the-environment-183159.

5. Ed Ram, "'In 10 years, we might not have forests': DRC struggles to halt charcoal trade—a photo essay," *The Guardian*, July 20, 2022, https://www.theguardian.com/global-development/2022/jul/20/in-10-years-we-might-not-have-forests-drc-struggles-to-halt-charcoal-trade-a-photo-essay.

6. Since 2006, various organizations, municipalities, and governments within Brazil, Bolivia, Colombia, Ecuador, India, Mexico, New Zealand, and the US have sought to protect the inalienable Rights of Nature. In September 2008, Ecuador became the first country in the world to recognize Rights of Nature in its constitution, while New Zealand granted the Whanganui River legal standing in 2017.

> *Rights of Nature is the recognition and honoring that Nature has rights. It is the recognition that our ecosystems—including trees, oceans, animals, mountains—have rights just as human beings have rights. Rights of Nature is about balancing what is good for human beings against what is good for other species, what is good for the planet as a world. It is the holistic recognition that all life, all ecosystems on our planet are deeply intertwined. Rather than treating*

> *nature as property under the law, rights of nature acknowledges that nature in all its life forms has the right to exist, persist, maintain and regenerate its vital cycles.*

"What Are the Rights of Nature?" Global Alliance for the Rights of Nature, accessed May 17, 2023. https://www.garn.org/rights-of-nature/.

7. Neema Namadamu, "Quitting The Game," *World Pulse*, September 26, 2011, https://www.worldpulse.com/community/users/neema/posts/18111.

8. John Dear, "Neema Namadamu, Congo's visionary peacemaker," *National Catholic Reporter,* October 15, 2013, https://www.ncronline.org/blogs/road-peace/neema-namadamu-congos-visionary-peacemaker.

9. Accessed May 5, 2023, https://whc.unesco.org/en/list/137/.

10. To hear more of this story, visit: https://www.worldpulse.org/story/congo-a-revolutionist-mind-39097.

Chapter Fourteen: Poison into Wisdom

1. For more on the Five Buddha Families and the five dakinis, see: Lama Tsultrim Allione, *Wisdom Rising: Journey Into the Mandala of the Empowered Feminine* (New York: Atria/Enliven Books, 2018).

Ken McLeod, "Dismantling Reactive Emotions," in *Wake Up To Your Life: Discovering the Buddhist Path of Attention* (New York: HarperCollins Publishers, 2002), 207–242.

Chogyam Trungpa, "Mandala" and "The Five Buddha Families," in *Journey Without Goal: The Tantric Wisdom of the Buddha* (Boulder: Prajna Press, 1981), 31–38 and 77–85.

Section Three: Becoming a Holy Vessel

Chapter Fifteen: Taking Refuge in the Earth

1. Thich Nhat Hanh, *Love Letter to the Earth* (Berkeley: Parallax Press, 2013), 27–28.

2. Hanh, *Love Letter to the Earth*, 100.

3. Miranda Shaw, *Buddhist Goddesses of India* (Princeton: Princeton University Press, 2006), 17.

4. Shaw, *Buddhist Goddesses of India,* 21.

5. Shaw, *Buddhist Goddesses of India*, 22.

6. The Three Refuges of Thich Nhat Hanh can be found in *Chanting from the Heart: Buddhist Ceremonies and Daily Practices* by Thich Nhat Hanh and the Monks and Nuns of Plum Village. Working with this as my foundation, I have integrated other strands from different sources, including from Thich Nhat Hanh's "Invoking the Bodhisattva's Names" for the ceremony called Touching the Earth (prostrations), along with some of my own language.

For Thay, the inclusion of Bodhisattva Gaia was a relatively new addition to "Invoking the Bodhisattva's Names" around 2010 to 2011. His original wording goes like this:

Mother of buddhas, bodhisattvas and all beings,
Nourishing, holding and healing all,
Bodhisattva Gaia, Great Mother Earth, precious jewel of the cosmos,
to whom we bow in gratitude.

Thich Nhat Hanh and the Monks and Nuns of Plum Village, *Chanting from the Heart: Buddhist Ceremonies and Daily Practices* (Berkeley: Parallax Press, 2007), 88–89.

Chapter Sixteen: Sacred Time

1. Arkan Lushwala, *The Time of the Black Jaguar: An Offering of Indigenous Wisdom for the Continuity of Life on Earth* (Ribera: Arkan Lushwala, 2012), 91, 96.

2. Lushwala, *The Time of the Black Jaguar*, 96.

3. Charles Eisenstein, *The More Beautiful World Our Hearts Know Is Possible* (Berkeley: North Atlantic Books, 2013), 234, 238.

4. Thich Nhat Hanh, *Touching Peace: Practice the Art of Mindful Living* (Berkeley: Parallax Press, 1992), 1.

5. We now know that the "2012 phenomenon" was a misrepresentation of Mayan lifeways and the meaning of the sacred change their calendar underwent at the 2012 winter solstice. December 21, 2012, did not herald the end of the Mayan Long Count calendar, as was put forth by various New Age teachers. These misconceptions are now being corrected by Mayan traditional elders. For more information, visit: https://www.instagram.com/p/CgURQtPMN27/.

6. Marianne Williamson, preface to *The Law of Divine Compensation: On Work, Money, and Miracles* (San Francisco: HarperOne, 2012).

Chapter Seventeen: Offerings

1. Miranda Shaw, *Buddhist Goddesses of India* (Princeton: Princeton University Press, 2006), 26.

2. The International Council of Thirteen Indigenous Grandmothers is an international association of Indigenous women who are deeply concerned with healing the Earth through projects of protecting the environment,

nurturing diverse cultures, praying, and educating children to live in Indigenous ways of life. For more information, see: https://www.grandmotherswisdom.org/.

3. To learn more about Evon Peter: Joaqlin Estus, "Evon Peter: Seeing Indigenous Success," *ICT*, July 7, 2021, https://indiancountrytoday.com/news/evon-peter-seeking-indigenous-success.

4. David Suzuki and Amanda McConnell, *The Sacred Balance: Rediscovering Our Place in Nature* (Vancouver: Greystone Books, 1999), 188.

5. Mary Oliver, "Wild Geese," in *New and Selected Poems* (Boston: Beacon Press, 1992), 110.

6. Thich Nhat Hanh, *Present Moment Wonderful Moment: Mindfulness Verses for Daily Living*, trans. Annabel Laity (Berkeley: Parallax Press, 1990), 3.

7. The reference to a lotus blooming with each step comes from the story of the Buddha's birth. It is said that when the baby Buddha was born, he immediately took seven steps and where his tiny feet touched the Earth, a lotus bloomed. Thay invited us to imagine this for ourselves.

During one summer retreat, Thay had little round stickers made for us to place inside our shoes. The stickers said "I walk for you" in English, French, or Vietnamese. Every time we slipped on our shoes to go outside for walking meditation, we were reminded to walk mindfully, not just for ourselves but for each other, too.

Chapter Eighteen: Becoming a Holy Vessel

1. To see whole interview with Joanna Macy, *Vessels of the Holy*, visit: https://www.youtube.com/watch?v=4HfQbUg1rS0.

Chapter Nineteen: Listening to the Elders

1. Alan Ereira, *The Elder Brothers: A Lost South American People and Their Message about the Fate of the Earth* (New York: Alfred A. Knopf, 1990), 10, 12.

Chapter Twenty: Welcome to Country

1. Robert Lawlor, *Voices of the First Day: Awakening in the Aboriginal Dreamtime* (Rochester: Inner Traditions, 1991), 1, 18.

2. "Acknowledgement of Country and Welcome to Country," Reconciliation Australia, https://www.reconciliation.org.au/acknowledgement-of-country-and-welcome-to-country.

3. *Kanyini*, directed by Melanie Hogan (Australia: Sand Hill Road Pictures and Reverb Films, 2017), https://www.amazon.com/s?k=Kanyini&i=instant-video&ref=nb_sb_noss.

4. The estimated time that the Aboriginal people have lived in Australia is disputed. While mainstream research usually dates only as far as forty thousand years, Aboriginal people confirm at least sixty thousand years or longer. Erin Blakemore, "Aboriginal Australians," *National Geographic*, January 31, 2019, https://www.nationalgeographic.com/culture/article/aboriginal-australians.

The website of Australia's national institution on Aboriginal People says upwards of sixty thousand years according to current research. "Australia's First Peoples," Australian Institute of Aboriginal and Torres Strait Islander Studies, accessed July 18, 2023, https://aiatsis.gov.au/explore/australias-first-peoples.

5. Mumma was totally at ease with fire. She'd had a relationship with fire all her life, as her people all do. Burning the undergrowth is their method of taking care of the land in the traditional ways. In North America we are deathly afraid of fire and have lost touch with how to take care of the land to prevent wildfires. Margaret was comfortable with and trusting of the elemental energy of fire. This was another profound teaching for me.

Section Four: Collective Awakening

Chapter Twenty-One: Indra's Net

1. Indra, a deity from Hindu mythology, is one of many such figures that were retained in Indian Buddhist teachings. The Tushita heaven of Buddhism corresponds to Indra heaven of Hinduism. Thich Nhat Hanh, *Understanding Our Mind*, (Berkeley: Parallax Press, 2006), 81–82.

Chapter Twenty-Two: Sacred Activism

1. Bayo Akomolafe, "Meeting the Inappropriate/d: The Liminality of Justice and Reconciliation in Canada," May 5, 2016, https://www.bayoakomolafe.net/post/meeting-the-inappropriate-d.

2. Thanissara, *Time to Stand Up: An Engaged Buddhist Manifesto for Our Earth—The Buddha's Life and Message through Feminine Eyes* (Berkeley: North Atlantic Books, 2015), 112.

3. Cynthia Jurs and Kim Spencer, "Turning Prayer Into Action: Indigenous Grandmothers Meet the Bioneers," September 25, 2016, documentary for Link TV, 25:21, http://www.prayerintoaction.com/.

4. Jurs and Spencer, “Turning Prayer Into Action,” 56:25.

5. Andrew Harvey, introduction to *The Hope: A Guide to Sacred Activism* (Carlsbad: Hay House, 2009), xviii.

6. David Nicol, introduction to *Subtle Activism: The Inner Dimension of Social and Planetary Transformation* (Albany: State University of New York Press, 2015), 4.

7. Thich Nhat Hanh, “Part Two: Mindfulness Must Be Engaged,” in *Peace Is Every Step: The Path of Mindfulness in Everyday Life* (New York: Bantam, 1991), 91.

8. Charles Eisenstein, *The More Beautiful World Our Hearts Know Is Possible* (Berkeley: North Atlantic Books, 2013).

9. The source of this quote has been challenged, but it appears to be a paraphrase by Ram Dass based on his interpretation of Einstein’s writings, accessed July 24, 2023. https://hsm.stackexchange.com/questions/7751/did-einstein-say-we-cannot-solve-our-problems-with-the-same-thinking-we-used-to#:~:text=124%2C%20is%20%22The%20world%20that,Ram%20Dass%20(who%20needs%20his.

10. Colin Schultz, “Is This the Oldest Cave on the Planet?,” *Smithsonian Magazine*, July 30, 2012, https://www.smithsonianmag.com/smart-news/is-this-the-oldest-cave-art-on-the-planet-9100329/.

11. Charles Eisenstein, *Climate: A New Story* (Berkeley: North Atlantic Books, 2018), 42.

Chapter Twenty-Four: Head over Heels

1. This vase was placed inside the stupa that marks the entrance to Tolu Tharling Monastery in 2019 by Lama Ngawang Tsultrim Zangpo when he did the initial rebuilding of the monastery. Along with the Earth Treasure Vase, this stupa also holds the remains of his father, Kyabje Kyaprok Tulku Rinpoche, the previous abbot of Tolu Gompa.

Chapter Twenty-Five: Buddha Gotami

1. Systems of power work in insidious ways to marginalize, silence, and devalue us. Very often, unequal power dynamics become invisible when women and others who struggle to be heard have unconsciously internalized those power dynamics. We erase ourselves and become co-opted by these systems. In this way, we become unconsciously complicit in destructive ways of life.

2. "Buddha Gotami," the name I am giving the Buddha if he were a woman, is not to be confused with the historical Buddha's step-mother and maternal aunt, who was named "Mahapajapati Gotami." Mahapajapati raised the Buddha as her own when her sister died shortly after giving birth. The name "Gotami" refers to the Gotama clan, which was the ruling clan of the Shakya tribe in northern India at the time.

Chapter Twenty-Six: The Oracle's Message

1. Catherine Brooks, "The Shrine of Gaia and Python at Delphi," on her personal blog, January 8, 2022, https://catherinebrooks.com/the-mysteries-of-gaias-shrine-at-delphi/.

2. For more information about the Corycian Cave, visit: https://via-hygeia.art/john-opsopaus-the-bee-nymphs-of-mount-parnassus/https://atemplewild.com/journal/delphi-and-the-corycian-cave.

Epilogue

1. "Thich Nhat Hanh," Profiles of Paris, https://profilesofparis.com/profiles/.

GLOSSARY

Ani: Ani is the Tibetan word for "nun." The suffix "la" is a term of respect which can be affixed to the end of a title, as in "Ani-la," or it can be affixed to the end of a personal name, as in "Tenzin-la."

Avatamsaka Sutra: A Mahayana Buddhist scripture, also called the Flower Ornament Sutra, renowned for the beauty in which it describes the interconnectedness and interpenetration of all phenomena. One such metaphor found in this sutra is Indra's Net.

Axis Mundi: From the Latin, meaning "the axis of the world," referring to the center of the world or the axis of connection between heaven and Earth. For some cultures, the axis mundi is embodied by a tree of life; for others, a mountain (such as Mount Olympus for the ancient Greeks, Mount Kailash for Hindus and Tibetans). In Pueblo cultures it is the place of the Peoples' emergence into this world. In Africa, Zulu sangoma Credo Mutwa taught that the Nilotic Meridian is the axis mundi.

Bardo: In Tibetan Buddhism, bardo is the transitional state between death and rebirth or reincarnation.

Beyul: In the Nyingma lineage of Tibetan Buddhism, beyul are hidden valleys that were blessed by Padmasambhava as holy places of refuge in Nepal, Tibet, India, and Bhutan. Protected by snowstorms, avalanches, mists, thunderstorms, and snow leopards, they are places where physical and spiritual worlds overlap and the effectiveness of our practices and prayers multiply.

Bodhicitta: From the Sanskrit *bodhi,* "awakened" or "enlightened," and *citta,* "heart-mind." Widely translated as "awakening mind," bodhicitta is the intention to awaken in order to help others awaken. It is the state of mind of a bodhisattva, who pursues Buddhahood in order to benefit others and is dedicated to freeing all beings from suffering.

Bodhisattva: From the Sanskrit *bodhi,* "awakened," and *sattva,* "being." Awakened being. A holy being, spiritual hero, or saint. Someone who has attained wisdom and enlightenment, and who has vowed to help all other sentient beings attain enlightenment before entering nirvana and becoming a Buddha oneself.

Charok Rinpoche: Also known as His Eminence Kushok Mangdon Rinpoche, he resided in his later years in a cave at Charok, hence the name *Charok* Rinpoche. Charok Rinpoche belonged to the Konchok Chidu lineage and was born at Thame Monastery, which is the oldest monastery in the Khumbu region of Nepal. This is the lama that gave Cynthia the Earth Treasure Vase practice.

Chokgyur Lingpa: Orgyen Chokgyur Dechen Lingpa was one of the major tertöns in Tibetan history. His termas are practiced widely in the Nyingma and Kagyu sects, and he is considered the last of the one hundred prophesied tertöns. The teachings he discovered, known as the "New Treasures of Chokgyur Lingpa," include his practice on the Twenty-One Taras.

Constituent Assembly: In May, 2008, the 601 members of the first Constituent Assembly (CA) of Nepal—elected through a system of proportional representation—gathered to write a new constitution and act as the interim legislature for a term of two years. On May 28, 2008, the CA voted to declare Nepal a federal democratic republic, abolishing the monarchy. The first CA failed to put a constitution into effect, and a second CA, later converted into a legislative parliament, was formed in 2013 to complete the task.

Copper-Colored Mountain: The pure land where it is said Padmasambhava (Guru Rinpoche) can be found until the end of time. Here, he manifests as a *vidyadhara*, or knowledge holder of spontaneous presence, and offers protection to the living.

Dakini: From the Tibetan *khandro,* meaning "sky dweller" or "sky dancer." A dakini is an embodiment of the sacred feminine who can appear as a human being, a meditational deity, or a protector. Depending on the situation, dakinis may appear as wrathful or peaceful, or as wisdom or worldly emanations. They are said to aid and protect practitioners striving to awaken.

Damaru: A small two-sided drum used as an instrument in Tibetan Buddhist meditation practices.

Dedication of the Merit: At the end of any dharma practice or virtuous action, practitioners will express their intention to share any merit or blessings that might have been accumulated during the practice with all living beings.

Deities of the Bardo: In Tibetan Buddhism, it is said that when one dies and enters the bardo, one passes through several different realms on the way to rebirth and can encounter a hundred different deities—forty-two peaceful deities and fifty-eight wrathful deities—along the way.

Devi / Deva: Devī is the Sanskrit word for goddess; the masculine form is deva. Devi and deva mean heavenly, divine, or anything of excellence.

Dharma: The teachings of the Buddha. *Dharma* is also a Buddhist, Hindu, and yogic concept referring to a divine law or principle governing the universe. To live out one's dharma is to live in accordance with this principle.

Dharmacharya: From the Sanskrit *ācārya*, meaning "Teacher," therefore, "Dharmacharya" refers to a "Teacher of the Dharma."

Didjeridu: An Australian wind instrument, cylindrical in shape, usually made from the branches of eucalyptus trees. When played, it creates a continuous drone through a unique technique called circular breathing. Measuring between three and ten feet long, didjeridus were first created by Aboriginal peoples in northern Australia at least a thousand years ago. Westernized spelling is usually "digeridoo," but Aboriginal people refer to this instrument as "didjeridu" or "magu."

Dorje: See "Vajra."

Dudjom Tersar: The cycles of teachings revealed first by Dudjom Lingpa (1835–1904), and then by his reincarnation, Dudjom Jigdral Yeshe Dorje Rinpoche (1904–1987), the supreme head of the Nyingma lineage and one of the most important lamas of the twentieth century.

Dzogchen: Meaning the "Great Perfection," these are the teachings at the heart of the Nyingma lineage. The "path" of *Dzogchen* is the realization of our primordial nature, which has always been perfect from the very beginning, just like the sky.

Five Buddha Families: The foundational nature of the mandala principle. These five families (called *buddha*, *vajra*, *ratna*, *padma*, and *karma*) are characterized by the five "poisons" or reactive emotions and their transformation into wisdom. Each of the five families also relates to a color, an elemental energy, and a direction within the mandala. In their transformed state, the Five Buddha Families embody an aspect of enlightenment, with the mandala depicting the whole of enlightened awareness.

Gabarnmung: Jawoyn for "[place of] hole in the rock." A sacred site in southwestern Arnhem Land, in the Northern Territory of Australia, inhabited for at least forty-four thousand years. Gabarnmung is in a remote location on the land of the Jawoyn people, the Buyhmi clan being the traditional owners. It is a cathedral-like rock shelter with thirty-six supporting pillars, featuring prehistoric paintings of fish, wallabies, crocodiles, humans, and spiritual figures.

Gaia: From the Greek *Gaia*, a poetical form of *gē,* "earth." One of the deities of the ancient Greeks, a personification of the Earth, she was seen as the ancestral mother of all life. In modern times, James Lovelock popularized the term when he wrote about the Gaia principle to raise awareness of the Earth as a dynamic, living entity.

Gatha: From the Sanskrit, meaning "song" or "verse." In the tradition of Thich Nhat Hanh, a gatha is a type of verse that is recited (most often silently, sometimes out loud) in rhythm with the breath as part of the practice of mindfulness.

Gompa: Tibetan word meaning "remote place," but it generally refers to a temple or a place for meditation and spiritual learning.

Guru Yoga: In the Vajrayana tradition, Guru Yoga is a devotional practice in which the practitioner unites their mindstream with the mindstream of their guru. One is instructed to regard one's guru as an awakened Buddha.

Indra: In Hindu and Buddhist cosmology, Indra was the king of the gods. His net of jewels or pearls hangs over his palace on Mount Meru.

Interbeing: A new verb, coined by Thich Nhat Hanh, meaning the state of all things being interconnected and interdependent.

Khata: A ceremonial scarf, usually of white silk, representing purity and compassion. In the Tibetan tradition, it is presented on special occasions, including births, weddings, funerals, graduations, and the arrival or departure of special guests.

Kiva: An underground chamber used by modern and ancestral Pueblo peoples for ceremonial purposes. Kivas are entered by a ladder from the roof down to the center of the kiva floor. The ritual emergence of participants from the kiva into the plaza in ceremonies still enacted today represents the original emergence by Pueblo Peoples from the underworld into the current world.

Konchok Chidu: A lineage of teachings (meaning the "Embodiment of the Precious Ones") that are an important cycle of treasure texts (terma) revealed by the great tertön Rigdzin Jatson Nyingpo (1585–1656) and practiced in the Nyingma and Kagyu traditions. Tolu Tharling Monastery is the seat of this lineage in Nepal.

Kundalini Shakti: Sanskrit term meaning "serpent power," first referenced in the Upanishads. In Hinduism, Kundalini is believed to be a goddess, whose power lies dormant and coiled at the base of the spine. This primal energy, representing the potential within us, can be awakened and cultivated through practices such as yoga, chanting mantras, and meditation.

Lama: A Tibetan word meaning "spiritual teacher" ("guru" in Sanskrit), often associated with monks or yogis who have completed a traditional three-year retreat.

Ley Lines: Ancient, invisible pathways in the Earth indicating powerful flows of energy between sites and structures. For example, a famous ley line known as the St. Michael line travels from Skellig Michael in Ireland through both St. Michael's Mount in England and Mont-Saint-Michel in France to Assisi in Italy; Dodona, Delphi, Athens, and Rhodes in Greece; and Mount Carmel, Israel. Ley lines have been compared to the dragon lines of Chinese feng shui, as well as to the *Te Ao Māori* of New Zealand.

Lineage Masters: The transmission of teachings in Tibetan Buddhism is dependent upon the concept of a lineage and lineage holders, or lineage masters. A lineage is an unbroken line of transmission, and lineage masters are lamas who have received the transmission of the dharma teachings and are therefore part of the lineage.

Lung: Lung (pronounced "loong") is Tibetan for "repetition." Lung is one of three types of initiation or empowerment in Tibetan Buddhism, which allow one to receive the transmission of a teaching or lineage. The first is called *tri* and is a full explanation of the transmission and the meaning of the text. The second is called *lung* and is an oral transmission whereby the teacher recites the entire text and gives authorization to do the practice. The third is called *wang*, which is an elaborate empowerment ceremony. The wang is most often bestowed first, to facilitate the receiver being able to absorb the initiation into a practice ceremonially, followed by the oral transmission, or lung, and then the explanation, or tri.

Mala: Prayer beads used for reciting mantras. Counting the movement of beads (usually there are 108 total) on a mala every time a mantra is recited is a way of tracking the accomplishment of a mantra. The recitation of a mantra one hundred thousand times is considered a good foundation for realizing a practice.

Mandala: From the Sanskrit mandala meaning "circle." A mandala is a geometric pattern that symbolically and metaphysically represents the universe, and at its most basic is made up of the center and the four directions. Each of the four directions and the center of a mandala can be seen to embody a quality or energy that is one aspect of the whole. *See also:* Five Buddha Families.

Mantra: A sacred sound, syllable, word, or phrase, usually in the Sanskrit language. The sound of the Sanskrit syllables when chanted are said to carry spiritual power and meaning. *Om* is the simplest and best-known mantra; many believe it to be the first sound, which blossomed into the creation of all things.

Mara: From the Sanskrit *māra,* meaning "demon" or "destroyer." In Indo-Tibetan Buddhism, there are several classes of mara; these are considered forces that act as obstacles to enlightenment. Mara, the Lord of Demons, tried to tempt Prince Siddhartha from attaining enlightenment as he sat beneath the Bodhi Tree.

Melissae: *Melissa* (singular) and *Melissae* (plural). A feminine proper name, from the Greek meaning "honeybee." The word "Melissae" also refers to the priestesses of Delphi, the oracular bee nymphs of ancient Greece. Originally, there were three bee nymphs, also known as the Thraia, who inhabited the springs within the Corycian Cave high on the slopes of Mount Parnassus. They were the first prophets and oracles at Delphi and were believed to have taught Apollo the art of divination.

Mo Tzu: A Warring States–period Chinese philosopher who lived from the late fifth to the early fourth centuries BC and taught that everyone is equal in the eyes of heaven. His teachings placed special value upon universal love, social order, the will of heaven, the sharing of wealth, and honoring the worthy.

Mudra: From Sanskrit, a mudra is a ritual hand gesture in Indo-Tibetan Buddhism. These gestures are thought to increase the efficacy of one's prayers.

Ngöndro: The preliminary, preparatory, or foundational practices of Vajrayana Buddhism, which offer a complete path to enlightenment. The practice begins with the contemplation on the four thoughts that turn the mind towards the dharma, then turns to taking refuge and awakening bodhicitta, purification with the Vajrasattva prayer, accumulating merit and wisdom with the mandala offering, and, finally, Guru Yoga (uniting one's mind with a guru as a living embodiment of the Buddha). It then ends with closing the visualization and dedicating the merit. Each section of the ngöndro is generally repeated one hundred thousand times.

Nyingma: From the Tibetan, meaning "old" or "ancient," Nyingma refers to the "Old School" (or lineage or tradition) of Tibetan Buddhism. It basically follows the teaching brought to Tibet by Padmasambhava and translated, mainly during the reign of King Trisong Detsen in the eighth century up to Rinchen Sangpo in the ninth century, by the great masters Padmasambhava, Vimalamitra, Shantarakshita, and Vairocana. The other three major schools of Tibetan Buddhism—the Gelug, Kagyu, and Sakya—together comprise the School of New Translations. There is also a prominent nonsectarian Rimé movement.

Omphalos: An ancient Greek term meaning "navel." According to myth, Zeus set two eagles free to find the center of the world. They flew through the skies westward and eastward, and their paths crossed in Delphi, which Zeus declared to be the center of the world. The Omphalos stone marks the spot that the ancients considered to be the navel of the world, the umbilicus of the Earth. Some say this sacred round stone may have been made from meteorite.

Ouroboros: A circular symbol that depicts a snake or dragon devouring its own tail and represents the eternal cycle of destruction and rebirth. Literally meaning "tail-devourer" in Greek, the ouroboros symbolizes nature's cycles and the mystery of cyclical time, which flows back into itself. In alchemy, the ouroboros represented the idea of eternity and endless return, the unity of time's beginning and end. From a Gnostic point of view, the opposing ends of the ouroboros were interpreted as divine and earthly human nature which exist in union, comparable to the Chinese yin and yang.

Padmasambhava: Known as Guru Rinpoche or Precious Teacher, born in the eighth century, Padmasambhava is the founder of Tibetan Buddhism. He was responsible for having brought the teachings of Vajrayana to Tibet from India and is known in Tibetan Buddhism as the "second Buddha."

Pecha: A Tibetan spiritual text in the form of a traditional loose-leaf "book" of long, thin, rectangular pages, with writing or printing on both sides and top and bottom covers made of firm materials.

Prasad: From Sanskrit, meaning "favor" or "grace." In Hinduism, during worship, food and water called *prasad* are offered to a deity.

Primordial Wisdom Awareness: Meaning "As it is, from the beginning." The fundamental state of consciousness before it is divided into "I" and "other" or into the various emotions; the innate wisdom present in all sentient beings.

Prithvi: From the Sanskrit, meaning both "earth" and "ground," as well as the name of a goddess called Prithvi Mata, or Mother Earth. Prithvi is revered in Buddhism for both protecting Gotama Buddha and serving as witness to his awakening. She dispelled the tempter Mara by attesting to Gotama Buddha's worthiness to attain enlightenment when he summoned her by touching the Earth.

Rigpa: A Dzogchen term referring to the experience of the nature of mind. Sometimes translated as "clarity," "wisdom," "intelligence," "awareness," or "knowledge," rigpa is our innermost nature of mind, our ultimate nature, a state of being that goes beyond all limits or concepts.

Rinpoche: An honorific title meaning "precious teacher."

Root Teacher: One's primary teacher in Tibetan Buddhism. The one who introduces you to the nature of mind.

Sa Chü Bumpa: The Tibetan term for Earth Treasure Vase, meaning "vase to invigorate the Earth." Most agree that the practice of burying an Earth Treasure Vase to bless and to empower the area where it is placed was given to us by Padmasambhava, but this practice could be even older, possibly dating back to the pre-Buddhist Indigenous Bön religion of the Zhang Zhung empire.

Sadhana: From Sanskrit, meaning "means of accomplishment." This is an Indian yogic term that refers to any type of spiritual practice that aims to bring practitioners closer to their goal. In Tibetan Buddhism, it usually means a ritual practice that outlines the means of accomplishing or realizing the nature of one or several deities.

Samsara: The seemingly endless cycle of birth and death. The Sanskrit term means "world," and the Tibetan means "wheel" or "cycle." It refers to wandering aimlessly through this life (or these lives) in this illusory world of suffering. When one awakens, one is no longer caught in the endless cycle of suffering.

Sangoma: From the Zulu, meaning "healer." In South Africa, a traditional healer is involved in physical and emotional healing, divination, counteracting witchcraft, etc., as well as carrying the oral history of their tradition. A sangoma is connected to the ancestral spirits and can guide and protect the living, both in this life and the next.

Seed Syllable: In Sanskrit, *bījā*, or "seed." A seed syllable is a mystical syllable that is both contained within and contains the entirety of a mantra or a teaching. A deity is said to be invoked from the sound of its seed syllable when the syllable is chanted. A seed syllable can appear in many sadhanas in order to increase the power and efficacy of the practice.

Shaktipat: From the Sanskrit, *shakti*, (psychic) energy, and *pāta,* to fall. The transmission or conferring of spiritual energy in the Hindu tradition from one person to another. It can be transmitted by a look, a touch, a word, or even a thought, and is considered a gift from the guru.

Siddhartha Gotama, Shakyamuni: From the Sanskrit, *Śākyamuni*, meaning "Sage of the Sakyas." The historical Buddha, Prince Siddhartha Gotama (alternatively spelled "Gautama") was born in the sixth century BC to King Suddhodana and Queen Mahamaya in Lumbini, in present-day Nepal. Seven days after the Buddha was born, his mother, Queen Mahamaya, died. The Queen's sister, Mahapajapati Gotami, then raised the child as if he were her own. After leaving behind the life of a prince and following ascetic practices for many years, he eventually came to sit beneath the Bodhi Tree and attained enlightenment. When the demonic figure Mara tried to prevent him from doing so, the Earth attested to his worthiness and supported his awakening. After that, he spent forty-five years teaching.

Sixteenth Karmapa: The sixteenth Gyalwa Karmapa, Rangjung Rigpe Dorje (August 14, 1924–November 5, 1981), was the spiritual leader of the Karma Kagyu lineage of Tibetan Buddhism. The sixteenth Karmapa was considered to be a "living Buddha" and was deeply involved in the transmission of Vajrayana Buddhism to Europe and North America following the Chinese invasion of Tibet.

Songlines: For the Aboriginal peoples of Australia, songlines are "dreaming tracks" or "energetic highways"—and refer to the energy system of the planet. They can travel across the land and through the sky, and mark the route followed by the creator-beings. Ancestors played a great role in the Dreaming, or Dreamtime, in the creation of all things on Earth and in heaven, as well as in the foundation of sacred sites, such as Uluru. The songlines connect creation events and sacred places through the song cycles, stories, dances, and art of the Aboriginal people, to which the songlines are known as the "footprints of the Ancestors."

Stupa: A geometric and circular structure symbolizing the enlightened mind and containing precious Buddhist relics. In Tibet, there are eight different types of stupas, each with its own meaning. They are objects of meditation, and to circumambulate a stupa is a devotional practice said to bring great merit. The stupa is similar to the pagoda in China and Japan.

Sutra: From the Sanskrit *sūtra*, meaning "thread," "string," and "discourse." In Buddhism, it refers to the teachings, or discourses, of the Buddha, which were given during the forty-five years that he taught. After his death, these were recorded by his disciple Ananda and the Buddhist councils.

Take Refuge: This is a practice or way to give ourselves over to something larger than ourselves. By taking refuge in the Three Jewels (the Buddha, Dharma, Sangha), one can receive the spiritual support we need to stay on the path and awaken from confusion.

Tara: From the Sanskrit *Tārā*, meaning "she who liberates." Tara is a female deity of compassion revered in all schools of Tibetan Buddhism who appears in twenty-one forms and guises—each of which has a different color, and purpose. The most popular is Green Tara, who is associated with accomplishment and protection, and White Tara, who is associated with long life.

Terma: Hidden spiritual treasure. Spiritual treasures are believed to have been hidden by Padmasambhava and Yeshe Tsogyal to be discovered at the appropriate time by "treasure revealers," or tertöns. There are two main types of hidden treasures: physical objects known as earth-treasures, like scrolls written in a special dakini script, statues, vajras, and phurbas; or, termas, discovered within the mindstream of the tertön, called mind-treasures, which depend on seeing, hearing, or understanding of words and sounds.

Tertön: A revealer of spiritual treasures, or termas. There have been numerous tertöns since the time of Padmasambhava. There are said to be one hundred great tertöns, which include the reincarnations of Guru Rinpoche's twenty-five main disciples, as well as one thousand minor tertöns—even some in the present time, including Kyabjé Dudjom Rinpoche and Chokgyur Dechen Lingpa, who were major tertön and gave us many important sadhanas still practiced today.

Three Jewels: There are three sources of refuge in Buddhism. They are the Buddha, the one who shows us the way in this life; the Dharma, the teachings of understanding and love; and the Sangha, the community that practices harmony and awareness. The Buddha, Dharma, and Sangha are called "jewels" because they are considered the most precious source of protection, guidance, inspiration, and wisdom. *See also:* Take Refuge

Tjukurrpa: An Aboriginal word used by the Pitjantjatjara people of central Australia to describe the Dreaming, which refers to the origins and powers embodied in the land, sacred places, objects, songs, and stories. It is a way of seeing and understanding the world and connects people to "Country" and to each other through shared social and knowledge networks.

Tonglen: A Tibetan word meaning "giving and receiving," or "taking and sending." It is the practice of taking on the pain and suffering of others with the inhale of one's breath and sending peace and well-being to them on the exhale.

Vajra: In Tibetan, "dorje." A mythical weapon originally associated with the Vedic deity Indra, the vajra is said to be as indestructible as a diamond and as powerful as thunder and lightning. Capable of penetrating anything, the vajra came to symbolize indestructible wisdom and is used as a ritual instrument along with a bell in Vajrayana ceremonies. Held in the right hand, the Vajra represents the male principle and symbolizes compassion; the bell, held in the left hand, represents wisdom and the female principle.

Vajrayana: The "diamond vehicle," from the Sanskrit, *vajra*, meaning "diamond," (see above) and *yāna,* "vehicle." This is the form of Buddhism that developed in India and blossomed in Tibet, and from there it was carried to other Himalayan states and on to China, Mongolia, and Japan. Its teachings are esoteric, and its practices include the use of mantras, mudras, mandalas, and the visualization of deities as personified aspects of our Buddha Nature.

Yeshe Tsogyal: An important historical figure in the Vajrayana, Yeshe Tsogyal was born a princess in Karchen, Tibet, in 777 AD, and attained enlightenment in her lifetime. Primarily known as the principal consort of Padmasambhava, she—through the power of her unfailing memory—collected all the teachings he gave in Tibet and concealed them as terma to be revealed at a later time. At the end of her life, it is said she flew through the air to find him in his pure land, the Copper-Colored Mountain.

Yoni: From the Sanskrit, meaning "source," "womb," or "vagina." In Hinduism, Yoni is an abstract representation of the goddess Shakti, the feminine pro-creative power.

Zen: A Japanese school of Mahayana Buddhism emphasizing meditation and insight into the nature of mind as the path to enlightenment.

EARTH TREASURE VASE LOCATIONS

The First Generation of Earth Treasure Vases as of September 2023

1. A cave above Los Alamos National Laboratory, in New Mexico, the birthplace of the atomic bomb
2. The Source of the Rio Grande River, Creede, Colorado
3. The Mouth of the Rio Grande at the Gulf of Mexico
4. On Mt. Baldy above Santa Fe, New Mexico
5. On Mt. Chicoma—known as Tsikumu to the Tewa People of New Mexico, the custodians of the sacred lands where this mandala began
6. The Indian Point Nuclear Reservation on the Hudson River in New York
7. The Headwaters Old Growth Redwood Forest in Northern California
8. Punta Cometa, on the coast of Oaxaca, Mexico
9. Vilcabamba, Ecuador
10. Djakova, Kosovo
11. The Lawrence Laboratory at the University of California, Berkeley
12. The Dtao Dum Forest, on the border of Thailand and Burma
13. The Village of Ein Karem in Israel/Palestine

14. Hiroshima, Japan
15. Inwood Park above the Cloisters in New York City
16. The Biosphere 2 in Oracle, Arizona
17. The Martin Luther King Jr. Freedom Center in Oakland, California
18. The Source of the Ganges in India
19. The Source of the Amazon in Peru
20. The Southern Pacific Ocean—93' down in Egum Atoll, the Trobriand Islands, Papua, New Guinea
21. The Arctic Circle, Alaska
22. The Kogi lands of the Sierra Nevada de Santa Marta, Colombia
23. Tellewoyan Village, Lofa County, Voinjama District, Liberia, West Africa
24. The Blyde River Canyon, Limpopo Province, South Africa
25. The Giza Plateau, Egypt
26. Haleakala, Maui, Hawaii
27. The Itombwe Forest, South Kivu Province, Democratic Republic of Congo
28. Avebury, England
29. Bindaluk, Jawoyn Country, Katherine, Northern Territory, Australia
30. The Mother Vase lives for now on Cynthia's altar and will be buried when all the others have been accomplished.

The Second Generation of Earth Treasure Vases

31. Gabarnmung, Arnhem Land, Australia
32. The MacKenzie King Park, Ottawa River Valley, Ottawa-Gatineau, Canada
33. The original garden in Findhorn, Scotland
34. The Great Stupa of Boudhanath in Kathmandu, Nepal
35. The Flint Hills of Kansas in the heartland of America
36. The Santa Cruz Mountains near Silicon Valley, California
37. The Valles Caldera of northern New Mexico
38. Purnululu (Bungle Bungles), the Kimberley Region, Australia
39. The village of Utiagvik at the edge of the sea in northernmost Arctic Alaska
40. The Hanford nuclear reservation on the shores of the Columbia River in the state of Washington
41. Mount Ryosen above Fukushima, Japan
42. Back to where it all began at the cave hermitage of Charok, Nepal
43. Margibi County, Liberia
44. In the base of an old Ironbark tree on Didthul Mountain in the Budawang wilderness of Walbunja Country, Yuin Nation, South-eastern Australia
45. Our root temple, Tolu Tharling Monastery in Nepal
46. The Munzur Valley near the source of the Euphrates River in Turkey
47. Serpent Mound, Ohio
48. The Border Peace School in Cheorwon, in the demilitarized zone (DMZ) between North and South Korea

49. The Ashaninka Spiritual Portal, Kampa do Rio Amonea Indigenous Land, State of Acre, Brazilian Amazon
50. The Arhuaco lands in the Sierra Nevada de Santa Marta, Colombia
51. Te Waipounamu, the South Island, Aotearoa-New Zealand
52. Mount Parnassus above Delphi in Greece

The Third Generation of Earth Treasure Vases

53. Antarctica
54. The Isle of Lewis, Outer Hebrides, Scotland
55. Saugatuck Dunes on Lake Michigan, USA
56. The Highwood Valley in Alberta, Canada
57. Southeastern USA Turtle Island, Shaconage, Tennessee
58. On the shores of Lake Washington in Kirkland, Washington
59. Permian Basin, New Mexico

Second Generation Earth Treasure Vases Being Stewarded (not yet buried)

60. Southwestern Australia
61. The Bering Strait in Russia
62. Altai, Russia
63. A vase dedicated to healing racism in the USA
64. Washington, DC
65. Italy
66. British Columbia
67. The Himalayas

68. Afghanistan
69. Auroville, South India
70. Luxembourg
71. Chile
72–77. Six Second Generation Earth Treasure Vases still awaiting their destination

Third Generation Earth Treasure Vases (not yet buried)

78. Taos, New Mexico
79. Little Shell Tribe territory, Montana
80. Paramo ecosystem of Colombia, for the waters of the world
81. Cape Cod, Massachusetts, for the whales
82–93. Twelve Third Generation Vases still awaiting their destination

RESOURCES

Alliance for the Earth is a 501(c)(3) nonprofit organization dedicated to global healing and collective awakening. We facilitate these intentions through the distribution of Earth Treasure Vases around the planet, and our regular meditations, teachings, retreats, pilgrimages and events. To learn about all of our programs, including working with the Earth Treasure Vases, go to **https://GaiaMandala.net**

Alliance for the Earth serves as the fiscal sponsor for the Earth Treasure Vase Global Healing Project and the international Gaia Mandala Community. We also support a peacebuilding program in Liberia and the rebuilding of our home temple, Tolu Tharling Monastery in Nepal.
To support our work, please go to: **https://GaiaMandala.net/donate**

Subscribe to our monthly Full Moon Newsletter here:
https://GaiaMandala. net/#newsletter-subscribe

Join our monthly Earth Treasure Vase Full Moon Global Healing Meditation by registering here: **https://GaiaMandala.net/ #full-moon-meditation**

To attend a retreat on the Sadhana of the Sublime Mother Gaia, let us know you are interested here: **https://GaiaMandala.net/ #sublime-mother-gaia**

Become a member of our private online community, The Gaia Mandala, on Mighty Networks here: **https://Gaia-Mandala.mn.co/ landing-page**

To learn more about our work of Sacred Activism, go to: **https://GaiaMandala.net/sacred-activism**

Contact us at: **info@EarthTreasureVase.org**

Additional Organizations to Know

Action Kivu
https://www.actionkivu.org

Biosphere Foundation
https://biospherefoundation.org

BuddhaPath
https://www.buddhapath.com

Global White Lion Protection Trust
https://whitelions.org

Hero Women Rising
https://www.herowomenrising.org

Honor Our Pueblo Existence (the work of Marian Naranjo)
https://shuffle.do/projects/honor-our-pueblo-existance-h-o-p-e

Plum Village (the practice community of Thich Nhat Hanh)
https://plumvillage.org

Tewa Women United https://tewawomenunited.org

The Work That Reconnects (the work of Joanna Macy)
https://workthatreconnects.org

Women's Earth and Climate Action Network (WECAN)
https://www.wecaninternational.org

World Pulse
https://www.worldpulse.org

ABOUT THE AUTHOR

Cynthia Jurs is a Dharmacharya in the Order of Interbeing of Zen Master Thich Nhat Hanh. In 2018, she was made an Honorary Lama in recognition of her dedication in carrying this practice all around the planet. Inspired by thirty years of pilgrimage into diverse communities and ecosystems with the holy vessels, today Cynthia is forging a new path of dharma in service to Gaia, deeply rooted in the feminine, honoring indigenous traditions, and teaching an embodied, engaged, sacred activism dedicated to global healing and collective awakening. Cynthia leads meditations and pilgrimages and through her non-profit, Alliance for the Earth, she works with former combatants in Liberia to build peace through mindfulness. She lives at the base of the Sangre de Cristo mountains in northern New Mexico where she often walks in the wilderness with her dog or gardens with her husband. You can find her offerings and join the global healing community she founded at: https://GaiaMandala.net